"Clearly written, assiduously researched, and never fantastical, *Democracy, the Courts, and the Liberal State* is a delight-filled primer for how to overhaul our thinking about constitutionalism to uphold liberal democratic values for the twenty-first century. If David Miles can imagine and explain taking democracy seriously, then surely we can conceive of the serious institutions to build it!"

Malik R Dahlan, *Professor of International Law and Public Policy at Queen Mary University of London*

"Electoral processes are a crucial yet curiously neglected feature of any constitutional system. Not only legal theorists but also constitutional courts often have had overly simple, not to say simplistic, views of how these processes might best operate so as to secure and support core liberal democratic principles. David Miles' excellent book breaks new ground in tackling this issue head on. In particular, he provides a critical and comparative examination of the core decisions on matters of electoral process of the US Supreme Court and the German Federal Constitutional Court. His analysis highlights both the importance of courts in fostering a flourishing liberal democracy, and the strengths and weaknesses of current judicial reasoning in the United States and Germany in this area."

Richard Bellamy, *Professor of Political Science, UCL*

Democracy, the Courts, and the Liberal State

Reformulating a problem of both constitutionalism and liberalism discussed in the works of Ernst-Wolfgang Böckenförde, Hannah Arendt, and Alexis de Tocqueville, the book examines one generally overlooked manifestation of constitutionalism: the role of the courts in shaping democratic politics and the inter-relationship between citizens and state.

Drawing on constitutional history, law, and political theory, David Miles argues that constitutionalism cannot be seen merely as an institutional mechanism to limit government, as it also has a crucial civic dimension upon which the liberal state depends. Utilising the works of Böckenförde, Arendt, and Tocqueville, constitutionalism is conceived in the book as part of a broader system of communal norms which sustains representative democracy and liberalism. Through an analysis of judicial interventions in the electoral processes of the United States and Germany, Miles explores the role of civil society actors in transforming constitutionalism through legal challenges to oligarchical or exclusionary practices. He assesses how, in adjudicating these cases, the US Supreme Court and the German Constitutional Court have mediated the tension between threats to stability and the imperative of democratic renewal.

Democracy, the Courts, and the Liberal State will be of interest to scholars, students, and practitioners interested in comparative politics, political theory, and constitutional law and history.

David Miles is a former Carnegie Scholar and teaches international relations at the University of St Andrews. His academic and research interests include comparative politics, political theory, American and German constitutional history, US foreign policy, international relations, and identity. He is Editor-in-Chief of *Global Politics Magazine*.

Routledge Innovations in Political Theory

Epistemontology in Spinoza-Marx-Freud-Lacan
The (Bio)Power of Structure
A. Kiarina Kordela

Aesthetics and Political Culture in Modern Society
Henrik Kaare Nielsen

Post-Fukushima Activism
Politics and Knowledge in the Age of Precarity
Azumi Tamura

Reconstructing Nonviolence
A New Theory and Practice for a Post-Secular Society
Roberto Baldoli

Rethinking Positive and Negative Liberty
Maria Dimova-Cookson

The Problem of Value Pluralism
Isaiah Berlin and Beyond
George Crowder

On Biopolitics
An Inquiry into Nature and Language
Marco Piasentier

Democracy, the Courts, and the Liberal State
A Comparative Analysis of American and German Constitutionalism
David Miles

Legislative Deliberative Democracy
Freedom of Speech During War
Avichai Levit

Democracy, the Courts, and the Liberal State

A Comparative Analysis of American and German Constitutionalism

David Miles

Routledge
Taylor & Francis Group
NEW YORK AND LONDON

First published 2021
by Routledge
605 Third Avenue, New York, NY 10017

and by Routledge
2 Park Square, Milton Park, Abingdon, Oxon, OX14 4RN

First issued in paperback 2022

Routledge is an imprint of the Taylor & Francis Group, an informa business

Publisher's Note
The publisher has gone to great lengths to ensure the quality of this reprint but points out that some imperfections in the original copies may be apparent.

Library of Congress Cataloging-in-Publication Data
A catalog record for this title has been requested

ISBN 13: 978-0-367-60932-0 (pbk)
ISBN 13: 978-0-367-20032-9 (hbk)
ISBN 13: 978-0-429-25925-8 (ebk)

DOI: 10.4324/9780429259258

Typeset in Times New Roman
by Wearset Ltd, Boldon, Tyne and Wear

For my Mother and Sister, and the memory of my Father

Turning and turning in the widening gyre
The falcon cannot hear the falconer;
Things fall apart; the centre cannot hold;
Mere anarchy is loosed upon the world,
The blood-dimmed tide is loosed, and everywhere
The ceremony of innocence is drowned;
The best lack all conviction, while the worst
Are full of passionate intensity.

(W. B. Yeats—'The Second Coming', 1920)

Contents

Acknowledgements

Far more friends, colleagues, family members, mentors, and others helped me in the process of writing this book than I will ever be able to thank. I will try and make a stab at doing so though.

Much of the research that has gone into the book was originally made possible by the generous financial support of the Carnegie Trust for the Universities of Scotland during my time as a Carnegie Scholar. Without this support, I would never have been able to begin the research that led to this book, let alone bring it to completion.

First and foremost, I need to thank Tony Lang for his support, friendship, company on the golf course, the great discussions, and the many books he's lent me over the years (some of which I still need to give him back). Tony was a constant source of guidance and encouragement, and his importance as a friend and mentor has not diminished since I finished my PhD. Working with Tony at the Centre for Global Constitutionalism as an Associate Fellow was professionally stimulating and gave me an important insight into the normative significance of constitutionalism in an increasingly fragmented and unstable global political context.

Nick Rengger was another hugely important influence on my thinking and, ultimately, the research that led to the book. Both as a friend and as a mentor, the conversations I had with Nick, inevitably over a glass or two of red, enriched my research, and my understanding of constitutionalism and political theory beyond measure. Michael Oakeshott wrote that a conversation needs no purpose, has no conclusion, and "its value lies in the relics it leaves behind in the minds of those who participate", a philosophy that encapsulated Nick's own approach to scholarship and life. Nick taught me the infinite value of a conversation as an end in itself. I miss him greatly.

I have discussed many of the ideas in the book, and the process of writing it, with friends and colleagues at St Andrews and other places over the years. With apologies to those I have inadvertently forgotten, I wish to thank John Anderson, Bernhard Blumenau, Michelle Burgis, Helen Chambers, Malik Dahlan, Sir David Edward, Colin Kidd, Natasha Saunders, John-Harmen Valk, and Andrew Williams. Richard Bellamy and Patrick Hayden also deserve huge thanks for their valuable advice and comments on my PhD project, much of which has found its way into this book with far fewer errors than there would have been otherwise. Helen Chambers and Bernhard Blumenau kindly looked at some of my German into English translations, advice which I have dutifully tried to follow. I owe a big thank you to Natalja Mortensen, Charlie Baker, and the editorial team at Routledge for their truly infinite patience and support in bringing the manuscript to completion and for making the whole process less confusing and daunting than I thought it would be. Claire Bell, Ashleigh Phillips, Emma Critchley, and others have done excellent work on the copy-editing and production side of things. Any of the mistakes or misunderstandings that remain, from which these friends, colleagues, and editors have heroically tried to save me, are mine alone.

I have been lucky to have some wonderful friends in St Andrews over the last ten years who have given me time and space to escape from the academic insanity, and to relax, recuperate, escape onto the golf course, or just have a good chat in the pub. Thanks for the good times and drams: Alasdair, Antonio, Felipe, John-Harmen (again), Lin, Natasha, Pinar, Quinn, and Rikard.

Finally, I must thank my mother, Helen, my late father, Wilf, and my sister, Jennie, for their love and years of interesting conversations. This book is dedicated to them.

Abbreviations and German Terms

Bundesverfassungsgericht/BVerfG	Federal Constitutional Court
CDU	Christian Democratic Union (the party of Konrad Adenauer and Angela Merkel)
Die Vergangenheitsbewältigung	A term used to describe the debate and the process of coming to terms with the Nazi past which began in the late 1950s and 1960s
ECHR	European Convention on Human Rights
EP	European Parliament
EPII	European Parliament II Case (2011)
EPIII	European Parliament III Case (2014)
FCCA	Federal Constitutional Court Act
FRG	Federal Republic of Germany (formerly West Germany)
Fünf Prozent Hürde	Five Percent Hurdle, a specific barring clause or electoral threshold which parties must clear to receive seats in the legislature
GDR	German Democratic Republic (East Germany)
Grundgesetz (Basic Law)	West Germany's constitution, promulgated in 1949 and, following reunification in 1991, the constitution of a reunified Germany
KPD	Communist Party of Germany (banned by the *BVerfG* in 1956)
LWV	The League of Women Voters
MEPs	Members of the European Parliament
NS Zeit	Commonly used German expression describing the National Socialist Period
Organstreitverfahren	Organ of State Proceedings/Complaints
PDS	Democratic Socialist Party (former ruling party of the GDR)

SPD	Social Democratic Party of Germany (the party of Willy Brandt and Helmut Schmidt)
Sperrklauseln	Barring Clauses, also known as electoral thresholds
SRP	Socialist Reich Party (banned by the *BVerfG* in 1952)
Verfassungsbeschwerden	Constitutional Complaints

Introduction

> A constitution is a standard, a pillar, and a bond when it is understood, approved and beloved. But without this intelligence and attachment, it might as well be a kite or balloon, flying in the air.[1]
>
> (John Adams)

Constitutionalism in the United States and Germany reflects different forces, threats, and unique historical experiences, yet common to both is Carl Friedrich's idea that it is "rooted in certain basic beliefs; the belief in the dignity of man and in the belief of man's inclination to abuse power" (1974: 123). American and German constitutionalism have been primarily concerned with the attempt to constrain public power in the name of the people. Stephen Griffin notes that "modern constitutionalism involves a tension between the constituent power of the sovereign people and the constitutional forms that are intended to express and check this power" (2007: 49). The manifestation of the people in constitutional, democratic, and social forces has shaped political and legal institutions and the evolution of states. Yet constitutionalism is also, as this book argues, oriented towards a view that 'the people' are an unpredictable force, sometimes requiring restraint, at other times in need of protection and representation.

The establishment of stability is generally common to constitutionalism in different countries, but the degree of stability a particular country seeks and the tools it uses to preserve it may differ. The ability of citizens in modern liberal democracies to plan their lives with minimal state interference presupposes a certain level of political stability. Since the late eighteenth century one clearly accepted basis for the establishment of both political stability and a sphere of private autonomy for citizens immune from state interference is the crafting of a written constitution. The "special virtue of constitutionalism", writes Richard Kay, "lies not merely in reducing the power of the state, but in effecting that reduction by the advance imposition of rules" (1998: 23). Such criteria allow the subject of state power

> to place every planned action in one of two categories, one subject to undoing by the state, the other immune to such authority … Within that second category, however narrow, a person may construct his or her own life.
>
> (Kay, 1998: 23–24)

Of course, while constitutionalism can provide some stability for the state and the individual, so too could a totalitarian system, albeit a stability geared far more to the interests and security of the state than the individual, for whom the midnight knock at the door from the authorities remains a remote but fearful prospect. Within a liberal democracy governed according to the precepts of constitutionalism, however, a civic space must also be permitted for the emergence of new opinions and the associated values which these opinions reflect, embody, and draw sustenance from. Moreover, the very concept of a liberal democracy presupposes that an opinion and the values it reflects should have a chance to become more widely accepted, even to become a majority opinion (Koopmans, 2003: 123). Constitutionalism, however, has something to say about how opinions emerge in a society, for as a philosophy of governance and as a concept it is not value neutral.

Threats to the stability of the liberal state can emerge when the civic and democratic space is allowed to 'boil over' with opinions which may be illiberal or aimed at attacking and destroying the existing constitutional order. In the eyes of the American founders, observes Arendt, "the rule of public opinion was a form of tyranny" (1973: 93). Equally, the liberal state may be at risk when democratic processes become debilitated through the absence of new political voices, or when oligarchical tendencies in a political system seek to exclude certain voters, parties, and minority groups, constitutionally and unconstitutionally, from democratic participation. This book argues that constitutionalism in both the United States and Germany has been oriented around mediating the political tensions generated between these two opposing poles of *stability* and *renewal.* One consequence of the stability and renewal dichotomy, I contend, is that the American and German 'constitutionalisms', as mediated by the United States Supreme Court and Germany's Federal Constitutional Court, the *Bundesverfassungsgericht* (*BVerfG*), have been primarily concerned with mitigating the threats to the liberal state, either from individuals and groups being able to participate in the democratic process without restraint, or from their not being able to participate enough.

This raises the question of how the particular characteristics of American and German constitutionalism shape the civic space within which political participation and the formation of majority opinions takes place. When people are excluded from that space by their communities or the state itself through the denial of the vote, what should the response of constitutionalism be? If too many of the wrong opinions are bad for the liberal state and too few of the right opinions are equally bad, how does constitutionalism determine what is 'just right'?[2] What is 'right', as will be assessed in Chapter 1, is greatly determined by whether opinions are in conformity with the particular precepts of America's liberty-oriented constitutionalism or Germany's dignity-oriented model (see also Eberle, 2002). In other words, the book's analysis is based not on a Dworkin type 'moral' or normative reading of constitutional principles, but on whether certain court decisions can be said to be in conformity with the understanding of American and German constitutionalism outlined in the succeeding chapters.

The book is conceptually divided on several levels. The balance between stability and renewal is a constant thread in the succeeding chapters, representing constitutionalism's orientation point, or rear-view mirror, against which it must adjust to possible democratic threats, or new social and political forces in need of recognition. Put slightly differently, the book is concerned with the *civic space* where individuals fight for access to the political process, contest constitutional meaning, and uphold, challenge, or destroy their government, and the *legal institutional* space within which particular conflicts over issues such as voter exclusion must be resolved in the courts. It is the civic space which is most central to the health of the democratic relationship between citizen and state, and to the survival of the constitutional order. The degree to which American and German constitutionalism, and each court, can exert influence over this civic space is a key question as the book proceeds. As I will suggest, this question is partly dependent on whether law and constitutionalism are accepted in the relevant national or local civic space within each political system.

A common theme with respect to both countries which holds in many Western liberal states is that representative democracy has become almost entirely detached from a civic and communal sphere. This carries serious implications if citizens cannot connect the significance of their votes in the ballot box every four years with their communities and their own lives. The book examines how the political and legal institutions of the United States and Germany have mediated the relationship between citizen and state. It does this primarily with reference to the ideas of Ernst-Wolfgang Böckenförde, Hannah Arendt, and Alexis de Tocqueville, and through a close reading of significant constitutional court cases. A key aim of the book's analysis is the much understudied question of why elements of the electoral processes in American and German representative democracy became subject to judicial scrutiny in the way they did, and how the historical development of constitutionalism in each country shaped that process.

The particular emphasis of each country has largely been determined by its approach to constitutionalism, and how the *polis*—upon which the survival of the state depended—was constituted. As will be examined in Chapter 1, America's liberty-centric constitutionalism sought to confine state power within a distinct area, thereby creating a space for the people to shape their *polis*. By contrast, Germany's normative dignity-oriented constitutionalism largely left the creation of the *polis* in the judicial hands of the *BVerfG*. This difference is central to how the values of the respective 'constitutionalisms' are mediated and interact with more traditional forces of identity and social cohesion. The liberty and dignity distinction also determines how interventions by the courts in the processes of representative democracy occur, and whether values arising from social struggles are merely 'formalised' as law in court decisions, or whether the values of a predominantly normative constitution are 'inculcated' in state institutions and society.

Constitutionalism: An Overview

> A constitutional government will always be a weak government when compared with an arbitrary one. There will be many desirable things, as well as undesirable, which are easy for a despotism but impossible elsewhere. Constitutionalism suffers from the defects inherent in its own merits. Because it cannot do some evil it is precluded from doing some good. Shall we, then, forego the good to prevent the evil, or shall we submit to the evil to secure the good? This is the fundamental practical question of all constitutionalism. It is the foremost issue in the present political world; and it is amazing, and to many of us very alarming, to consider to what insufferable barbarities nation after nation today is showing a willingness to submit, for the recompense it thinks it is getting or hopes to get from an arbitrary government.[3]
>
> (McIlwain, 'The Messenger Lectures' 1938–1939, quoted in 2005: 32)

Any study on the paradoxical relationship between constitutionalism and representative democracy must acknowledge that tension will be an unavoidable by-product of their interaction, especially during times of political change or upheaval. Representative democracy aims to ensure that the institutions and policies of government broadly reflect the popular will as shown during elections. By contrast, constitutionalism fundamentally seeks, as McIlwain observed, to prevent "some evil" at the cost of being unable to do "some good" (2005: 32), thereby setting distinct limits on what the people and their institutions of government can do. Understandably, this can be a tough pill for some citizens to swallow, particularly at times of economic crisis when demands for action and energy in government will be loudest. This book is concerned with one distinct and often overlooked manifestation of constitutionalism—the role of the courts in shaping democratic politics. What is central to all forms of constitutionalism, though, is the importance of rules to organise, limit, and enable state power, and establish a framework which permits a political system to function. An important goal for such rules is to protect the fundamental rights of individuals and the democratic rights of groups of voters from a legislative majority which might seek to change the constitutional ground rules in its favour. Constitutions seek to somehow reconcile these divergent goals and aims of different groups and interests, and, as Kautz notes, "to thwart the unjust rule of a part over the whole" so as to "establish a moderate politics where the rulers serve the common good" (2011: 2).

One of the challenges for constitutionalism is establishing a constitutional charter to keep a government in order, but also allowing a state to update its prevailing value orientations through a process of mediating the institutional and civic space within which opinions become more widely held, or more widely rejected. Michael Brenner argues that

> the modernity and success of a constitution … depends on whether it proves able to facilitate social and political changes and thus the formation of the future quite independently from daily political routine and changing times.
>
> (Brenner, 1999: 136)

The development of American constitutionalism has been driven to a far larger extent than its German counterpart by evolving currents in society and politics. A glance at the 27 ratified constitutional amendments reveals a historical record of the struggles for equality, the fruits of a slowly expanding suffrage, and of a government that slowly responded to the developments of a 'maturing society'.[4] That part of the egalitarianism of America's founding documents was, as Justice William Brennan put it, "more pretension than realised fact" (1990: 23) is hardly contentious. Yet if the divergence between the values suggested by the Constitution and those emanating from political and societal practice is so plain, we are left with the simple but crucial question of whether theory and ideals have the political force to drive praxis or vice versa?[5] German constitutionalism in the form of the militant democracy might suggest this question is irrelevant because it assumes that constitutional institutions such as the *BVerfG* are there for precisely those moments when illiberal forces are in the ascendancy. Yet for such institutions to have the force to be able to suppress illiberal tendencies, even in opposition to the popular will, necessarily means, as Böckenförde pointed out, that the liberal state can only guarantee itself by sacrificing its liberalness (1991: 45). If a society's values are the driving force behind law and politics, then the fate of a constitutional order will be determined largely by whether the society's direction of travel is towards ideals of greater emancipation and human dignity, or towards more malignant impulses. One fundamental question at the heart of constitutionalism, this book argues, is the extent to which the values of a society shape its law and politics, or whether law can direct a society in a more emancipatory direction?[6]

Reduced to its core, this is essentially a question of value strength: whether citizens identify more with their liberal constitutional values or "internal bonding forces" (Böckenförde, 1991: 46) such as religion, nation, or other forms of identity. As will be illustrated, these internal bonding forces can sometimes reinforce constitutional values and principles of democratic engagement, or they can weaken them. Where they point in significantly different directions, such as during the Weimar Republic—where nation was a more potent force of social cohesion than constitutional values—then, as Böckenförde notes, the liberal state is vulnerable, particularly in a "time of crisis" (1991: 46). This discussion will be expanded upon in Chapter 2, which examines the contestation and interdependence between constitutional and traditional values, and their effects in reinforcing or weakening the liberal state and its democratic relationship with its citizens.

A constitution is a legal as well as political instrument. For constitutionalism to be sustained, it has to enjoy the confidence of enough people in society who must be willing to sacrifice their will on some issues to ensure that their own rights are protected on some issues where they might not be in the majority. This highlights, of course, the problem of how one assesses majoritarianism in practice since theoretical accounts tend to elide the reality of how groups in society coalesce on some issues and break apart on others (see, for example, Bishin, 1977: 1103). As Richard Bellamy puts it, "most majorities turn out to be shifting coalitions of minorities" (2007: 75). For the members of any political community, as Lawrence Sager notes, "there is the certainty that some questions of considerable importance will be decided against their interests" and this includes democracies where someone may be on the losing side in elections or in legislative votes (1998: 251).

This picture reflects the experience in Western liberal democracies since 1945, where being on the losing side over a particular issue did not result in incarceration or a more unpleasant fate. For the purposes of the present enquiry, however, the elephant in the room remains 1930s Germany. Hitler never secured a majority of the popular vote, either in the election before or after the National Socialist power grab in January 1933.[7] One lesson that post-1949 German constitutionalism learned from 1930s Germany is that tyrannies can take hold even absent majority support. The Nazis required only the legitimacy which the organs of state authority conferred to complete their dismantling of constitutional democracy. The 1960s reapportionment cases examined in Chapter 4 tell a similar story. While the malapportioned state legislatures fell some way short of Nazi tyranny, a crisis of legitimacy in American democracy was growing. By January 1962, 45 states across the United States were under the control of state legislatures where majority control of at least one house could be theoretically achieved with legislators representing less than 40 percent of the state population (see Smith, 2014: 17).

As we will see in Chapter 2 and later chapters in the context of Germany's recovery after 1945, constitutional dangers for the fledgling Federal Republic were identified in 1964 by Ernst-Wolfgang Böckenförde, a political theorist and justice on the *Bundesverfassungsgericht* from 1983 to 1996. Böckenförde's concern was how the liberal democratic state could sustain itself in a secular age without the type of indoctrination of the citizenry which would make a mockery of the idea of 'liberal' democracy. Böckenförde's question was directed at the same problem addressed in different ways by Tocqueville and Arendt: how the bond between the emancipated citizen and the state could be maintained. Thomas Jefferson's concern, according to Arendt, was about how the bond between citizens and state could be maintained through civic participation and increasing the presence of the state in the lives of the citizens. By contrast, Böckenförde's concern—reflecting the modern difficulty of broad civic participation in large complex states—was about whether that same bond could be maintained in a secular age through liberal constitutional values alone. Böckenförde's critique was aimed at the 'objective value order' of the *BVerfG*—the Court which he would later sit on—a value system which he thought, first, sacrificed some "liberalness" in the interests of the "prescribed state ideology, the revival of the Aristotelian *polis* tradition", and, second, might be insufficiently cohesive to bind Germans to what was in 1964 a fragile liberal democracy (1991: 45–46). Böckenförde's view on the bonds of social cohesion, Arendt's interpretation of Jefferson, and Tocqueville's view on how despotism occurs are all pointing to the same general conclusion. That representative government, or the liberal secular state, as Böckenförde puts it, are at risk when citizens and the state become foreign to one another, either through a lack of participation in government or when the values and interpretations of each diverge.

The focus of the book's legal case studies is on citizens who have been excluded from the civic space either by local political majorities and their representatives, or excluded by the state in the interests of stability. The first scenario reflects the debasement of urban citizens' votes in the US prior to the 1970s due to malapportionment, and the second, the German electoral threshold cases in 2011 and 2014 related to European Parliament elections, where the votes of German citizens for parties garnering less than 5 percent of the vote are effectively nullified because the parties do not gain a seat in parliament. Although the legal cases are argued in the legal institutional space, the effects of the decisions have the potential to be felt in the civic space in terms of whether they improve electoral participation, the constitutional culture, the overall quality of the polity, and the relationship between the citizen and the state.

Beyond the issue of how specific court decisions in the legal institutional space affect democratic politics is the central question of how American and German constitutionalism in the guise of the US Supreme Court and *Bundesverfassungsgericht* shape and influence the important civic space? This question raises multiple difficulties, not least whether the creation and maintenance of a civic space by judges in the context of a liberal democracy is itself a non-sequitur. Does a judicially created 'civic space' constitute a negation of liberalism itself? Germany is, following Böckenförde's critique (1991: 45–46), the most obvious example of such a judicially created *polis*. As I examine in Chapters 2 and 5, the very idea that the *BVerfG* can create a *polis* stems principally from the dignity-oriented nature of German constitutionalism, the Court's objective value order, its wide-ranging powers under the Basic Law, and its control over public and private law.

The legal cases and the effects of American and German constitutionalism in their respective civic spaces reveal some paradoxical conclusions, but ones which nevertheless follow from the liberty-dignity dichotomy. Through its decisions in the reapportionment cases, *Baker v Carr* and *Reynolds v Sims*, the Supreme Court was able in the legal institutional space to successfully correct flaws in the political process to end malapportionment. This had a broadly positive effect on the civic space due to a rebalancing of political power from rural to urban areas. Moreover, the knowledge of urban and suburban voters that their votes were no longer being debased could only improve democratic participation. However, the positive long-term effects of the reapportionment cases in the civic space were limited. The Court's inability to deal with the issue of gerrymandering, to bridge differences between urban and rural areas, and to positively improve American democratic practices illustrates its limited reach in the civic space. By contrast, in the legal institutional space, the *BVerfG*'s interventions in the European Parliament electoral threshold cases have sometimes been methodologically suspect, counter-productive, and potentially a risk to stability at the EU level. Yet in the civic space the *BVerfG* has been more successful than the Supreme Court at shaping a strong democratic and constitutional culture (see, for example, Collings, 2015: xxxvi). Some possible reasons I offer for this success include the *BVerfG*'s objective value order, the high respect for law in Germany, the Court's powers under the Basic Law, and the positive effect on Germany's constitutional culture from the constitutional complaint mechanism.

The intervention by the Supreme Court in the reapportionment cases and its 'one person, one vote' decision can be explained through a changed understanding of the idea of equality within American constitutionalism, and of the groups and persons to whom equality applies. The Supreme Court's formalisation of this 'equality' narrative of constitutional development concealed increasing geographic and regional tensions between urban and rural areas, and northern and southern regions after the 1930s, which came to a head during the period of the Warren Court (1953–1969). Malapportionment was ostensibly a power battle between state legislatures dominated by rural lawmakers representing a declining number of voters, and urban politicians and civil society actors demanding more equal numerical representation between electoral districts. The conflict over malapportionment also reflected a clash of interests and values. On one side were the wealthy rural areas supported by big business interests that were vehemently opposed to the social reforms ushered in by the New Deal. On the other side were cities with underrepresented and growing populations, where unionisation created a political consensus demanding improved rights for employees (see Smith, 2014: 4–5).

While interventions in American representative democracy by the US Supreme Court have been generally episodic to deal with specific issues like malapportionment, those of the *BVerfG* have been as constant as they have been significant. The German judicial involvement in representative democracy represents a paradox. It is characteristic of the militant democracy at the heart of the constitutional order since 1949, but this *stretibare Demokratie* also marks the maturation of Germany's liberal constitutionalism that was extinguished in 1849, and which was again snuffed out with the demise of the Weimar Republic. The Court's intervention in the European Parliament electoral threshold cases thus represents an attempt to balance fundamental goals which lie at the heart of Germany's constitution, the Basic Law (*Grundgesetz*): upholding the architectonic principles of human dignity and the free democratic basic order and preventing the constitutional order from committing democratic suicide. The title of Chapter 1 with its main focus on constitutionalism is 'Taking Democracy Seriously'. In Germany, this has meant a reliance on the *BVerfG* and the defence mechanisms of the militant democracy to maintain stability. The Court's role as guardian of the Basic Law means that it must decide whether new political parties represent forces of renewal which can be safely integrated within the constitutional order as the Greens were in the 1980s, or whether they must be banned in the interests of stability as two political parties were in the 1950s; see *Socialist Reich Party Case* (1952) and *Communist Party Case* (1956).

Understanding how both countries have mediated this balance requires a focus on how the values of constitutionalism have developed through interpretation and social struggle in society, and the extent to which citizens and groups in both countries identify with these values, or only with what Böckenförde calls "internal bonding forces" (1991: 46), such as religion or nation. The emancipation of the individual from the state, which the French 'Declaration of the Rights of Man and of Citizens' of 1789 ushered in, was initially short-lived as the rise of nationalism in the nineteenth century provided a means to reintegrate individuals into the state. However, the relative decline of nation since 1945 raises the question of how representative democracy and liberal values can maintain the connection between citizen and state absent other bonding forces such as religion or nation. Individualism too has increasingly alienated people from one another, leaving societal cohesion and the liberal democratic constitutional state reliant on those values of human dignity, equality, and fundamental rights, reflected in the post-1945 human rights instruments and in the rulings of the Supreme Court from the late 1930s onwards. As Böckenförde notes:

> The recognition and diffusion of a spiritual-ethical pluralism in the wake of the realisation of the modern idea of liberty, as reflected in individual fundamental rights as rights of liberty, bears within it the tendency to erode religion as a homogeneity-conveying force. Under the banner of religious freedom, religion loses the general obligatoriness for the political order and social coexistence; within the context of society it becomes one offering without a normative status of its own.
>
> (Böckenförde, 2017: 334)

The 'international' dimension of human rights is highlighted in Chapter 1 because of its relevance to two recurring ideas which will be referred to in the following chapters. First is the question, unique to Germany, of whether the Federal Republic (FRG) after 1949 was simply a 'fair-weather' democracy, blessed with economic growth and an international Cold War context which provided stability, but which disguised the absence of a supportive framework of liberal values or democratic inclination in German society? Second is the question which, I contend, has implications for all liberal constitutional democracies, of whether the liberal democratic state, following Böckenförde, rests "on presuppositions that it cannot itself guarantee" (1991: 45)? The fact that the values being promulgated in the Basic Law and other new constitutions after 1945 also reflected the principles found in the Universal Declaration of Human Rights (UDHR) and European Convention on Human Rights (ECHR) was cause for optimism, but also caution. Was the dialectic of rights and human dignity at the international level simply a veneer which masked the innate fragility of liberal values *within* states?

Enquiry

The scholarly interest in democracy in the early years of the twenty-first century was palpable. Partly this was a response to the end of the Cold War and the burgeoning of democratic forces in Eastern Europe. Democracy was, as one writer put it, "the only game in town" (Scheppele, 2005: 1). This academic focus reflected the underlying reality that "there have been more governments that would be termed 'democratic' in place over the past two decades than at any point in human history" (Issacharoff, 2010: 965). Yet even as democracy appeared to enjoy a resurgence with the collapse of Soviet communism in Eastern Europe, concerns were raised about the illiberal nature (see Zakaria, 1997) of some of these emergent democracies.

Since World War II, *democracy* and *liberalism* in the guise of 'liberal democracy' became almost interchangeable as labels for a government committed to upholding the civil, individual, and political rights of its citizens. As Chantal Mouffe has cautioned, however, the liberal tradition "constituted by the rule of law, the defence of human rights and the respect of individual liberty", and the democratic tradition "whose main ideas are those of equality, identity between governing and governed, and popular sovereignty" represent two incompatible logics (2000: 2–5). The oppositional nature of the two concepts creates "a tension that can never be overcome but only negotiated in different ways" (Mouffe, 2000: 5). The increasingly clear disjuncture between the two concepts in recent years caused by growing illiberalism—illustrated by the current anti-liberal trajectory of Hungary and Poland, and the unpredictability of the Trump presidency—brings into sharp relief the role of the courts in maintaining rights when political channels either become corrupted or actively hostile to individual liberty and democracy itself. The ongoing threats to constitutionalism in Hungary and Poland from their ruling parties, countries where the roots of liberalism have been only recently planted, are a reminder of the challenge of entrenching liberal values against nationalist and other extremist forces. That Germany's post-war constitution served as a model for Hungary and Poland (see Kokott, 1999) is a further reason to assess whether the successful German model of constitutionalism—as manifested in fundamental rights, restrictions on state power, and a powerful constitutional court—remains effective at preventing a country from succumbing to anti-democratic or illiberal forces.

Even compared to perennial questions over the legitimacy of judicial review, which lay at the heart of Alexander Bickel's 'Countermajoritarian Difficulty' (1986), judicial involvement in the processes of representative democracy raises additional concerns about the justification for such interventions, confidence in democratic processes, and the substantive values that a constitutional order stands for. Constitutionalism adds a further layer of complexity to these questions of democratic legitimacy by seeking to ensure that political processes are conducted in conformity with duly enacted law and are compatible with the higher law values that a constitutional order recognises through its courts. To what extent do fundamental values of human dignity and equality eclipse the right of democratic participation, or justify the courts intervening in rules governing democratic or electoral processes, even to protect minority groups? And if participating in the democratic process is itself an intrinsic mark of human dignity, under what circumstances may that right be restricted in the interests of either stability or the survival of the state?

In the US, footnote four of the Supreme Court's decision in *United States v Carolene Products* (1938) captures a number of the book's central concerns including: voter exclusion from the political process, the susceptibility of democratic processes to oligarchical control, and the threat to opposition parties and minority interests from those in the majority. Footnote four signalled a process of more searching judicial review where legislation had excluded minority groups from participation in the political process. In the US malapportionment cases, voter exclusion through the debasement of voting strength was manifestly unconstitutional as a consequence of the failure of many state legislatures to reapportion for almost 60 years.

There are essentially two forms of malapportionment: *numerically* based, which is referred to as 'malapportionment' hereafter; the second is *geographically* based malapportionment, which is known as 'gerrymandering'. The main focus of Chapter 4 is on numerically based malapportionment, which was the primary problem in the United States prior to the 1960s reapportionment cases, including *Baker v* Carr (1962). This form of malapportionment occurs when there are significant variations in the populations of legislative districts in a state, resulting in some legislators representing many more constituents than other lawmakers. After numerically based malapportionment was declared unconstitutional by the Supreme Court in the 1960s, gerrymandering became more common. The latter is characterised by the attempt to gain electoral advantage for one party by the drawing of the boundaries of electoral districts to include certain preferred voters and exclude other voters.

Since the *BVerfG*'s establishment in 1951, it has seen its role as giving support to the parliamentary opposition in discharging their responsibilities and in support of the integration of parties like the Greens. A shift in the *BVerfG*'s jurisprudence can be observed from some aspects of the traditional stability-oriented 'militant democracy' stance of German constitutionalism to a more renewal-centric focus on electoral equality between voters and equal opportunity between parties. In *European Parliament II Case* (2011) and *European Parliament III Case* (2014), which will both be assessed in Chapter 6, the Court made a controversial decision to strike down the 5 percent hurdle for elections to the European Parliament.[8] The decisions were contentious because such electoral hurdles have been seen as an important tool in preventing the sort of legislative fragmentation that fatally weakened the Weimar Republic. The spectacle of a constitutional court taking steps to reduce voter inequality and widen the plurality of democratic choices available, against the wishes of, and to the consternation of, Germany's democratic legislature and government, is only one of the paradoxes of constitutionalism that these cases raise.

Institutions and the Civic Space

Constitutionalism in its post-1787 American and post-1949 German manifestations was fundamentally built around institutions. Even if human virtue was absent or corrupted, what mattered was that the institutions held firm (Waldron, 2016b: 6). Institutions form the bedrock of the American and German experiments in constitutional government. Both sets of institutions were intended to control the more venal instincts in human nature, whether they emanated from the rulers or the people. With the failed liberal legacies of the Weimar Republic (1918–1933) and the constitution of 1849 offering stark warnings from the past, Germany's institutions after 1949 had to contain the continuing political dangers emanating from National Socialism.

Jeremy Waldron, for one, thinks institutions matter a great deal for political theorists and for democracy.

> We need institutions to frame the hard choices and decision-making that our disagreements give rise to. And we need to find ways of respecting one another in our politics in the environment that those institutions provide.
> (Waldron, 2016b: 7)

Moreover, institutions are not simply frameworks for argument, or restraints on a tyrannical government or corrupt individuals; they can also help deliver positive goods. Even if principles such as justice, liberty, security, and equality remain our main preoccupation, Waldron adds, we must understand the institutions, (or "mechanisms"), through which these 'ideals', as he calls them, are pursued (2016b: 6).

Waldron's emphasis on the importance of institutions is reasonable. This book adopts an analytical-historical approach that assesses American and German constitutionalism through three understandings of institutions: as a restraint on government and the people; as a framework for ongoing deliberation among people of different views; and as a mechanism through which the state may attempt to advance certain values including justice, liberty, security, and equality.

However, institutions are not enough.

The presence of institutions does not tell us what is happening in the civic space, or reveal the health of the relationship between a people and their constitutional government; nor do institutions sufficiently explain why some constitutions succeed and others fail. In the context of the central enquiry, a concentration on institutions alone does not explain the value systems, ways of life, forms of identity and "internal bonding forces" (Böckenförde, 1991: 46) in the civic space, and the ways in which they may reinforce or undermine the enunciation of constitutional values in the legal institutional space. Put differently, an institutions-centric view of constitutionalism presents a dangerously incomplete picture if it neglects the crucial civic space in which citizens participate in their democracy, or challenge it. The increased utilisation of constitutional mechanisms and constitutional amendments by authoritarian and semi-authoritarian governments in recent years to undermine both democratic processes and protections on individual rights illustrate the problem of relying on institutions alone (see, for example, Landau, 2013). As Mark Tushnet argues, while the requirements of constitutionalism can be met by a variety of institutional designs, what matters is "political support for constitutionalism itself" (2007: 1488).

A number of other writers have also highlighted the importance of democratic practice, political culture, and civil society in supporting formal political institutions. In his study of 22 democracies that have remained steadily democratic since at least 1950, Robert Dahl noted that the key factors which seem to favour democratic stability include "effective control by elected leaders over the military and police, a political culture supportive of democratic beliefs, and a relatively well functioning economic order" (2003: 94). If some conditions in a country are favourable to democracy while some are unfavourable, then Dahl argues that the specific features of constitutional institutions could tip the balance one way or the other, "toward democratic stability or democratic breakdown" (2003: 95–96). Dahl's study indicates that "no constitutional system can preserve democracy in a country where these and other favourable conditions are absent" (2003: 95). In other words, institutions may sometimes tip the balance "where the underlying conditions make democracy rather chancy" (Dahl, 2003: 95), but they are only part of the picture.

With Dahl's somewhat bleak take duly noted, it would seem that constitutionalism will often have its work cut out in certain countries at certain times. Dahl's emphasis on a "political culture supportive of democratic beliefs" highlights the need for an analytical approach that recognises the importance of both the civic space, and legal institutional space. This is the approach that will be adopted in the succeeding chapters.

One writer who addressed the need for a structure within which political conversations and participation could take place is Hannah Arendt. As Waldron notes, Arendt "invokes the imagery of construction outside the house: fences and boundary walls, which make politics possible by securing a space for the public realm" (2016a: 293). Waldron emphasises Arendt's idea of *isonomy*—the "capacity of positive laws to make people equal in the political realm, even if they are in other respects different and unequal" (2016a: 299). This idea of law creating a common language within which citizens can relate to one another as equals is one I will return to in the following chapters. Arendt's focus on *persona* (or the role of law in the act of citizenship) seems particularly relevant for both the United States and Germany, although in different ways. The influence of law has been central to the institutional development of both countries and, to a greater or lesser degree, to their national narratives.

The term 'civic space' used throughout the book refers to the place where citizens participate in politics and their democracy by voting, or where they uphold or contest the values of their society through discourse and argument. For a civic space to exist, I argue that it must be based, as Arendt observed, on an "exchange of opinion between equals" (1973: 93). Law occupies an important place in the book that I have called the 'legal institutional space', which is an important part of constitutionalism. It is primarily the courtroom, but also wherever the influence and value of law and the constitutional interpretations of the respective courts are accepted. Thus, the law may be, in Böckenfördean terms, an internal bonding force of civic and societal cohesion, or a common language within which citizens can regard one another as equals. John Finn's contrast between the 'Civic' and 'Juridic' constitutions is also a useful model for thinking about how the interplay and tension between legal and societal interpretations of constitutional meaning can lead to a constant contestation and renegotiation of constitutional identity (see 2014: 2–3). Here, I argue that debate and discussion over the meaning of law can provide a framework and nomenclature which helps citizens see themselves as embodying and sharing certain values.

Although written about England in the 1940s, George Orwell's description of constitutionalism and law as cultural and social artefacts, and a language of cohesion, is exactly how I see the potential for the legal institutional space to extend into the civic space.

> Here one comes upon an all-important English trait: the respect for constitutionalism and legality, the belief in 'the law' as something above the State and above the individual. … Everyone takes it for granted that the law, such as it is, will be respected, and feels a sense of outrage when it is not. Remarks like "They can't run me in; I haven't done anything wrong", or "They can't do that; it's against the law", are part of the atmosphere of England. … Everyone believes in his heart that the law can be, ought to be, and, on the whole, will be impartially administered. The totalitarian idea that there is no such thing as law, there is only power, has never taken root.
>
> (Orwell and Davison, 1986: 397)

This understanding of the structural, cultural, and societal influence of law, and the potential consequences when it is corrupted to serve particular ends reflects both McIlwain's view (2005: 32) and also Justice Felix Frankfurter's observation about Justice Robert Jackson's role in prosecuting the Nazi leadership at Nuremberg.

> Nuremberg, I believe, had a profound influence on his endeavour to understand the human situation. An essentially good-natured, an even innocently unsophisticated temperament, was there made to realise how ultimately fragile the forces of reason are and how precious the safeguards of law so painstakingly built up in the course of centuries.
>
> (Frankfurter, 1955: 437)

Those safeguards, echoing Orwell, are those deeply embedded norms within society about the actions and behaviour that law and constitutionalism require of institutions and individuals. Germany's post-war founders drew similar conclusions to Jackson regarding the importance of law to the country's political and moral rehabilitation. As will be shown in Chapter 5, law in the Federal Republic of Germany after 1949 was no longer a means to an end as it was during the Nazi period, but became the basis of the inter-relationship between state and society. Without acceptance of this sense of law and constitutionalism in the civic space, the influence of the US Supreme Court and the *Bundesverfassungsgericht* remains largely institutional and effectively limited to the courtroom. Court decisions still have the force of law and must be obeyed, but the courts' potential to improve the processes and values of democratic politics and support the relationship between citizen and state is greatly reduced.

One apparent problem in the US currently is that there no longer seems to be any civic (or civil) language that is able to fill the gap that the decline of civic, religious, and associational activity has left. Richard Bellamy's argument that democracy "embodies and upholds" the values of "constitutionalism, rights [and] the rule of law" (2007: 260) provides an important framework for conceptualising what I see as a key question which orients the distinction between America's 'liberty'-oriented constitutionalism, and Germany's 'dignity'-infused model. This is the question of whether democratic ideas and practice provide the conditions for rights and the rule of law to emerge, or the reverse: whether fundamental rights and the rule of law are the *sine qua non* for the emergence of liberal democracy? The latter view is embodied in the principles and practice of German constitutionalism since 1949.

Some of the roots of this understanding lie in the Kant-infused development of the *Rechtsstaat* in the early nineteenth century. The translations 'rule of law' state or the 'law-governed state' do not adequately reflect the original idea of the *Rechtsstaat* as a "state governed by the law of reason" which

> insisted on the freedom, equality, and autonomy of each individual within the framework of a unified legal order defined by legislation and administered by independent courts of law.
>
> (Kommers and Miller, 2012: 48)

As will be addressed in Chapters 5 and 6, after 1949, this older focus on the *Rechtsstaat* was fused with a set of constitutional values derived from "the dialectic between … liberal, socialist, and Christian natural-law traditions" (Kommers and Miller, 2012: 70). Moreover, the older emphasis on law and natural rights as a precondition for democracy found fertile ground in the widely held German cultural view that politics was "a dirty business" and law a "clean one" (Schlink, 1994: 210–211).

In the US by contrast, the free space that the constitutionalism of liberty initially provided opened up boundless possibilities for the development of various forms of self-government and various value systems, including malignant ones like slavery. The fencing off of government which created this zone of liberty created a profound divergence between what Wolin saw as the "sophisticated theory of a Constitution" represented by *The Federalist Papers*, and the "flourishing political cultures and practices" represented by the colonial and revolutionary history of the several states (1989: 86–87).

There is, though, an important difference between the US and Germany which takes us back to Waldron's point about how institutions can be a means to pursue certain "ideals". American constitutional institutions were fundamentally conditioned by the idea of restraining the state—what I call 'liberty' constitutionalism—and thus leaving a zone of freedom for the citizen. By contrast, the highly normative 'dignity' constitutionalism of Germany's Basic Law and its institutions sought to establish, as the *BVerfG* noted in its *Investment Aid Case* judgment, a relationship between the individual and their community based on "a person's dependence on and commitment to the community, without infringing upon a person's individual value" (1954). In other words, American constitutionalism sought to fence off the institutional space (i.e. government) from the civic space, whereas German constitutionalism has sought to reunite them. This understanding shapes the context within which judicial interventions in representative democracy occur, and the extent to which the respective 'constitutionalisms' are able to influence the civic space.

Situating the Book

Historical institutionalism provides a useful way of conceptualising how constitutionalism can be understood as part of a broader system of norms and understandings of what constitutes legitimate authority. Judges follow the law because "it persuades as an authoritative conceptual system in which they as officeholders are bound to operate" (O'Neill, 2009: 291). This view is rooted in the historical institutionalist tenet that "institutions, especially government institutions, are defined by a distinctive mission or responsibility that is tied to a conception of legitimate authority" (O'Neill, 2009: 292). According to this view, the roles of political and legal institutions in society, and judicial understandings of those roles, are shaped by wider normative understandings within a community regarding their purpose and legitimacy. The permissible scope of the judicial role and the choices available to judges are therefore circumscribed by the norms that the political community has chosen to instil in its institutions over time.

Due to the inevitable constraints inherent in any comparative analysis it is important at the outset to highlight the scope and aims of the book. The book seeks to address the problem of how a state can establish the conditions for liberal values to endure without imposing them on its citizens, and thereby negating liberalism itself. In doing so, my aim is to illustrate how an analysis drawn from history, political theory, law, and constitutionalism can help us better understand the complex relationship between democracy, liberalism, and the courts, and the constitutional choices of societies over extended periods of time. The book does not substantively address the question of the legitimacy of judicial review of legislation (see, for example, Waldron, 2006; Bellamy, 2007), nor does it seek to retrace the well-trodden debates between procedurally oriented constitutionalism (see Ely, 1980) and substantive constitutionalism (see Dworkin, 1985, 1999). Rather, the aim is to explain the role of the courts in the democratic processes of Germany and the United States, how that role has assisted or, sometimes, hindered the exercise of democratic rights, and, ultimately, how it has shaped the relationship between citizen and state. Although the book does not examine the legitimacy of judicial review, it does engage with Bickel's concept of the 'countermajoritarian difficulty'. This is to illustrate how that mid-twentieth-century American debate on the democratic legitimacy of judicial review fits into the historic development of constitutionalism, how the balance between majority rule and individual rights has changed, and what that shift portends for the ability of individuals within liberal democratic states to coalesce around a common set of norms. Further, the extreme salience of the countermajoritarian difficulty within American constitutional scholarship for decades offers a useful conceptual device for the comparative analysis since questions about the legitimacy of judicial review are almost entirely absent from German scholarship due to the clarity of the judicial role within German constitutionalism.

Although the book's approach is predominantly analytical and historical, there are some normative difficulties that must be addressed. In arguing that the strength of the relationship between citizen and state also depends on whether each court can influence the civic space and inculcate the values of the respective constitutional orders in the political culture, judgments must inevitably be made in terms of whether the influence of these prominent courts has been positive or negative. Ostensibly, such an evaluation might appear to be normative if it was based on some notion of 'the good'. Stephen Elkin argues that "political institutions are educative and thus have an ethical dimension" (1993: 118). Although an ethical evaluation of institutions is not a concern of the present enquiry, such a possibility nevertheless raises the question of whether the legal institutional space and the civic space have a normative function or disposition that is intrinsic to them? The clear answer offered here is that they do not. While institutions may be designed to better achieve certain normative values as, indeed, those established by Germany's Basic Law *were*, the value orientation of institutions is, I contend, principally based on the actions of those operating within them. If the policies flowing from state institutions are flawed it is predominantly because the people inside them are flawed. This should not come as a surprise.

The American and German constitutions were both designed with a pessimistic view of human nature in mind (see, for example, *Federalist 51* by Madison). Passion will often prevail over reason, interests over principles, and, as Finn notes, a civic constitutional project will "not always showcase our best constitutional selves" (2014: 224). What perhaps matters most is a set of constitutional institutions that are capable of organic improvement in response to social struggle and the demands of citizens. As Judith Shklar suggested, one redeeming feature of America's "tragically flawed institutions" was that they were at least capable of becoming more democratic and liberal over time (1991: 4, 15).

A key focus of the book's approach is understanding constitutionalism as a process of historical development, within which emancipatory advances take place. As Stanley Katz puts it, "true constitutionalism … is the product of political struggle within particular societies, not a set of universal values or prescribable institutions" (2007). Constitutionalism is a legal and a political idea; both will be brought forth in the chapters ahead through an analysis based on political theory, but which also assesses the historical context within which each of these important courts developed. Overall, the analysis seeks to understand how a changing emphasis on stability or renewal within American or German constitutionalism can affect interactions between the respective courts and litigants in cases, and more broadly how constitutional values can be reinforced or undermined by more traditional value systems and forms of identity in the civic space and society.

One reason, it is suggested, that the Supreme Court has not been able to positively influence all of the multiple civic spaces in a continent-sized country such as the US is the liberty-centric nature of American constitutionalism with its hyper-individualism and its deep ambivalence towards government. Thus, the predominant value orientation operating within a given American civic space at any time is likely to be determined as much, if not more, by the value orientations of those citizens and civil society actors who are active in that civic space. As I will illustrate in Chapter 4, it was the activities and values of civil society actors such as the League of Women Voters in the United States that reached across from the civic space into the legal institutional space and precipitated the litigation that resulted in malapportionment being declared unconstitutional. A further aspect of the analysis in Chapter 6 involves assessing the decisions of the *BVerfG* in the European Parliament (EP) electoral threshold cases against the stability-oriented account of German constitutionalism that I will set out in Chapter 5. Such an assessment inevitably involves an evaluative judgment of those EP decisions, particularly given the normative orientation of German constitutionalism (see, for example, Kommers and Miller, 2012: 45). The book posits that the *BVerfG*'s normative exuberance in advancing one value in the Basic Law, equality, is in tension with the Court's prior emphasis on stability.

In Germany, the fundamental respect for law in German society, the principle of the *Rechtsstaat* from the early nineteenth century, and the unfulfilled liberal principles of the country's 1849 constitution which militarism had crushed for almost a century, all contributed to the strong resurgence of constitutionalism after 1949. Additionally, and to a far greater extent than the US, the values of German constitutionalism were influenced by comparable principles emerging from the post-1945 rights instruments and regimes, particularly the European Convention on Human Rights (ECHR). The founders of the Federal Republic who established the Basic Law in 1949 were especially concerned with binding the country to international institutions. This was partly because they shared the values of these instruments and wanted Germany to rejoin the community of nations, sentiment that is clearly expressed in the Basic Law's preamble. However, a secondary motive behind binding Germany to the Western alliance, the ECHR, and the emerging European community was also to reinforce the country's fragile democratic institutions (see Moravcsik, 2000).

The analysis of the German Constitutional Court, *the BVerfG*, has intentionally relied on criticisms made within Germany, since to anyone outside Germany the placing of so much trust in a court might seem problematic. However, the Court has undoubtedly worked for Germany. Although the Court is *sui generis* in terms of its power over the German political and legal system, the flaws in constitutional democracy that it was created to counter have existed from classical times to the present day, but at no point in human history have those flaws been as badly exposed, and with such an ultimately heavy human cost, as in the Weimar Republic.

Why the United States and Germany?

Issacharoff notes that there is "a recurring pattern through which courts in many different constitutional regimes have had to confront surprisingly similar issues, regardless of the precise constitutional regime at play" (2010: 963). While rejecting any claim of universal applicability, important lessons can be drawn from the United States and Germany given that both countries' constitutions have acted as models for constitution formation in scores of states around the world. The cases studies are drawn from the period during which the courts have existed in parallel: from 1951, when the *Bundesverfassungsgericht* was established, to the present day. Although the case studies will be drawn from this period, the analysis of the development of American and German constitutionalism will cover the period from the late eighteenth century to today. The focus on the period beginning in 1951 is not merely for reasons of temporal convenience. As Lietzmann notes,

> the orientation of judicial activities on topics such as freedom of speech and assembly, the dignity of men and women, and the putative values of the constitution, in short, the manifestation of the traditional civil-democratic rhetoric, is formative for both courts.
>
> (Lietzmann, 2002: 94)

The cases examined are instances where the courts have responded to a demand for relief from civil society groups, political actors, and individual voters. In *Baker v Carr* and the other reapportionment cases, legal action was preceded by years of demands from civil society and the federal government's executive branch for action by state legislatures to end the malapportionment. No actions were forthcoming since legislators elected by a minority of the population were reluctant to reapportion themselves out of employment. In the German cases, *EPII* (2011) and *EPIII* (2014), a challenge was made to the 5 percent hurdle for electoral success for EU elections, which came through a combination of constitutional complaints from German citizens (*Verfassungsbeschwerden*) and complaints made by organs of the state (*Organstreitverfahren*). These cases, which were brought by individual voters and smaller political parties, provide a useful illustration of the Court's influence over the German political system, but equally highlight the central themes of the book: of voter exclusion, and how constitutionalism mitigates the dangers to the system of either too much of the wrong participation, or not enough of the right kind.

Outline of the Book

From here, then, the book will proceed as follows. In Chapter 1, I will begin by establishing some parameters for understanding American and German constitutionalism as being broadly rooted in the principles of liberty and dignity, respectively. The development of a predominantly normative constitutionalism after 1945 grounded in human rights norms and the individual in law will be considered, particularly with respect to Germany where the international context was more keenly felt than the US Although post-1945 constitutionalism reinforced the idea of the rise of the individual, it also contributed to a further weakening of the homogenising bonds between citizen and state which are an important part of this enquiry.

The question of civil association, civic participation, and the values of the civic space will be considered in Chapter 2. Do political activities and more traditional forms of association and identity in the civic space serve to reinforce or undermine constitutional values, and the relationship between citizens and their state? Through particular reference to the writing of Ernst-Wolfgang Böckenförde, the chapter addresses whether liberal constitutional values such as human dignity and fundamental rights are sufficiently potent to hold a political community together and fashion an affinity between citizens and their state without "internal bonding forces" (Böckenförde, 1991) or traditional forms of identity. Differences in interpretation between institutions and civil society are unproblematic provided the majority still obeys the interpretations of the courts. The problem for a state is when its values and institutions are challenged by parts of its population, as during the Weimar Republic.

Chapter 3 considers the legal institutional context within which constitutional values have been interpreted by the Supreme Court. The chapter then assesses the problematic concept of majoritarianism in a country like the United States with various local and regional majorities, whose views can often differ starkly from national majority opinion, as the Civil War and segregation illustrate. Madison's and Jefferson's fears about the threats arising from 'local majorities' in state legislatures illustrated the divide in the United States between constitutional value systems and those which threatened the rule of law. Ultimately, it is the very flexibility in the Constitution which provides for the possibility of renewal, but which can also prompt such intense arguments over constitutional meaning. Through an assessment of the Court's complex relationship with national majoritarian politics we can observe its shifting jurisprudence in incorporating the Bill of Rights, and better understand the significance of footnote four of *US v Carolene Products* (1938) in protecting political processes and minority groups. The outcome of these developments was a seismic change between the late 1930s and 1960s in the idea of equality and an expansion of the groups and individuals to whom the principle of equality applied.

In Chapter 4, the book addresses the reapportionment cases that Chief Justice Earl Warren regarded as the most important during his time on the Supreme

Court. It was the concerted political action of civil society actors for two decades in the civic space which was instrumental in getting *Baker v Carr* heard in the Supreme Court, the only place where a remedy to malapportionment could be secured. In its reapportionment decisions the Court fulfilled the principles embodied in footnote four, and by doing so unblocked the stoppages in the democratic process, illustrating what Ely saw as the Court's main purpose (1980: 117). As significant as the decisions were at the time, and remain in hindsight, they were, though, unable to correct the fundamental value differences between urban and rural areas in the civic space which caused malapportionment.

The successful emergence of German constitutionalism and the country's representative democracy depended greatly on the high regard for law within German society. This deep respect for law boosted the standing of the *BVerfG*, allowing it to consolidate its position as guardian of the Basic Law and German democracy. Chapter 5 will assess the theoretical, historical, and jurisprudential supports for stability and renewal within the Basic Law, with a particular focus on how the 'value of law' was important in establishing the *BVerfG*'s legitimacy in 1951. This was at a time when Germans had little faith in political institutions, a sentiment which was reciprocated in the Federal Republic's constitutional institutions which were designed to counter what many of the country's post-war founders perceived to be the anti-democratic and illiberal inclinations of the German people.

Chapter 6 assesses the relationship between German representative democracy and the German people as it is shaped by the *BVerfG*. I will assess how the Court has involved itself in Germany's political and electoral processes, often on behalf of opposition groups and smaller political parties. In the European Parliament electoral threshold cases, the Court controversially struck down the long-standing 5 percent hurdle that parties have to clear to gain a seat. Overall, the chapter takes a more critical look at the role of the *BVerfG* in its interventions in these cases, even as the Court's standing and respect among the German people remains unequalled by any other institution in the German state.

Germany's post-1949 dignity-oriented constitutionalism has been able to influence the civic space, and the mechanisms by which majority opinion is formed, to create a mature liberal democracy. By contrast, the more liberty-centric emphasis of American constitutionalism has allowed scope for a range of variations in majority sentiment to emerge. One consequence of this constitutional flexibility has been that although the conditions which sustain liberal democracy have not been actively nurtured as they were in Germany, the ability of individuals in the US to live their lives within a broad tableau of constitutional meaning has, thus far, prevented either democratic or constitutional collapse. Understanding how the 'liberty' and 'dignity' orientations of American and German constitutionalism have shaped the relationship between citizens and their democratic processes is the question to which we now turn.

Notes

1 Adams wrote the comment in his copy of Mary Wollstonecraft's book of 1795 'An Historical and Moral View of the Origin and Progress of the French Revolution'.
2 The men of the American Revolution, wrote Arendt, "knew that the public realm in a republic was constituted by an exchange of opinion between equals, and that this realm would simply disappear the very moment an exchange became superfluous because all equals happened to be of the same opinion" (1973: 93).
3 Drawn from 'the Messenger Lectures', given by McIlwain at Cornell in 1938–1939.
4 The Reconstruction amendments after the Civil War, and the Seventeenth and Nineteenth Amendments are some examples (see also Bellamy, 2007: 135). The Supreme Court has used the 'maturing society' phrasing in its Eighth Amendment jurisprudence—see *Trop v Dulles* (1958) and *Rhodes v Chapman* (1981), and the analysis in Chapter 3.
5 See also (Huntington, 1981: 1–4) on the gap between principles and practice, ideals and reality, in American politics.
6 This question resonates with Gitta Sereny's observation about Germany in Chapter 2 (see 2000: 85).
7 In the election of November 1932, the National Socialists (NSDAP) won 33.9 percent of the vote, and in the March 1933 election following the Reichstag fire and a campaign of terror against their opponents, they only managed to get 43.9 percent of the vote.
8 The 2014 decision struck down the 3 percent threshold that the *Bundestag* had passed in response to the 2011 decision.

References

United States v Carolene Products Company, 304 US 144, 1938
Socialist Reich Party Case, 2 BVerfGE 1, 1952
Investment Aid I Case, 4 BVerfGE 7, 1954
Communist Party Case, 5 BVerfGE, 1956
Trop v Dulles, 356 US 86, 1958
Baker v Carr, 396 US 186, 1962
Rhodes v Chapman, 452 US 337, 1981
European Parliament II Case 2 BVC 4/10, 2011
European Parliament III Case 2 BvE 2/13, 2014

Arendt, H., *On Revolution* (Harmondsworth: Penguin, 1973).
Bellamy, R., *Political Constitutionalism: A Republican Defence of The Constitutionality of Democracy* (Cambridge: Cambridge University Press, 2007).
Bickel, A. M., *The Least Dangerous Branch: The Supreme Court at the Bar of Politics*. 2nd edn (New Haven: Yale University Press, 1986).
Bishin, W. R., "Judicial Review in Democratic Theory", *Southern California Law Review*, 50 (1977), 1099.
Böckenförde, E. W., "The Rise of the State as a Process of Secularisation", in *State, Society, and Liberty: Studies in Political Theory and Constitutional Law* (New York: Berg Pub Ltd, 1991).
Böckenförde, E. W., *Constitutional and Political Theory: Selected Writings*. Vol. 1 (Oxford: Oxford University Press, 2017).
Brennan Jr, W. J., "The Constitution of the United States: Contemporary Ratification", in *Interpreting the Constitution: The Debate over Original Intent*, ed. by Jack N. Rakove (Boston, MA: Northeastern University Press, 1990).

Brenner, M., "The Constitutional Framework of Democratic Representation", in *Constitutionalism, Universalism and Democracy: A Comparative Analysis*, ed. by Christian Starck (Baden-Baden: Nomos-Verlag-Ges., 1999).

Collings, J., *Democracy's Guardians: A History of the German Federal Constitutional Court, 1951–2001* (Oxford: Oxford University Press, 2015).

Dahl, R. A., *How Democratic is the American Constitution?* 2nd edn (New Haven, CT: Yale University Press, 2003).

Dworkin, R., *A Matter of Principle* (Cambridge, MA: Harvard University Press, 1985).

Dworkin, R., *Freedom's Law: The Moral Reading of the American Constitution* (Oxford: Oxford University Press, 1999).

Eberle, E. J., *Dignity and Liberty: Constitutional Visions in Germany and the United States* (Westport, CT: Praeger, 2002).

Elkin, S. L., "Constitutionalism's Successor", in *A New Constitutionalism: Designing Political Institutions for a Good Society*, ed. by Stephen L. Elkin and Karol Edward Soltan (Chicago: University of Chicago Press, 1993).

Ely, J. H., *Democracy and Distrust: A Theory of Judicial Review* (Cambridge: Harvard University Press, 1980).

Finn, J. E., *Peopling the Constitution* (Lawrence: University Press of Kansas, 2014).

Frankfurter, F., "Foreword: Robert H. Jackson", *Columbia Law Review*, 55(4) (1955), 435–437.

Friedrich, C. J., *Limited Government: A Comparison* (Englewood Cliffs, NJ: Prentice-Hall, 1974).

Griffin, S. M., "Constituent Power and Constitutional Change in American Constitutionalism", in *The Paradox of Constitutionalism: Constituent Power and Constitutional Form*, ed. by Martin Loughlin and Neil Walker (Oxford: Oxford University Press, 2007).

Huntington, S. P., *American Politics: The Promise of Disharmony* (Cambridge, MA: Harvard University Press, 1981).

Issacharoff, S., "Constitutional Courts and Democratic Hedging", *Georgetown Law Journal*, 99 (2010), 961.

Katz, S. "Who's Afraid of Senator Byrd? The Constitution and the Uses of American History" (2007), available at: www.princeton.edu/~snkatz/papers/snkatzConstitution.pdf [last accessed 15 May 2014].

Kautz, S., "Introduction", in *The Supreme Court and the Idea of Constitutionalism*, ed. by Steven Kautz, Arthur Melzer, Jerry Weinberger, and M. Richard Zinman (Philadelphia: University of Pennsylvania Press, 2011).

Kay, R. S., "American Constitutionalism", in *Constitutionalism: Philosophical Foundations*, ed. by Lawrence A. Alexander (Cambridge: Cambridge University Press, 1998).

Kokott, J., "From Reception and Transplantation to Convergence of Constitutional Models in the Age of Globalization—With Special Reference to the German Basic Law", in *Constitutionalism, Universalism and Democracy: A Comparative Analysis*, ed. by Christian Starck (Baden-Baden: Nomos-Verlag-Ges, 1999).

Kommers, D. P. and R. A. Miller, *The Constitutional Jurisprudence of the Federal Republic of Germany*. 3rd edn (Durham, NC: Duke University Press, 2012).

Koopmans, T., *Courts and Political Institutions: A Comparative View* (Cambridge: Cambridge University Press, 2003).

Landau, D., "Abusive Constitutionalism", *UC Davis Law Review*, 47 (2013), 189.

Lietzmann, H., "Constitutional Courts in Changing Political Systems", in *Constitutional Courts in Comparison: The US Supreme Court and the German Federal Constitutional Court*, ed. by Ralf Rogowski and Thomas Gawron (New York: Berghahn Books, 2002).

Madison, J., "Federalist Number 51", in *The Federalist Papers*, ed. by Isaac Kramnick (Harmondsworth: Penguin, 1987).

McIlwain, C. H., *Constitutionalism: Ancient and Modern* (Clark, NJ: The Lawbook Exchange, 2005).

Moravcsik, A., "The Origins of Human Rights Regimes: Democratic Delegation in Postwar Europe", *International Organization*, 54(02) (2000), 217–252.

Mouffe, C., *The Democratic Paradox* (London: Verso, 2000).

O'Neill, J., "Carl J. Friedrich's Legacy: Understanding Constitutionalism as a Political System", *European Legacy*, 14(3) (2009), 283–300.

Orwell, G. and P. H. Davison, *The Complete Works of George Orwell*. Vol. 12 (London: Secker & Warburg, 1986).

Sager, L., "The Domain of Constitutional Justice", in *Constitutionalism: Philosophical Foundations*, ed. by Lawrence A. Alexander (Cambridge: Cambridge University Press, 1998).

Scheppele, K. L., "Democracy by Judiciary. Or, Why Courts Can be More Democratic Than Parliaments", in *Rethinking the Rule of Law After Communism*, ed. by Adam Czarnota, Martin Krygier, and Wojciech Sadurski (Central European University Press, 2005).

Schlink, B., "German Constitutional Culture in Transition", in *Constitutionalism, Identity, Difference, and Legitimacy: Theoretical Perspectives*, ed. by Michel Rosenfeld (Durham, NC: Duke University Press, 1994).

Sereny, G., *The German Trauma: Experiences and Reflections, 1938–2001* (London: Penguin, 2000).

Shklar, J. N., "Redeeming American Political Theory", *American Political Science Review*, 85(1) (1991), 3–15.

Smith, J. D., *On Democracy's Doorstep: The Inside Story of How the Supreme Court Brought "One Person, One Vote" to the United States* (New York: Hill and Wang, 2014).

Tushnet, M., "Some Skepticism About Normative Constitutional Advice", *William and Mary Law Review*, 49 (2007), 1473.

Waldron, J., "The Core of the Case Against Judicial Review", *The Yale Law Journal* (2006), 1346–1406.

Waldron, J., "The Constitutional Politics of Hannah Arendt", in *Political Political Theory: Essays on Institutions* (Cambridge: MA: Harvard University Press, 2016a).

Waldron, J., "Political Political Theory", in *Political Political Theory: Essays on Institutions* (Cambridge: MA: Harvard University Press, 2016b).

Wollstonecraft, M., *An Historical and Moral View of the Origin and Progress of the French Revolution: And the Effect it Has Produced in Europe. By Mary Wollstonecraft. Volume the First* (J. Johnson, 1795).

Wolin, S. S., *The Presence of the Past: Essays on the State and the Constitution* (Baltimore, MD: Johns Hopkins University Press, 1989).

Zakaria, F., "The Rise of Illiberal Democracy", *Foreign Affairs*, 76(6) (1997), 22–43.

1 Taking Democracy Seriously

> What has changed since the Second World War is the acceptance that there is an overriding body of legal principle which limits the powers of the sovereign state; and that, in the German perspective, is very fundamental precisely because they saw what could be done with an unscrupulous government, using conventional legislative methods. So the idea of an overriding and encircling body of 'law' is something which has developed and constitutionalism is part of it.
>
> (Judge David Edward,[1] interview with author, October 2013)

> It ought not to be regarded as slavery to live according to the constitution, but rather as self-preservation.
>
> (Aristotle, *The Politics*, Bk V. ix)

The Waldronian focus on constitutional institutions considered in the introduction is an important aspect of constitutionalism. However, a concentration on constitutional mechanisms alone can neglect important aspects of the electoral politics of the United States and Germany. In terms of numerical malapportionment in the 1960s, what happens when the spirit and letter of constitutional rules and democratic processes are deliberately ignored by self-serving politicians, and that malfeasance is then compounded due to non-enforcement of those rules by the federal courts? What happens when, as in 1930s Germany, a political party is elected democratically according to the constitutional rules, but then uses those same constitutional institutions to dismantle democracy and the rule of law, leaving only the empty edifice of positive law to justify state power?

These questions highlight some of the historical reasons why constitutionalism matters, but there is also a more functional reason for constitutionalism. It provides a structure and framework for normal politics to unfold. Constitutionalism is intended to remove from the table those issues which might be a source of violence, such as occurred in previous centuries, so that the main topic of politics becomes competition over differing interests (Kautz, 2011: 2). This logic of continuity and stability from one generation to another is one that made sense to the ancient Greeks. Stephen Holmes notes that most early-modern theorists of politics, Rousseau included, recognised that the great achievements of the ancient world would have been impossible had "one generation been unwilling or unable to create a difficult-to-change political framework within which subsequent generations could predictably live" (Holmes, 1995: 148). "To live according to the constitution", as Aristotle noted, should be regarded not as "slavery", but as "self-preservation" (Bk V. ix). Indeed, the very essence of constitutionalism, this book argues, is that the trade-offs and limitations intrinsic to it must be understood and accepted by citizens, as Aristotle implies.

This 'security' or 'survival' element of constitutionalism highlights its complex role in mediating between the state's function of ensuring civil peace and the role of politics to allow different groups and factions to pursue certain interests and, when they form a majority, to enact particular policies without injuring the rights of those in the minority or in opposition. The understanding of where an 'unrestrained' politics could lead was as clear to the post-1945 German founders and to the American constitutional framers as it had been to Aristotle. Diagnosing the problems of an unrestrained American majoritarian politics in 1787, Madison wrote in *Federalist 10* that:

> Complaints are everywhere heard from our most considerate and virtuous citizens … that our governments are too unstable, that the public good is disregarded in the conflicts of rival parties, and that measures are too often decided, not according to the rules of justice and the rights of the minor party, but by the superior force of an interested and overbearing majority.
>
> (Madison, *Federalist 10*, 1987a: 123)

At the core of Madison's fear is that an unrestrained politics can lead to extremes and enmities that can imperil the rights, interests, and liberty of individuals in a society. Without such restraints, Madison observed that

> A zeal for different opinions concerning religion, concerning government, and many other points, as well of speculation as of practice; an attachment to different leaders ambitiously contending for pre-eminence and power; or to persons of other descriptions whose fortunes have been interesting to the human passions, have, in turn, divided mankind into parties, inflamed them with mutual animosity, and rendered them much more disposed to vex and oppress each other than to co-operate for their common good. So strong is this propensity of mankind to fall into mutual animosities, that where no substantial occasion presents itself, the most frivolous and fanciful distinctions have been sufficient to kindle their unfriendly passions and excite their most violent conflicts.
>
> (Madison, *Federalist 10*, 1987a: 124)

It is hard to read Madison's warning about unrestrained politics without recalling Carl Schmitt's friend-enemy dichotomy in the *Concept of the Political*. Schmitt's view that 'the political' can often lead to enmity (2008: 28) animates his focus on the Hobbesian role of state authority in controlling the effects of this animosity. Commenting on the significance of Schmitt's work, Ernst-Wolfgang Böckenförde observes:

> How do you want to understand the political world today without the insight that the political can lead to enmity time and again? It doesn't have to, but it can, and often does. It is only this that reveals the importance and function of the state as a political entity and the guarantor of peace within the state. One must know about this peculiarity of the political so that one can engage in sensible politics.
>
> (Böckenförde, 2017: 372)

The keys to this 'sensible politics' are the written and unwritten rules that constitutionalism imparts. Yet citizens are more likely to overlook the importance of such a rule-based politics at times of economic uncertainty, and to retreat instead into the comforting certainty of identity based allegiances and affiliations. This point about how a constitution reflects, or shapes, the nature of its political system and society is addressed in the chapters ahead. Central to the experience of American and German constitutionalism has been a more dynamic inter-relationship where American and German identity and society have been shaped as much by the values enunciated in their constitutional texts as the other way around. However, support for the values of constitutionalism among political elites is crucial at the establishment of a constitutional order. As Mark Tushnet notes, without support for constitutionalism from the political system of a country, neither institutional design nor normative principles will count for much (2007: 1488). Important considerations, then, in assessing the relationship between constitutionalism and democratic politics are the circumstances surrounding a constitution's birth, and the attitudes and motivations of the individuals establishing the constitutional instruments.

In this chapter, the degree to which a polity tolerates the emergence of certain values and opinions in the formation of majority rule will be considered in the context of an American constitutionalism characterised more by liberty, and a German constitutionalism which has been oriented more to dignity. As will be addressed, this distinction shapes how in the United States most values and opinions are able to form, while in Germany there are absolute checks on whether opinions and values hostile to the constitutional order may emerge. One consequence of the liberty-dignity dynamic is that while the US Supreme Court has tended to formalise emerging majority opinion on issues like desegregation and reapportionment, the role of the *Bundesverfassungsgericht* (*BVerfG*) as the guardian of Germany's highly normative constitution has been more pedagogic in inculcating the values of the Basic Law in civil society.

The chapter then sets out the 'stability renewal' paradigm and how German constitutionalism has balanced the challenges of threats to the state, the integration of new political parties into the political system, and whether to maintain aspects of the militant democracy such as the thresholds for electoral success. A fine line exists between stability and ossification, which the *BVerfG* has not always mediated successfully. American constitutionalism has also come to recognise equality and human dignity in important court rulings such as *Brown v Board of Education* (1954a), *Baker v Carr* (1962), and *Reynolds v Sims* (1964a). Unlike in Germany, though, where rights are seen as anterior to the state and a precondition *of* democracy, in the US the emergence of these constitutional values has been largely the result of the free development of democratic principles in civil society and the parallel expansion of the suffrage and democratisation of political institutions.

The chapter then briefly assesses what I term 'post-1945 constitutionalism', including the establishment of international human rights instruments and a clear view of the centrality of the individual in law. This post-war period was characterised by the establishment of constitutional courts in Germany, Italy, and then later in Spain, which signified an effort to re-establish constitutionalism in countries where malignant legislative enactments and the tenets of legal positivism had conspired to undermine human rights. Yet the dialectic of human rights at the international level also had consequences in terms of growing individualism within liberal democratic states, challenging their ability to maintain societal cohesion and uphold their constitutional values (Böckenförde, 1991: 45). The role of constitutionalism in shaping those domestic values is considered now.

Constitutionalism

Martin Loughlin writes that "constitutionalism involves the attempt to subject all governmental action within a designated field to the structures, processes, principles, and values of a 'constitution'" (2012: 47). According to McIlwain, constitutionalism "in all its successive phases" from ancient Greece onwards has "one essential quality: it is a legal limitation on government; it is the antithesis of arbitrary rule; its opposite is despotic government, the government of will instead of law" (2005: 24). According to Walter Murphy,

> constitutionalism ... enshrines respect for human worth and dignity as its central principle. To protect that value, citizens must have a right to political participation, and their government must be hedged in by substantive limits on what it can do, even when perfectly mirroring the popular will.
>
> (Murphy, 1993: 6)

In other words, constitutionalism—meaning the constitutional rules and values of a political order and legal order—is better seen not as a limitation, but as a necessary condition for establishing democratic politics and ensuring rights of participation. Constitutionalism facilitates genuine democracy by securing democratic rights and puts in place measures to protect the minority[2] against the dangers of majoritarian excess. Parts of McIlwain's seminal account from the late 1930s are tinged with his obvious awareness of the threat that constitutionalism was facing from European totalitarianism (see 2005). The definition advanced by Murphy has incorporated the notion of protecting fundamental rights, human worth, and dignity, reflecting the new human rights priorities in constitutionalism which arose after 1945.

Keith Whittington writes that "the rise of the modern notion of constitutionalism was intertwined with liberalism, the belief that there were limits to the legitimate power of government, and that those limitations should be made effective and real" (2011: 221). Where constitutionalism ought to come into its own is, first, when the values of the constitutional order (i.e. justice, equality, liberty, human dignity) are challenged by individuals or groups in society, and, second, when voters elect representatives to power who are indifferent to the constitution's values or actively hostile to them, as the Nazis were to those of the Weimar Republic. This view of constitutionalism is that it provides a safety mechanism to prevent democracy becoming a conduit for the infringement of rights as was the case during the National Socialist period in Germany. Put simply, this view sees constitutionalism principally as a limitation on government.

Although restraint is certainly an important aspect of constitutionalism, particularly in its American manifestation, constitutionalism can also have some positive content in terms of specifying the substantive ideals of a polity and the overall context within which the relationship between citizen and state is shaped. German constitutionalism reflects both conceptions of constitutionalism, as a limiting and empowering mechanism. Alexander Somek argues that the "reasonable recognition concerning the supreme value and authority of human dignity and human rights" which emerges after 1945—what he calls 'Constitutionalism 2.0' and which is embodied in the constitutional practice of Germany's Basic Law—helps us understand constitutionalism as a "project of emancipation" (2014: 9). The assumption of many after World War II was that constitutionalism had secured, à la Fukuyama, the permanent ascendancy of liberal values with no possibility of a return to the barbarity of the past. But as Somek observes, "no emancipation is possible without political action" (2014: 283). Somek's view helps us see that constitutionalism is not merely a neutral vehicle into which any values (emancipatory or regressive) can be poured. The "project of constitutionalism", writes Kautz, is in some cases "an avowedly partisan project, whose aim is to establish a liberal polity in the face of a political culture that is at least somewhat resistant to liberalism" (2011: 4). We can see, then, a potential contradiction between constitutionalism as a mechanism to restrict the popular will, yet also facilitate the political action necessary to emancipate citizens and secure rights.

The portrait of democracy and the possibility of constitutionalism offered in this chapter and in the chapters ahead is a guarded one, reflecting the inherent challenge of building institutions which, to paraphrase Carl Friedrich, can preserve human dignity while controlling the worst aspects of human nature (1974: 123). However, the view that democracy *should* be taken seriously in no way suggests that there is any preferable form of government on the horizon to representative democracy. Taking democracy seriously means recognising its flaws and drawbacks as well as its obvious merits. It means recognising that in the US reapportionment cases examined in Chapter 4, it was the concerted political action of civil society actors over almost two decades that raised the profile of the issue, and managed to get the Supreme Court to accept the justiciability of the issue. In Germany, it was political action that propelled the German Green Party from a pressure group to a political party represented in the German Parliament in the 1980s, and eventually into government as junior coalition partners of the Social Democrats (SPD), with its leader Joschka Fischer becoming foreign minister and vice-chancellor of Germany.

While the experience of the classical world, of Germany in the 1930s, and the increasing prevalence of illiberal democracies since the end of the Cold War are salutary warnings of where democracy *can* lead, the correlation between democracy, on the one hand, and liberal constitutionalism and the rule of law, on the other, has been more constant in the twentieth century than that between democracy and illiberalism. What this correlation does not automatically reveal is whether it is the emphasis on rights-based constitutionalism, and strong political and legal institutions which leads to a vibrant democratic society, or whether democracy is the key to stable constitutionalism. What the historical evidence suggests, as Koopmans observes, is that democracy and the rule of law go hand in hand, and "where one of the two disappears, the other is in danger of being abandoned" (2003: 123). The reason, writes Koopmans is probably that

> Majority rule, in the democratic sense of the word, implies that different political opinions can compete for the voters' favour. Every opinion must have a chance to become more generally accepted, so that the minority of today can be the majority of tomorrow. Freedom of expression and protection of minority feelings are part of the prerequisites of democratic government.
>
> (Koopmans, 2003: 123)

Not stated until the final sentence are the ends that democratic government seeks. In other words, which *values* or social goods does the polity seek to advance and protect (i.e. freedom of expression, the rights of minority groups, equality, liberty, human dignity, justice)? The values that a polity stands for can be as crucial in determining the orientation of a constitutional order, and its relationship to individuals and groups in society as the institutional mechanisms which advance those values. Koopmans' statement encapsulates the dilemma of how a liberal constitutional democracy establishes the institutional and societal conditions to sustain itself over time, and why some fail.

Within constitutionalism we can say that values can be both the essential currency as well as the framework within which opinions shift from being a minority to a majority view. In other words, this is about debate, contestation and, sometimes, conflict between different interests and groups in society. Values inform and orient these debates but are inevitably shaped by them as well. One example would be how segregation increasingly became unacceptable in the United States during the 1940s and 1950s; another would be how gay marriage gradually came to be accepted by a majority of Americans between the early 2000s and today. Overall, constitutionalism provides a mechanism within which these debates and, sometimes, conflicts on rights and values take place. However, as will be shown in the chapters ahead, the emphasis in German and American constitutionalism over how and whether opinions are able to form and become 'the majority of tomorrow' on a given issue is very different.

American and German Constitutionalism

The risk of placing too much faith in human nature, or in the power of intellectual progress to make individuals more rational and tolerant of others has been a familiar refrain in constitutionalism. By the early nineteenth century the Enlightenment had left much of European intellectual thought with a clear sense of modernity. That so many fundamental strands of constitutional liberalism could become unravelled in 1930s Germany illustrates the extent to which the idea of any inevitable sense of progress may be a chimera without struggle or Somekian political action (see 2014: 283) to secure it.

Can the liberal democratic state simply be a neutral observer as liberal values and opinions compete with illiberal and intolerant ones in Justice Holmes' 'marketplace of ideas'?[3] Joseph Goebbels wrote unashamedly: "This will always remain one of the best jokes of democracy, that it gave its deadly enemies the means by which it was destroyed" (quoted in Fox and Nolte, 1995: 1). Post-1949 German constitutionalism has emphatically rejected the notion that the state can ever be neutral when popular and democratic forces were advocating policies hostile to either fundamental rights or the constitutional order itself. Put differently, German constitutionalism and its militant democracy is grounded in a total rejection of Koopmans' premise that "every opinion must have a chance to become more generally accepted", since the experience of the 1930s demonstrates that some of those 'opinions' may seek to destroy the values of the constitutional order, and democracy itself.

Rapid and unpredictable shifts in opinion are not merely theoretical possibilities, and the solution that constitutionalism offers is not theoretical either. Mechanisms such as a constitutional requirement for a qualified majority for certain types of major political change reduce the risks of badly informed voters sending a society over a cliff edge. While not eliminating such dangers entirely, mechanisms such as qualified majorities serve to "make the system less vulnerable to random fluctuations and political manipulation" (Elster, 1992: 40). This is not to say that constitutionalism is a panacea which can always keep a political system on an even keel. As I have indicated, the line between stability and oligarchy, on the one hand, and between renewal and chaos, on the other, can be fine. This delicate sense of equilibrium is captured well by Lally-Tollendal's remarks in the French Assemblée Constituante of 1789–1791 that

> In a given space of time the Constitution may be destroyed by a lack of change just as much as by too many changes. It must be neither easy nor impossible to modify it.
>
> (Quoted in Elster, 1992: 44)

Elster focusses significantly on the role of constitutional mechanisms to promote stability, but also addresses the issue of how well a particular constitution is suited to its society. "Does a changing society need a stable constitution as a flywheel—or a flexible constitution that can adjust to the changing environment" (Elster, 1992: 43)? The implications of this question for constitutionalism and how a constitutional order balances forces of stability and renewal is a central focus in the analysis that follows.

As we will see in the following chapters, constitutionalism can play a role not only in excluding issues from debate that can cause violence, but also institutionally in terms of establishing rules and parameters to enable opposition views to be heard, protected, and empowered in the formation of democratic opinion. The formation of democratic opinion and, ultimately, legitimate representative government requires open, transparent, forthright, and reasoned debate in which opposition and dissent play an essential role. As Stephen Holmes puts it:

> Democracy is government by rational and free public discussion among legally equal citizens, not simply the enforcement of the will of the majority. Public disagreement itself, conducted with Rawlsian civility, is an essential instrument of popular government. Not any 'will' but only a will formed in vigorous and wide-open debate should be given sovereign authority. The legally guaranteed right of opposition is therefore a fundamental norm of democratic government; it provides an essential precondition for the formation of democratic public opinion.
>
> (Holmes, 1995: 171)

This view on the role of open debate and the role of dissent sits at the heart of democratic theory and supports the book's idea of the civic space where opinions can take shape and, sometimes, become democratic decisions. It is a view that also lies at the heart of the reasoning of the Warren Court in the reapportionment cases, and, as will be shown in later chapters, led to important rulings by the *Bundesverfassungsgericht* that protected the role of opposition parties in the post-1949 landscape of German constitutionalism.

German constitutionalism is far more in tune with Koopman's final sentence (see 2003: 123) that democracy depends on respect for fundamental rights including human dignity and the protection of minority groups. Thus, in Germany, only through respect for rights—including freedom of speech and human dignity—could the minority of today become the majority of tomorrow. Since 1951 when the *BVerfG* began hearing its first cases, the formation of democratic opinion has been conditional on it being neither a threat to the country's free democratic basic order (*die freiheitliche demokratische Grundordnung*), nor the fundamental rights guarantees in the Basic Law. This prioritisation of the principles of human dignity and the free democratic order in the Basic Law trumps liberty and all other rights, whereas in the US, liberty would often trump values like human dignity (Kommers and Miller, 2012: 49). In the US, the formation of majority opinion was never so tightly regulated, due in large part to the free speech guarantees of the First Amendment, and the important American emphasis on voluntary associations and liberty.

Liberty and Dignity

The liberty-dignity dichotomy with respect to the United States and Germany provides a useful framework for assessing the interplay between constitutionalism and the civic space, and in determining how citizens engage in their democracy. To orient the subsequent analysis of how the judicial decisions of the American and German courts can be understood within the dichotomy of 'liberty' and 'dignity' constitutionalism, a brief elaboration and definition of these concepts is necessary. This should also allow for a better understanding of how and why judicial interventions in the processes of representative democracy have occurred in each country.

The emphasis on liberty in American constitutionalism has meant that struggles for rights, and the slow emergence of equality and human dignity as constitutional values have been driven primarily by social forces, and only incrementally have come to be recognised by the federal government and Supreme Court. By contrast, the emphasis on human dignity in German constitutionalism is grounded in the view of the autonomous individual as part of a community. The paradox, then, is that the state has a duty to ensure that the freedom of the individual is realised but, according to the *BVerfG*'s jurisprudence, that is only possible through "synthesis with the community" (Durham, 1993: 45). The influence of human dignity means, as will be shown, that rights in German constitutionalism are a precondition for democracy, not ancillary to it.

Primarily, the utilisation of liberty and dignity within the book is contextual, representing the predominant value orientations of each polity, and within which the respective courts act and interpret. The emphasis on liberty in American constitutionalism has shaped constitutional jurisprudence with respect to freedom of speech, and has tended to place an onus on the federal courts to ensure that a particular constitutional right has been infringed before acting. The primary concern of American constitutionalism has therefore been with "limiting the reach of state authority in order to preserve private liberty" (Eberle, 2002: 257). By contrast, the emphasis on dignity in German constitutionalism has placed an emphatic duty on the *BVerfG* to ensure that certain rights are realised, particularly in the realm of equality. Thus, as Eberle notes, human dignity sits at the apex of the Basic Law's value structure and "naturally radiates throughout the legal system, in both public and private law" (1997: 1049). The key difference in the United States is that while human dignity was an ideal implicit, but not realised at the American founding, and which only became realised belatedly through the struggles in a society conditioned by liberty, in Germany, human dignity is *the* key value of the constitutional order which shapes state action and the relationship between citizen and state. Rights and democracy can only be exercised within the dignity-shaped constitutional landscape established by the Basic Law and the *BVerfG*.

The juxtaposition between the American Constitution's emphasis on liberty and the Basic Law's greater emphasis on human dignity is not absolute, as will be shown in the subsequent analysis, but it is a good starting point for understanding the role of the US and German courts in adjudicating value conflicts in their respective systems. One result of the liberty-dignity dichotomy, as already stated, is that in American constitutionalism the US Supreme Court has tended to formalise value changes *already* taking place in society, while in German constitutionalism the *BVerfG* has played a key role in *inculcating* the fundamental values of the Basic Law in German politics and society. Why this difference exists will be expanded on throughout the succeeding chapters, but is partly grounded in the American Constitution's authority only over public authority. In other words, liberty was indirectly established as a corollary of a constitution which had nothing to say about the private sphere of life. This compares to the Basic Law's comprehensive applicability to all political and legal institutions of the state, and the entire legal system encompassing public and private law.

Summarising the principle of liberty in the United States, Eugene Rostow wrote: "the root idea of the Constitution is that man can be free because the state is not" (1952: 195). America's 'liberty'-orientated constitutionalism reflected the initial configuration of the relationship between citizen and state; that government was restrained so the individual could be at liberty. That theoretical restraint on government was to be achieved indirectly through the institutional fragmentation of the government into separate and competing branches of government. As Madison hoped in *Federalist 51*, "ambition must be made to counteract ambition" (1987b: 319).[4] Fundamental to Madison's conception of government, then, is the idea of distrust in human nature and in the capacity of individuals to check their own power. Distrust, as Dana Villa notes, is "a constitutive element not only of our system of checks and balances, but any and all forms of liberal constitutionalism" (2008: 10). In the American experience this distrust has also been manifested in a somewhat paradoxical consensus on basic political values and beliefs. These values, according to Huntington, constitute what is sometimes called 'the American Creed' and are "liberal, individualistic, democratic, egalitarian, and hence basically anti-government and anti-authority in character" (1981: 4). Yet this anti-government and anti-authority aspect of the American character has traditionally concealed more subtle, horizontal collective social belief systems and structures rooted in communities and other forms of civil association. Tocqueville's view that "freedom of opinion does not exist in America" (1998: 104) speaks to this curious replacement of governmental authority with more invisible value systems and structures of social control within political communities.

The establishment of the American Constitution after the near anarchy experienced under the Articles of Confederation presupposed a need to both limit state power and channel the energy and purposes of government in a way that left citizens a wide sphere of liberty where civil society might be able to flourish. As Eberle observes, "in American law, the Constitution only applies when government acts" (2002: 29). It ostensibly has nothing to say about the relationship of Americans to one another or to their society. Only if a space was provided for the people and for civil society to grow and renew itself, it was thought, would America's constitutional experiment be secure. That meant that Americans were free to decide in the course of two centuries of struggle whether principles like dignity and equality were important to them or not (see for example, Goodman, 2006: 745). Eberle notes that Americans believe in individual liberty more than any other value. "For Americans, this means freedom to do what you choose. From a legal standpoint, such freedom actually means freedom from government and official control" (Eberle, 2002: 6).

It is this view of liberty which shapes the ongoing discussion in the succeeding chapters. Liberty in American constitutionalism has meant that the individual was protected from government interferences through the clear enumeration of the powers of the latter, and through the protections of the Bill of Rights. Thus, the notion of liberty constitutionalism in the subsequent analysis is one based on the idea of the freedom of the individual from interference by the state in their private life. In Supreme Court decisions, the notion of liberty was perhaps best described by Justice Louis Brandeis in *Olmstead v United States* as "the right to be let alone" (1928: 478). To some, however, implicit in the idea of being left alone was "being alone" (Palmer, 2007: 23). Thus, liberty meant that the individual was essentially isolated in the community; once emancipated from the state in this way, the particular challenge for American government was how to avoid the atomisation of society, and ensure a citizenry that would uphold their government and their liberty.

Establishing a wall between the public and private spheres may protect liberty, but how can that wall then be surmounted to maintain the connection between the people and their republic? This was the crucial issue that animated Jefferson's fears about whether Americans could sustain self-government if they only encountered it at election times, and will be discussed in Chapter 2. The Constitution, so it was thought, guaranteed the liberty of the people and in return the people would preserve it in order to defend their *own* liberties. Here, there are shades of Gouverneur Morris' admonition that "the French want an American Constitution without realising they have no Americans to uphold it" (Walther, 1934: 76; quoted in Hartz, 1991: 38). Morris' words sound rather hollow in the era of Donald Trump, while the very idea of 'renewal' can no longer be assumed to mean 'progress'. For citizens who value the liberty that American constitutionalism provides, but also cherish a sense of belonging to society, there is often an unbridgeable tension where "freedom and community can be reconciled only in the nostalgic dream of an idealized past" (see Palmer, 2007: 24).

The original conception of liberty in American constitutionalism, as Rostow conceives it above, caused two problems that are central to our discussion. One, as already mentioned, was that the separation of the public and private spheres might cause citizens and state to become alienated from one another. The other problem which could result from strict non-interference by the state in social life was, as Stephen Holmes notes, "private injustice and oppression" and "an outcropping of brutal monopolies" (1995: 244). The evolution of American constitutionalism over more than two centuries of social struggle and injustice has been a gradual coming to terms with the reality that government also had a role in preventing private injustice. Here, Sager notes that "the most active and secure ingredients of our liberty-bearing constitutional jurisprudence fit … with the broad concerns of equal membership, on the one hand, and fair and open government, on the other" (1998: 259–260). At the heart of the Progressive Movement and the New Deal, according to Rorty, was a quasi-communitarian rhetoric "in which the government ensures equality of opportunity as well as individual liberty" (1998: 8). As will be shown in Chapters 3 and 4, this narrative provided the context for the changing jurisprudence of the Supreme Court regarding equality, the protection of minorities, and electoral participation from the late 1930s to the 1960s. However, the traditional resonance of liberty remained strong, and meant that when the Supreme Court got involved in electoral processes in *Baker v Carr* and the other reapportionment cases in response to the demands of civil society, it was extremely tentative about its intervention and proceeded cautiously. It was notable that those opposed to numerically equal representation (or 'one person, one vote') used the liberty argument. Opponents of a 1948 California ballot initiative on reapportionment claimed that equal numerical representation would ensure the trampling of minority rights by unscrupulous urban majorities (Smith, 2014: 26). The battle against reapportionment was waged by civil society—as befits the US conception of liberty—but it was unable to make progress against state legislatures that refused to reapportion. A clear national consensus had emerged against malapportionment after over a decade of civil society activism, and the Court's decisions in the reapportionment cases were generally well received across the country (Smith, 2014: 233). The Supreme Court's role was, then, largely one of formalising existing value changes within society, and will be examined in Chapters 2 and 4.

The German Constitution, or Basic Law (*Grundgesetz*), could hardly be more different. By contrast with Rostow's view that liberty is secured in the United States through the restraint of government, in Germany it is only through government that freedom can be established. Liberty as understood in the American context has no meaning because, in the jurisprudence of the *BVerfG*, the Basic Law views the individual not as an isolated, autonomous person but as part of a community.[5] Freedom in the Federal Republic of Germany can only come from a recognition of the dignity of the individual person as part of their community. "Rather than being the key power that needs to be restrained if liberty is to be preserved, the state is seen as the vehicle for achieving freedom" (Durham, 1993: 45). Ernst-Wolfgang Böckenförde has noted that "the *Rechtsstaat* serves to secure freedom, namely, through fundamental rights and the separation of powers, and the elaboration of liberty-protecting forms and procedures" (2017: 376).

While the constitutional meaning of liberty may be contested, that of dignity is even more so. Ronald Dworkin notes that "the idea of dignity has been stained by overuse and misuse" and that attempts to define it are invariably challenged owing to the fact the dignity is an interpretive concept (2011: 204). It is important to say that the principle of human dignity has been cited by the Supreme Court as representing an American ideal (see, for example, Goodman, 2006: 745), so as a value it is certainly not absent from American constitutionalism. However, human dignity is particularly central to German constitutionalism and means that "each person must always be treated as an end in himself or herself" (Eberle, 2002: 7). The basis of human dignity in Germany's Basic Law was not grounded in any particular religious or philosophical tradition, but the jurisprudence of the Court has sometimes adopted "a Kantian view in regarding persons as ends and not merely the objects of manipulation" (Kommers and Miller, 2012: 358). The *BVerfG* has articulated a view of human dignity which "while protecting an inner core of personal freedom, concurrently binds the individual to certain norms governing the whole of society" (Kommers and Miller, 2012: 384).

Human dignity represents the highest value of the Basic Law and is protected from constitutional amendment by the 'eternity clause' of Article 79(3). Article 1(1) of the Basic Law states that "Human dignity shall be inviolable. To respect and protect it shall be the duty of all state authority." In the Court's first two decades, it understood and presented itself as a fundamental rights tribunal (Collings, 2015: 64). This emphasis by the Court on human dignity and fundamental rights as a precondition for social and political life reinforced the notion that nothing in the German state was superior to fundamental rights, not even democracy. Germany's tolerance of the *BVerfG* as the guardian of democracy reflects, writes Collings, "a substantive, value-laden definition of democracy, rather than a flaccid valuation of it" (2015: 219). Nevertheless, the early tolerance for the *BVerfG* as the guardian of the Basic Law also reflected an old German view that politics was a "dirty business" (Schlink, 1994: 210–211), and an even older respect for law in Germany rooted in the *Rechtsstaat*. This perspective will be assessed more fully in Chapter 5.

Stability and Renewal

Germany is the ultimate embodiment of a state in which constitutionalism has played a significant role in aiding the recovery from extreme nationalism, genocide, and totalitarianism. These reasons alone might justify this book's focus, but a further reason is the significance of Germany's Basic Law for constitutionalism around the world after World War II (see Ackerman, 1997: 773), and particularly in the Eastern European states which were reconstituted after the end of the Cold War (see, for example, Eberle, 2002: 12). The German Basic Law remains one of the world's most influential constitutions based on the frequency with which its provisions and institutions have been replicated by newly emerging states around the world (Kokott, 1999). Some states which adopted German constitutional structures such as Hungary and, more lately, Poland, have taken a distinctive turn towards the illiberal and ideological right in recent years with attacks on the independence of each country's respective constitutional courts intensifying. One scholar has observed that "Poland and Hungary now offer a toxic ideological brew that is reminiscent of interwar Europe" (Müller, 2016).

These developments highlight the inherent challenge for liberal democratic states in maintaining their fundamental constitutional values and rights protections when voters opt for parties or politicians intent on undermining them.

Maintaining some equilibrium between the forces of stability and renewal is crucial to ensure a polity can adjust to a changing social context. During the Parliamentary Council, which drafted the Basic Law in 1948, some delegates were opposed to the idea of electoral thresholds (*Sperrklauseln*) because they felt they would exclude the types of vibrant political forces that a polity needs to renew itself (see Wenner, 1986: 91). The emergence of the Greens in democratic politics in the 1980s—after they finally managed to overcome the 5 percent hurdle—was precisely the type of new political blood that the rather conservative German political system needed according to some.[6] The *BVerfG* played a role in this process of integration through several court decisions which arose out of constitutional complaints made by the Greens.[7] The ability of a constitutional system to integrate new political parties within its existing institutions in a stable manner—even ones initially viewed with suspicion as the Greens were—is fundamental to the health of a polity. If rising political parties are seen to have been unreasonably excluded from political power there is a risk, first, of increased alienation between voters and their elected representatives, and, ultimately, the danger is that voters lose faith in their democratic institutions.

While this may be true of most democracies, the risk calculation in Germany's case over whether certain parties are acceptable is materially different given its history, its constitutional values, and the concept of the militant democracy. Thus, political ossification must be balanced against the existential threat posed to a constitutional order if hostile political forces or parties are integrated within its institutions. If such parties enter parliament there are two principle risks: one is that they can gain enough leverage to compromise the values of the polity; another is they can prevent the parliament from functioning, potentially bringing democratic institutions into disrepute. The latter situation can also occur not only through the malicious intent of a party to wreck democratic processes, but through the entry of many innocuous smaller parties into a parliament, thus precipitating legislative gridlock and preventing it from functioning. This is exactly what happened during the Weimar Republic, the experience of which is still used as justification for maintaining electoral thresholds for elections to the *Bundestag*. As will be examined in Chapter 6, the criterion that a legislature must be able to function is still important. However, the Court has seemingly viewed this test as being less important at the EU level, which has caused considerable consternation in the federal government (*Bundesregierung*) and among MEPs in Strasbourg (see Amann et al., 2014).

One notable feature of the development of an American constitutionalism which belatedly came to recognise the dignity of man, the expanding scope of equality, and individual rights is that its trajectory has exactly paralleled the expansion of the suffrage and the increased democratisation of political institutions, not run counter to it. In *Rhodes v Chapman*, the US Supreme Court has described "the evolving standards of decency that mark the progress of a maturing society" (1981). Clearly, however, different societies and different sub-sections of society as well as the political branches of government may have their own ideas about how standards of decency may have evolved (Koopmans, 2003: 121). It is in the different interpretations between the judiciary, politics, and society that political and constitutional tensions—manageable or dangerous—are generated. Certain contexts and problems strongly favour judicial scrutiny of political institutions. Chief among these are cases where the constitutional system has become ossified, where democratic representation is failing, and where individual rights are being infringed, concerns present in footnote four of the Court's decision in *US v Carolene Products*.

The connection between democracy and rights is common to both Germany and the United States. As the Supreme Court noted in *Wesberry v Sanders*, "other rights, even the most basic, are illusory if the right to vote is undermined" (1964b). If a group of politicians or a political party were able to gain power through malapportioned constituencies, or limits on free speech (or, as the Court declared in *Citizens United* (2010), no limits!), then they would be able to both disenfranchise some citizens and effectively strip them of their constitutional rights. While the inter-relationship between democracy and rights has only emerged occasionally in the Supreme Court's jurisprudence in the twentieth century, in Germany, this inter-relationship is inherent in the Basic Law and has been further developed in the *BVerfG*'s jurisprudence. Fundamental rights in the Basic Law are seen as anterior to the state and as being an absolute precondition for democratic life (see Collings, 2015: 219).

A fundamental legal differentiation between American and German constitutionalism is that while the American Constitution only protects individuals against public authority, since the famous *Lüth Case* decision of the *BVerfG* in 1958 the German Basic Law has also protected the fundamental rights of German citizens against other citizens through the principle of 'Third Party Effect'. In the US the strictly public purpose of constitutional law maintains the separation between the public and private spheres that was deemed necessary for liberty to flourish. However, the Constitution's focus only on acts of public power meant that it provided no guarantee against one individual abusing the rights of another.[8] As White notes, "in 1876 the Court held that the Fourteenth Amendment did not preclude the infringement of a citizen's rights by another individual acting privately" (1959: 183). Crucially, the Constitution opened up the possibility of vastly different value interpretations between the Supreme Court and the federal government on the one hand, and those of local groups and local majorities on the other.[9] These value differences between local and national majorities explained, at their most extreme, the Civil War; however, they also explained segregation and the difference in attitudes to malapportionment between urban majorities and rural ones. The former wanted the equal representation which they believed the Fourteenth Amendment promised, while the latter felt that the very liberty that the Constitution guaranteed would be swept away by the numerical superiority of the urban areas under a system of equal numerical representation between electoral districts. Ultimately, as will be seen in the next chapter and later ones, these differences—first, between the values of national and local majorities, and, second, between the judicial interpretation of values and the interpretations held by members of either a national or local majority—can leave the liberal state perilously exposed.

The constitutional wall of separation between the public and private spheres was central to the fears of Thomas Jefferson about how to sustain a citizen democracy. Jefferson's fears in this regard also parallel both Böckenförde's concerns and the ideas of Tocqueville on civil association. Following the *Lüth* decision of 1958, the *BVerfG* held that the Basic Law governs the entire legal system including private law. Stern summarised the effect of this:

> The constitution takes on central significance for the legal system as a whole. State power may only be exercised in conformity with the Constitution. The Basic Law, then, lays claim to a comprehensive validity, for it directly shapes the political and social life of the community, a feature that is new to German constitutionalism.
>
> (Stern, 1993: 21)

Lüth will be assessed in more detail in Chapter 5, but its effect was to define a civic republican vision of the individual as part of the community. This vision, which was both legal and civic in a broad sense, laid the foundations for German constitutionalism's all-embracing influence over German democracy. The post-1945 human rights consensus was driven especially strongly by the US, although its effects on US domestic politics or constitutional law were minimal. However, the new normative outlook shaped the international and European context within which the Basic Law was established.

Post-1945 Constitutionalism

The international context of constitutionalism that emerged after 1945 was characterised by the promulgation of human rights regimes such as the ECHR and the development of a new conception of the individual in law and were used as a basis to lock in domestic political and legal institutions, especially in Europe. Although the United States was one of the key actors driving many of these international developments, including the establishment of dedicated constitutional courts in Europe, the impact and influence of these developments on domestic American constitutionalism are less marked. Nevertheless, these influences were not negligible and this section highlights some of the international influences driving constitutionalism after 1945.

If one of the fundamental questions for judges engaged in constitutional interpretation before 1945 was 'what sort of polity does the Constitution envisage?', in the decades after 1945 the increasingly normative hue in both German and American constitutional jurisprudence seemed to ask instead 'what sort of polity *should* the Constitution envisage?' While the reasons for this increased normative influence on American and German constitutionalism were, as will be shown in later chapters, of primarily domestic origin, the international context cannot be neglected, particularly with respect to Germany. Here, the creation of Germany's powerful constitutional court, with its strong jurisprudential concern for human rights, and its emphasis on the centrality of the individual in law, reflected emerging European and international trends in these areas. International factors in the United States were far less significant. However, as will be shown in Chapter 4, the developing domestic understandings of equality and human dignity which shaped the Supreme Court's decisions from the late 1930s to the 1960s—including Harlan Stone's opinion in *United States v Carolene Products* (1938) and the decision in *Brown v Board of Education*—were not immune to the international context (see, for example, Goodman, 2006: 745).

In the aftermath of World War II we can discern two separate strands of thinking within constitutionalism. One emphasised a focus on judicially enforceable constitutional norms as seen in the ECHR and the German Basic Law which had binding legal teeth; the other strand sought to release law and justice from the prison of legal positivism, and place the individual at the centre of all law (see, for example, Lauterpacht, 1943; Radbruch, 1957). The belief that German legal positivism had partly facilitated the National Socialist assault on justice drove the creation of powerful constitutional courts in Europe. These courts would come to prioritise values inherent in their new constitutions, even over the letter of the text itself (see MacCormick et al., 1997: 484–5). Aside from this emphasis on higher law values, and the decline in the relative importance of positive law, Hersch Lauterpacht went one step further. Lauterpacht's insight in 1943 that "the individual human being … was the fundamental unit of all law" (1943: 31) shaped the perspective of a generation of lawyers and judges on the law.[10]

Stone Sweet notes that "the inclination to construct and then secure normative hierarchies is a central focus of European constitutional theory" (2003: 2751). Germany since the establishment of the Basic Law is perhaps the best example of such a hierarchy—what the *BVerfG* referred to in *Elfes* as a "value-oriented order that limits public authority" (1957). This emerging normative orientation of constitutionalism presupposed the idea of what Judge David Edward called "an overriding and encircling body of 'law'" (Interview, 2013), containing fundamental rights principles which determined how state power would be applied within the constitutional systems of these countries. Somek notes that "modern constitutionalism is the project to establish and to constrain public power [and] law is the means thereto" (2014: 1). Law has had a dominant place in American constitutionalism back to the founding period (see, for example, *Federalist 78* by Hamilton). Due to its enhanced status after World War II, law has also come to play a more central role in governance and the protection of rights. In this respect, what was common to almost all forms of constitutional review in Europe after 1945 was the detachment of the new specialised constitutional courts from the ordinary judiciary so as to "ensure the normative superiority of the constitutional law" (Stone Sweet, 2003: 2745).

Stone Sweet sees constitutionalism as referring to "the commitment, more or less operative in any polity, to the idea that the interactions that take place within it are to be governed by a set of authoritative rules—the constitutional law" (2000: 20). This definition reflects the evolving importance of constitutional law after 1945 as the highest of legal norms. This changed view, which mirrored the path taken by Germany after 1949, also pointed towards an Aristotelian conception of political life where constitutional law also encompassed the interactions of the citizens with one another—the issue of Third Party Effect—according to legally enforceable rights norms.[11] Echoing the "overriding and encircling body of law" that Judge Edward referred to, Stone Sweet's use of the word 'commitment' highlights the metamorphosis in constitutionalism since 1945, and reflects a clearer conception of what can count as permissible action within a state, judgements which come not only from a written text but the entire value orientation of a state's constitutional order.

The successful post-war development of German constitutionalism was strongly influenced by wider European debates of the period. In the Council of Europe, these debates were primarily centred on the emerging human rights framework which was to become the ECHR as well as on the need to create political stability by learning lessons from the immediate past. Post-war human rights regimes were concerned as much with dealing with the prospect of a communist future as responding to the recent fascist past (Moravcsik, 2000: 237). Here, there was a clear understanding of the linkage between a country having stable democratic institutions and a non-aggressive outlook towards its neighbours. The Democratic Peace proposition, which dates from the work of Kant in the eighteenth century, was, says Moravcsik, "a central tenet, arguably *the* central tenet of postwar Western planning, as it had been in the thinking of Woodrow Wilson and other liberal statesmen a generation before" (2000: 237; emphasis in original). The chief French advocate of the ECHR in the assembly, Teitgen, saw the Convention's purpose as "assuring the stability of German democracy and thereby the security of France" (Moravcsik, 2000: 237). Unsurprisingly, the most fervent advocates of the ECHR as a bulwark against future tyranny were the representatives from Germany and Italy (see Moravcsik, 2000: 237–238). The intention was that these external legal institutional structures would reinforce Germany's domestic constitutional institutions in establishing an internal militant democracy. As Blankenburg notes, "constitutions gain increased importance in newly established democratic regimes where politics and law have to be institutionalised from scratch" (2002: 157).

Stone Sweet links the spread of the Kelsenian Constitutional Court to Italy and Germany after the war to a combination of domestic disenchantment with legislative power unique to those countries and an international trend towards the prioritisation of individual rights over state power. At the domestic level, the experience of fascism before the war and the American occupation after it, observes Stone Sweet, "conspired to fatally undermine the view that parliaments could do no wrong" (2003: 2769). Legislatures which had rubber-stamped National Socialist programmes before the war had illustrated the vulnerability of democratic systems to abuse if public power was not constrained by a higher constitutional law. Thus, the international dimension provided an institutional safety blanket of regimes that acted to consolidate domestic attempts to restore constitutionalism in Germany and Italy. The emphasis of states and the international community on constitutionalism and human rights after 1945 ostensibly marked a seismic shift. This shift, prominent in the work of the German legal scholar Gustav Radbruch after 1945, signified that neither legal positivism nor value neutrality could excuse the abuse of individual rights by the state (Radbruch, 1946).

Yet efforts to entrench rights, justice, and human dignity within domestic constitutional orders may face resistance if they are not accepted and understood by both state and society. This was the glaring weakness of the secular liberal state identified by Ernst-Wolfgang Böckenförde in 1964. Böckenförde posed his dilemma in the context of Germany's fragile constitutional order, and as a means of appealing to his fellow Catholics to integrate into a Federal Republic some were suspicious of. As welcome as the international emphasis on human rights was, the danger in Böckenförde's eyes was that its very individualism emancipates individuals "not only from religion but also … from the national idea as a homogenizing force" (1991: 45). Thus, the post-1945 focus on human rights and on the individual reinforced important legal principles, but they also reinforced forces of individualism which do not necessarily lend themselves to a dialectic of social cohesion and the imperative of states to remain stable and intact. As much, then, as the post-1945 narrative of human rights was welcome after what had gone on before, the 'locking in' of democracy and constitutionalism through mechanisms such as the ECHR merely reinforced the pertinence of Böckenförde's dilemma regarding how liberalism could secure itself domestically without negating its purpose. American and German constitutionalism offer very different answers to this question.

Conclusion

This chapter has primarily examined the domestic influences on American and German constitutionalism reflecting the overall focus of the analysis in the following chapters. As noted by Böckenförde, however, the significance of the rise of the individual since the French Revolution and embodied in human rights covenants posed challenges for the liberal secular state in how to maintain societal cohesion and its own constitutional values as associational activities gave way to an ethos of individualism.

The far more comprehensive role that the *BVerfG* has in German politics helps explain why for all the importance of the US reapportionment cases at the time, the German court has been able to exert a far more positive influence over Germany's democratic institutions and constitutional culture since 1949 than the Supreme Court has been able to over American democracy. In the US and Germany, the particular 'liberty' or 'dignity' aspects of American and German constitutionalism have broadly shaped how the Supreme Court and *BVerfG* have responded to the stability and renewal imperative in their democratic political processes. This liberty-dignity dichotomy has also shaped the response of each court as to how it deals with voters being excluded from the political process, and whether it is able to establish conditions favourable to a vibrant liberal democracy, including a supportive constitutional culture. Whether the state is more inclined towards liberty or dignity has determined the nature of the *polis* that has been established. This, in turn, has determined how interventions in the processes of representative democracy occur, and whether values are 'formalised' by the state as they emerge in society, or whether values are 'inculcated' in society by the state.

When this dichotomy is applied to the legal case studies examined in Chapter 4 and Chapter 6, what emerges is a US Supreme Court which at rare moments is able to correct flaws in the political process, as seen in the reapportionment cases. However, the overtly liberty-oriented nature of American constitutionalism means that the Court was unable to materially improve the civic space which is essential for a vibrant liberal democracy based on equal respect. As will be seen in Chapter 4, this is best illustrated by the Court's unwillingness to tackle gerrymandering, an issue which has had such a corrosive effect on the centre-ground of American politics. The Supreme Court's domain is primarily a legal one, which has limited the lasting impact of its interventions in the political process. By contrast, while the *BVerfG*'s interventions in specific aspects of Germany's electoral processes (such as the legal cases examined in Chapter 6) have sometimes been methodologically confused and counter-productive, its long-term influence on rebuilding a democratic constitutional culture in Germany has been significant. The *BVerfG*'s domain is all-encompassing, embracing legal, political, and civic functions. This comprehensive role has been instrumental to its ability to restore to Germany the liberal constitutional values which Prussian militarism, the *Kaiserreich*, and Nazism had, in turn, supressed for over a century. As a result, it now becomes necessary to examine whether such apparently fragile liberal constitutional values and the relationship between citizen and state can be maintained in the absence of supportive identity-heavy value systems such as religion or nation, or without the reinforcement provided by civil and associational practices.

Notes

1 Former judge, European Court of Justice.
2 'Minority' is used here to refer to groups which may be losers in the political process sometimes, but may equally be successful at other times.
3 Justice Holmes argued that "the best test of truth is the power of the thought to get itself accepted in the competition of the market" (see *Abrams v United States*, 1919: 630).
4 Madison was clearly referring to all three departments including the judiciary and noted: "Were the executive magistrate, or the judges, not independent of the legislature in this particular, their independence in every other would be merely nominal" (Madison, 1987b: 319).
5 This conception of the individual is expressed in *Life Imprisonment Case* BVerfGE 187 (1977) and *Investment Aid I Case* (1954b).
6 See the critique of the established German parties from Ernst-Wolfgang Böckenförde and Richard von Weizsäcker in Chapter 6.

7 One of the most notable cases was the *Green Party Exclusion Case* 70 BVerfGE 324 (1986).
8 This resonates with the earlier point on private injustice (see Holmes, 1995: 244).
9 Justice Oliver Wendell Holmes' dissent in *Lochner v New York* (1905), and the comments of Justice Stephen Breyer (2016), are relevant here, and are assessed in Chapters 2 and 3.
10 Philippe Sands QC calls Lauterpacht's book "one of the transformative legal works of the twentieth century" (Lauterpacht and Sands, 2013: vii).
11 'Third-party effect' refers to the emerging relevance of fundamental rights for private law—an entirely new development in Germany since 1949. See Chapter 5 and *Lüth Case* (1958).

References

Lochner v New York, 198 US 45, 1905
Abrams v United States, 250 US 616, 1919
Olmstead v United States, 277 US 438, 1928
United States v Carolene Products Company, 304 US 144, 1938
Brown v Board of Education of Topeka, 347 US 483, 1954a
Investment Aid I Case, 4 BVerfGE 7, 1954b
Elfes, 6 BVerfGE 32 (1957), 1957
Lüth Case, 7 BVerfGE 198, 1958
Reynolds v Sims, 377 US 533, 1964a
Wesberry v Sanders, 376 US 549, 1964b
Life Imprisonment Case, 45 BVerfGE 187, 1977
Rhodes v Chapman, 452 US 337, 1981
Green Party Exclusion Case, 70 BVerfGE 324, 1986
Citizens United, No. 08–205, 2010

Ackerman, B., "The Rise of World Constitutionalism", *Virginia Law Review* (1997), 771–797.

Amann, M., D. Hipp, R. Pfister, and C. Schult, "Is Germany's High Court Anti-European?", *Spiegel Online*, 13 March 2014, available at: www.spiegel.de/international/germany/the-eu-critical-course-of-the-german-high-court-a-958018.html [accessed 18 October 2016].

Aristotle, *The Politics*, Translated by T.A. Sinclair, Revised by T. Saunders. Rev. edn (London: Penguin, 1992).

Blankenburg, E., "Mobilisation of the German Federal Constitutional Court", in *Constitutional Courts in Comparison: The US Supreme Court and the German Federal Constitutional Court*, ed. by Ralf Rogowski and Thomas Gawron (New York: Berghahn Books, 2002).

Böckenförde, E. W., *Constitutional and Political Theory: Selected Writings*. Vol. 1 (Oxford: Oxford University Press, 2017).

Böckenförde, E. W., "The Rise of the State as a Process of Secularisation", in *State, Society, and Liberty: Studies in Political Theory and Constitutional Law* (New York: Berg Pub Ltd, 1991).

Breyer, S. "Interview with Justice Stephen Breyer—With Charlie Rose (Transcript)", (2016), available at: https://charlierose.com/episodes/29278 [last accessed 6 October 2016].

Collings, J., *Democracy's Guardians: A History of the German Federal Constitutional Court, 1951–2001* (Oxford: Oxford University Press, 2015).

De Tocqueville, A. and P. Renshaw, *Democracy in America* (Herts: Wordsworth Editions Limited, 1998).

Durham, C., "General Asseessment of the Basic Law—An American View", in *Germany and its Basic Law: Past, Present, and Future: A German-American Symposium*, ed. by Paul Kirchhof and Donald P Kommers (Baden-Baden: Nomos, 1993).

Dworkin, R., *Justice for Hedgehogs* (Cambridge, MA: Belknap Press of Harvard University Press, 2011).

Eberle, E. J., "Human Dignity, Privacy, and Personality in German and American Constitutional Law", *Utah Law Review*, (4) (1997), 963.

Eberle, E. J., *Dignity and Liberty: Constitutional Visions in Germany and the United States* (Westport, CT: Praeger, 2002).

Elster, J., "Intertemporal Choice and Political Thought", in *Choice Over Time*, ed. by George Loewenstein and Jon Elster (New York: Russell Sage Foundation, 1992).

Fox, G. H. and G. Nolte, "Intolerant Democracies", *Harvard International Law Journal*, 36 (1995).

Friedrich, C. J., *Limited Government: A Comparison* (Englewood Cliffs, NJ: Prentice-Hall, 1974).

Goodman, M., "Human Dignity in Supreme Court Constitutional Jurisprudence", *Nebraska Law Review*, 84 (2006).

Hamilton, A., "Federalist Number 78", in *The Federalist Papers*, ed. by Isaac Kramnick (Harmondsworth: Penguin, 1987).

Hartz, L., *The Liberal Tradition in America: An Interpretation of American Political Thought Since the Revolution* (San Diego: Harcourt Brace Jovanovich, 1991).

Holmes, S., *Passions and Constraint: On the Theory of Liberal Democracy* (Chicago, IL: University of Chicago Press, 1995).

Huntington, S. P., *American Politics: The Promise of Disharmony* (Cambridge, MA: Harvard University Press, 1981).

Kautz, S., "Introduction", in *The Supreme Court and the Idea of Constitutionalism*, ed. by Steven Kautz, Arthur Melzer, Jerry Weinberger, and M Richard Zinman (Philadelphia: University of Pennsylvania Press, 2011).

Kokott, J., "From Reception and Transplantation to Convergence of Constitutional Models in the Age of Globalization—With Special Reference to the German Basic Law", in *Constitutionalism, Universalism and Democracy: A Comparative Analysis*, ed. by Christian Starck (Baden-Baden: Nomos-Verlag-Ges, 1999).

Kommers, D. P. and R. A. Miller, *The Constitutional Jurisprudence of the Federal Republic of Germany*. 3rd edn (Durham, NC: Duke University Press, 2012).

Koopmans, T., *Courts and Political Institutions: A Comparative View* (Cambridge: Cambridge University Press, 2003).

Lauterpacht, H., "The Law of Nations, the Law of Nature and the Rights of Man", *Transactions of the Grotius Society*, 29 (1943), 1–33.

Lauterpacht, H. and P. Sands, *An International Bill of the Rights of Man* (Oxford: Oxford University Press, 2013).

Loughlin, M., "What is Constitutionalism?", in *The Twilight Of Constitutionalism?*, ed. by Petra Dobner and Martin Loughlin (Oxford: Oxford University Press, 2012).

MacCormick, N., Z. Bankowski, L. Morawski, and A. Migue, "Rationales for Precedent", in *Interpreting Precedents: A Comparative Study*, ed. by Neil MacCormick and Robert Samuel Summers (Aldershot: Ashgate Publishing, 1997).

Madison, J., "Federalist Number 10", in *The Federalist Papers*, ed. by Isaac Kramnick (Harmondsworth: Penguin, 1987a).

Madison, J., "Federalist Number 51", in *The Federalist Papers*, ed. by Isaac Kramnick (Harmondsworth: Penguin, 1987b).

McIlwain, C. H., *Constitutionalism: Ancient and Modern* (Clark, NJ: The Lawbook Exchange, 2005).

Moravcsik, A., "The Origins of Human Rights Regimes: Democratic Delegation in Postwar Europe", *International Organization*, 54(02) (2000), 217–252.

Müller, J.-W., "The Problem with Poland", *New York Review of Books*, 11 February 2016, available at: www.nybooks.com/daily/2016/02/11/kaczynski-eu-problem-with-poland/ [accessed 22 May 2016].

Murphy, W. F., "Constitutions, Constitutionalism and Democracy", in *Constitutionalism and Democracy: Transitions in The Contemporary World*, ed. by Douglas Greenberg (New York: Oxford University Press, 1993).

Palmer, B., "The Pursuit of Happiness", in *Habits of the Heart: Individualism and Commitment in American Life*, ed. by Robert N Bellah, Richard Madsen, William M Sullivan, Ann Swidler, and Steven M Tipton (Berkeley: University of California Press, 2007).

Radbruch, G., "Gesetzliches Unrecht und Übergesetzliches Recht", *Süddeutsche Juristen-Zeitung*, 1(5) (1946), 105–108.

Radbruch, G., *Der Mensch in Recht* (Göttingen: Vandenhoeck and Ruprecht, 1957).

Rorty, R., *Achieving Our Country: Leftist Thought in Twentieth-Century America* (Cambridge, MA: Harvard University Press, 1998).

Rostow, E. V., "The Democratic Character of Judicial Review", *Harvard Law Review*, 66(2) (1952), 193–224.

Sager, L., "The Domain of Constitutional Justice", in *Constitutionalism: Philosophical Foundations*, ed. by Lawrence A. Alexander (Cambridge: Cambridge University Press, 1998).

Schlink, B., "German Constitutional Culture in Transition", in *Constitutionalism, Identity, Difference, and Legitimacy: Theoretical Perspectives*, ed. by Michel Rosenfeld (Durham, NC: Duke University Press, 1994).

Schmitt, C., *The Concept of the Political: Expanded Edition* (Chicago, IL: University of Chicago Press, 2008).

Smith, J. D., *On Democracy's Doorstep: The Inside Story of How the Supreme Court Brought "One Person, One Vote" to the United States* (New York: Hill and Wang, 2014).

Somek, A., *The Cosmopolitan Constitution* (New York: Oxford University Press, 2014).

Stern, K., "General Asseessment of the Basic Law—A German View", in *Germany and its Basic Law: Past, Present, and Future: A German-American Symposium*, ed. by Paul Kirchhof and Donald P. Kommers (Baden-Baden: Nomos, 1993).

Stone Sweet, A., *Governing with Judges: Constitutional Politics in Europe* (Oxford: Oxford University Press, 2000).

Stone Sweet, A., "Why Europe Rejected American Judicial Review: And Why it May Not Matter", *Michigan Law Review*, 101(8) (2003), 2744–2780.

Tushnet, M., "Some Skepticism About Normative Constitutional Advice", *William and Mary Law Review*, 49 (2007), 1473.

Villa, D., *Public Freedom* (Princeton, NJ: Princeton University Press, 2008).

Walther, D., *Gouverneur Morris: Witness of Two Revolutions* (New York: Funk & Wagnalls Company, 1934).

Wenner, U., *Sperrklauseln im Wahlrecht der Bundesrepublik Deutschland* (Frankfurt am Main: Peter Lang, 1986).

White, J. P., "Warren Court under Attack: The Role of the Judiciary in a Democratic Society", *Maryland Law Review*, 19 (1959), 181.

Whittington, K. E., "Constitutional Constraints in Politics", in *The Supreme Court and the Idea of Constitutionalism*, ed. by Steven Kautz, Arthur Melzer, Jerry Weinberger, and M. Richard Zinman (Philadelphia: University of Pennsylvania Press, 2011).

2 Mediating the Values of the Civic Space

> When we are dealing with words that also are a constituent act, like the Constitution of the United States, we must realize that they have called into life a being the development of which could not have been foreseen completely by the most gifted of its begetters. It was enough for them to realise or to hope that they had created an organism; it has taken a century and has cost their successors much sweat and blood to prove that they created a nation. The case before us must be considered in the light of our whole experience, and not merely in that of what was said a hundred years ago.
>
> (Oliver Wendell Holmes Jr, *State of Missouri v Holland*, 1920)

While some accounts of constitutionalism see it as an antidote to, or a restraint on, representative democracy, this tends to neglect constitutionalism's important role in establishing the democratic rights of citizens, and the rules by which democratic processes can function. One of the key questions for Ernst-Wolfgang Böckenförde was understanding "the conditions for a democracy and a democratically organised statehood to be cohesive and possess the capacity for action" (2017: 328). Democracy assumes, he argues, that "authority and the exercise of power are indispensable for the orderly coexistence of people, and that individuals cannot do what they like" (Böckenförde, 2017: 328). Such authority and exercise of power

> lie with the very people who form a political entity and community. Thus democracy does not mean the absence of government, but the self-government of a people, constitutive participation and a share in the decisions and measures to which each individual is subject.
>
> (Böckenförde, 2017: 328–329)

Two key words here are 'cohesive' and 'community'. The sources that "nourish" this commonality can be rational "in the sense of a political and economic cost-benefit analysis and enlightened self-interest", but the sources can also be what Böckenförde calls 'pre-rational' (2017: 331). Böckenförde is clear here that he does not mean irrational sources, rather those sources through which commonality is mediated:

> Established mental traditions, practiced customs and ways of life, as well as myths, religious convictions, and not least a common language and a certain cultural consciousness. These sources create a togetherness and commonality that is also emotional and tends to assume some kind of existential character, to affect the mind and soul of a people. It is the 'sense of belonging' [English in original] that sustains and shapes the cohesiveness of a group of people, a population, a society united and ordered in a state.
>
> (Böckenförde, 2017: 331)

At the heart of the Böckenförde Dilemma is the question of whether a society characterised by the intrinsic individualism of liberalism can cohere without the reinforcement provided by other sources of values and identity including religious affiliation, nationalism or patriotism, or civil associational practices. A more recent critic of the liberal project has noted that

> the belief that liberalism could achieve *modus vivendi* by encouraging privatism has culminated in the nearly complete disassociation of the governing class and a citizenry without a *cives*.
>
> (Deneen, 2019: 9)

One of the key issues Böckenförde is grappling with is how the liberal state maintains sufficient *authority* to ensure an environment conducive to the maintenance of liberal values without, first, enforcing those values, and second, without the legitimacy derived from the underlying historical and religious justifications that gave rise to that authority?

This chapter will assess whether the liberal constitutional state can be sustained in the absence of either internal sources of identity or homogeneity, or a citizenry that participates in their government. This question will be examined with respect to the thoughts and writing of Ernst-Wolfgang Böckenförde on the survival of the liberal secular state. I will also draw on Hannah Arendt's interpretation of Thomas Jefferson's fears for republican government, Judith Shklar's ideas on liberal thought, and Alexis de Tocqueville's arguments on civil association as the basis for maintaining representative democracy. To better understand how American and German constitutionalism shape the relationship between citizen and state, and the significance of Böckenförde's ideas, we must first understand the differences and tensions between the liberal and civic republican traditions, both of which are represented within the constitutional frameworks of each country. Although my primary point of reference will remain the United States and Germany, the ideas of Böckenförde on internal bonding forces in the liberal state have implications beyond these countries. The chapter will first examine how the liberty-dignity dichotomy in American and German constitutionalism plays a key role in whether emerging societal values are formalised or whether constitutional values are inculcated in society. The chapter then considers how the public-private separation that is so essential to liberty also creates a possibly fatal weakness at the heart of republican government: how to keep the emancipated citizen engaged in upholding their constitutional order. Conversely, German constitutionalism and the *BVerfG* ran a risk from another perspective: that in inculcating a normative value orientation on the rest of the constitutional order including its political institutions, citizens would see democracy as an empty vessel, and might disengage from politics and political activity.

Stephen Kautz writes that the radical individualism of liberal political philosophy—seen as the basis of liberal ideas about "consent, individual (inalienable) rights, limited government, and the rest seems to be both sociologically and psychologically untrue" (2011: 42). "The image of solitary, free and equal individuals in a state of nature", he notes, "does not do justice to the evidence that we are constituted in various important ways by history, by culture, by family, by religion, and so on" (Kautz, 2011: 42). Citizens may therefore find solace in other forms of identity, social cohesion, and value systems that have more resonance in their lives, including religion or nationalism. This does not mean that religion or attachment to country will be antithetical to liberal constitutional values; sometimes they may reinforce them, which was Böckenförde's hope in 1964 (see Rath, 2009). As was the case during the Weimar Republic, though, it is where 'traditional' values and the interpretations of a national majority (or a significant minority of the population) run counter to the values of the constitutional order on *an issue of significance* to both that the liberal state is at risk. A liberal democratic state which is largely homogeneous and which has less variation between national and local majority sentiments may have fewer political divisions than the United States, but where individuals turn against the values of their constitutional order then the state is in far more serious danger. As Learned Hand put it

> Liberty lies in the hearts of men and women; when it dies there, no constitution, no law, no court can save it; no constitution, no law, no court can even do much to help it.
>
> (Judge Learned Hand, quoted in Griswold, 1960: 226)

Ultimately, German and American constitutionalism both have the potential to have a negative impact on liberty: Germany's from doing too much and smothering out democratic activity; America's from doing too little and letting republican government die out through anti-democratic practices like malapportionment or gerrymandering that entrench oligarchical interests.

There is a tendency to conceptualise political societies as static entities where public and majority opinion changes in response to shifting political dynamics, changing circumstances, and new information. Consequently, our judgements and analysis as to the degree of cohesion or fragmentation of a particular society are seen as merely a snapshot of an unchanging static society at a certain point in time. In fact, while public and majority opinion may indeed change due to the factors highlighted above, intergenerational change as older citizens die and new ones come of age can also be immensely consequential for the health of a polity and for the political and electoral choices it makes. Germany's rebirth after World War II illustrates that relationships between the generations can be complex and fraught, but that tension can also pave the way for a fundamental re-evaluation of a society's value commitments.

The fundamental rights provisions at the start of the Basic Law set out a clear value framework which is further buttressed through the 'eternity clause' of Article 79 which prevents changes to those values or to Germany's democratic and federal structure. Thus, the Basic Law's architectonic principles of human dignity and free democratic basic order are eternal according to this logic. Provisions without any scope for constitutional amendment would have doubtless horrified Jefferson by striking at his belief in the possibility of constitutional renewal and a tabula rasa moment.[1] Although Jefferson never used the word 'renewal' in describing his 'sovereignty of the living generation' idea where constitutions would lapse at the end of 19 years,[2] a reasonable interpretation would seem to be that he wanted to ensure continued popular acceptance for a constitution, and a continuing bond between the citizens and their republic to avoid political ossification. This last point—that republican government would fail because Americans would become aloof from the need to participate in government—will be assessed later in this chapter through Hannah Arendt's interpretation of Jefferson's concerns.

Part of the reason that Jefferson's maddening and whimsical inconsistencies endure is because constitutions seemingly strike at the heart of a fundamental human impulse: the ability to correct mistakes and to alter governing arrangements in response to changing circumstances. This, however, was precisely what Chief Justice John Marshall declared that "a Constitution intended to endure for ages to come" should be capable of doing: "being adapted to the various crises of human affairs" as he put it in *McCulloch v Maryland* (1819: 415). It was the mutability of constitutional form over time in response to societal developments and events that provided for this, Marshall said. Thus, Marshall's conception of an evolving constitutional understanding may provide a happy medium between Jefferson throwing the baby out with the bath water after 19 years and Germany's post-war aversion to throwing anything out. How this balance is struck, though, requires an appreciation of the role of constitutionalism in inculcating values in society or formalising values emerging from society. This process by which values in a society are diffused and mediated contributes, in turn, to the formation of opinions which can become more widespread and, as Koopmans noted (2003: 123), even become tomorrow's majority.

Inculcation or Formalisation

Commenting on the role of authority and values in state cohesion, Friedman notes (in terms that are counter-Schmittian and counter-Habermasian in equal measure) that "neither coercion nor rational argument, nor both together, seem capable of accounting for the coordination of wills required for a society to exist" (1990: 57–58). Friedman invokes Tocqueville's idea that "without common belief, no society can exist" (quoted in 1990: 58). This perhaps raises the question of whether a spirit of individualism, such as is associated with the United States, can itself become a source of cohesion and homogeneity? Maintaining a stable inter-relationship between citizens and state in a liberal polity requires some fundamental agreement on the acceptable values within a state, within its political culture, and within its society. Here, as Judith Shklar notes, liberalism does not have "to depend on specific religious or philosophical systems of thought"; provided liberalism does not choose between these systems, all that matters is that "they do not reject toleration" (1989: 24). Of particular relevance to the Böckenförde Dilemma and post-1949 German constitutionalism is Shklar's view that "no theory that gives public authorities the unconditional right to impose beliefs and even a vocabulary as they may see fit upon the citizenry can be described as even remotely liberal" (1989: 24). Shklar's view intersects with many of the concerns expressed by Böckenförde about the *Bundesverfassungsgericht*'s objective value order, before and after he sat on the Court, that a state that imposes values on its citizens is hardly *liberal*. As Böckenförde put it in a 2011 interview, "a use of liberty that remains within the boundaries of the law cannot be declared illegitimate because it adheres to values that are rejected" (2017: 376).[3] In order to fully understand the significance of Böckenförde's analysis for the endurance of certain value systems, it is perhaps useful to first examine what we mean by authority and whether certain types of authority are likely to be recognised by citizens as more legitimate than others, and, in terms of identity, as more relatable to their own interests, values, and community.

Sheldon Wolin asked of the American Constitution whether the "we" in its preamble was not so much the creator of it, but its "creature" (1989: 83). While the answer in America's case may be 'somewhere in between', the creature view is much easier to discern in the case of Germany after 1949. As much as the Basic Law resurrected elements of the Weimar Constitution and the country's liberal constitution of 1849, it also resonates with Jefferson's tabula rasa view of societal rebirth based on a clean break with the norms (and crimes) of the past. If American constitutionalism in the twentieth century has rested predominantly on a formalisation of value changes already occurring in society, German constitutionalism's normative bent since 1949 has relied on the inculcation of values from political and judicial elites downwards. Put slightly differently, America created a constitution which matched its political culture, while in Germany over the last 60 years a political culture has gradually developed which matches its constitution. The process of conditioning Germany's post-war constitutional culture was driven by a multiplicity of factors, including the normative aims of Germany's framers, then by the political leadership of Konrad Adenauer, and ultimately through the judgments of the *BVerfG*. The presence of the Court in public life and a growing awareness on the part of German citizens of its role as guardian of the Basic Law contributed to the civic education of Germans regarding the values of their constitutional order (see Collings, 2015: xxxvi).

What remained in doubt, as we shall see, was whether the values of constitutionalism were sufficient to uphold the liberal democratic state, absent some other source of societal and civic cohesion which could bind citizens to their states and to one another. The American and German constitutional cases looked at in Chapter 4 and Chapter 6 both illustrate the involvement of civil society groups and citizens in attempting to ensure their voting rights and constitutions were upheld. The political campaign against malapportionment in the US, which initially went nowhere due to the intransigence and vested interests of lawmakers who refused to reapportion themselves out of a job, eventually became a legal struggle in the federal courts. In Germany it was the constitutional complaint mechanism which provided the means for citizens and political parties in the two European Parliament cases to petition the *BVerfG*.

Justice William Brennan noted that the act of interpretation is "undertaken with full consciousness that it is, in a very real sense, the community's interpretation that is sought" (1990: 25). Depending on the particular case or controversy before the Court, Brennan is correct that a majority of the society may clearly favour the decision that the Court eventually reaches. *Brown v Board of Education* (1954), *Baker v Carr* (1962), and *Obergefell v Hodges*, the 2015 case which recognised gay marriage, are all cases where there was either a clear or emerging national consensus, even a bare one, in favour of the decisions that the Court reached. However, as will be outlined in Chapter 3, the notion of a national consensus can be more problematic in a continent-sized country such as the US where *local majorities* in different regions may have very different views from the *national majority*. The 'which majority?' question matters a great deal where competing value systems and competing interpretations may be antithetical to each other. Samuel Huntington argued that what has distinguished American politics from that of other countries is not some fundamental disagreement over principles, but rather how those principles should be applied in practice (1981: 3–4). Huntington's point is broadly correct, but it is also possible for a principle to be applied so differently in particular cases and between different communities as to make it meaningless. Citizens of Georgia and New York state in 1860 and 1960 may all have fervently believed in the idea of equality, but it is likely that majorities in each state would have differed significantly when it came to the question of which Americans that principle should apply to.

Keith Whittington's observation that "constitutionalism only binds the willing" (2011: 224) is relevant here. Constitutionalism gives the courts an important role to play in the application of principles, but this may often be in ways that local or national communities may disagree with. Seeking the community's interpretation may be all well and good if it respects universal principles of liberalism and human dignity. However, if its values are akin to Germany's in the late 1930s, or Alabama's in the 1950s, then this is ostensibly where and when constitutionalism matters the most. In other words, constitutionalism comes into its own at those moments when the decision of a court or indeed the political branches is *not* one that a majority of the population would likely have come to. Yet such decisions are likely to be the ones which are most essential and difficult for a court to make. Alexander Hamilton put the point best when he noted that

> It would require an uncommon portion of fortitude in the judges to do their duty as faithful guardians of the Constitution, where legislative invasions of it had been instigated by the major voice of the community.
>
> (Hamilton, *Federalist 78*, 1987: 440–441)

Justice Robert Jackson's majority opinion in *West Virginia v Barnette*[4] contains perhaps the most cogent definition of constitutionalism enunciated by a US court in the twentieth century. The First Amendment case, which Friedman regards as "one of the most notable pro-liberties decisions of the era", prompted the *New York Times* to write in response that "when the court rises to its full height it proves its claim to be regarded as one of the great prides of American democracy" (quoted in Friedman, 2002: 180). Jackson's majority opinion, which ruled that schoolchildren could not be compelled to salute the flag or be expelled from public schools for not doing so, came at a time when the United States was fighting totalitarianism abroad, and required precisely the sort of fortitude that Hamilton referred to.

> The very purpose of a Bill of Rights was to withdraw certain subjects from the vicissitudes of political controversy, to place them beyond the reach of majorities and officials, and to establish them as legal principles to be applied by the courts. One's right to life, liberty, and property, to free speech, a free press, freedom of worship and assembly, and other fundamental rights may not be submitted to a vote; they depend on the outcome of no elections.[5]
>
> Justice Robert Jackson, *Virginia v Barnette* (1943: 638)

Jackson's opinion is an important yardstick for it represents an example of what I describe below as *heightened constitutionalism*. In other words, this is a decision which is correct precisely because it would not be, in Justice Brennan's words, the "community's interpretation". *Barnette* speaks to one of the fundamental principles at the heart of constitutionalism, the placing of certain controversies beyond the power of democratic change. Jackson's opinion in *Barnette* represents a powerful statement of constitutionalism because it is the Court saying to the state and "the major voice of the community" during a time of war that the right to free speech requires that no citizen can be forced to salute the flag. Johnson notes that "rather than grounding his opinion in terms of freedom of religion, Jackson analysed the case as one of freedom of speech and expression" (2003: 953). I would agree with John Finn that *Barnette* was not a rejection of the "interest in national cohesion" that every constitutional regime has in the creation of citizens, but rather the case emphasised that "overly aggressive efforts to promote it", such as compelling citizens to salute the flag against their will, "may do damage to other bedrock constitutional ideals" (2014: 83–84).

The Court's authority to resist the will of the community in this sense nevertheless requires the community and the other branches of government to accept the importance of the constitutional principles at issue—be it freedom of speech, the rule of law, or human dignity—as fundamentally important, even if they might disagree with how the Court has applied these principles in a given case. What constitutionalism can do is to make moments of constitutional resistance and crisis transparent, providing the possibility for opposition to be mobilised against those resisting or rejecting the constitutional constraints (Whittington, 2011: 224). As Whittington points out, constitutional courts are particularly useful in this regard for publicising constitutional transgressions (2011: 224–225). Perhaps just as important, even if the government and community disagree with the relative importance of the principles or how the Court has applied them, constitutionalism requires that the community and legislators recognise the authority of the courts to make the call. One example of this is the enforcement of the Supreme Court decision in *Brown*, which was vigorously supported by President Eisenhower during the Little Rock controversy.

> The overwhelming majority of our people in every section of the country are united in their respect for observance of the law—even in those cases where they may disagree with that law. ... A foundation of our American way of life is our national respect for law.
>
> (Eisenhower, 1957)

John Finn's conception of 'the Civic Constitution' captures the dilemma in how to establish a dialogue over the meaning of law, and the extent to which questions of law can become values capable of binding a community or society together. The purposes of such a 'Civic Constitution' are to "establish a community, a civic culture, that prizes questions about the fundamental principles and purposes of constitutional life, principles that include, among others, the meaning of liberty, equality, and justice" (Finn, 2014: 2). For Finn, ensuring that the Constitution and law are accepted by citizens paradoxically means recognising the limitations of exclusively legal understandings of the Constitution, while demanding citizens exercise a role in realising a more expansive purpose to the constitutional text (2014: 2).

The values of constitutionalism—as enforced in the Supreme Court decision in *Barnette* or other cases—may often be antithetical to the forces of societal cohesion, be they religion or nation. Inevitably, politicians rarely take kindly to their key policies being subject to legal scrutiny, and the predictable cry goes up about unelected judges overriding policies which a party or politician was elected to implement. Nevertheless, citizens rarely enjoy having their political or civil rights curtailed either. A better understanding among citizens and officials that "part of constitutionalism is the rule of law, and part of the rule of law is allowing courts to decide issues"[6] (Judge David Edward, Interview) would minimise such disputes. This requires, as Wolfgang Friedmann notes, "the purposeful collaboration and the constant interplay between legislators, administrators and courts in the articulation and implementation of social change" (1972: 74). In times of normal political and social consensus within a liberal polity the interplay between society, the political branches, and the judiciary will be rather predictable with the values of each tending to reaffirm or only slightly alter the predominant normative orientations of the other groups. It is during times of crisis or extreme social and political flux that the formalisation of values versus inculcation of values dichotomy becomes more pertinent and crucial for the stability and even survival of a polity. In other words, the state, through the courts and the political branches, must decide whether the ideas of new and burgeoning social forces and political parties are ones that it is willing and able to incorporate into the permitted spectrum of constitutional values in the polity.

When values are formalised, as when the Supreme Court voted to desegregate schools in *Brown v Board of Education*, the Court is acting as a guide of sorts. In *Brown*, the Court saw the direction of travel of the national majority, or near majority of the population, and formalised that emerging national consensus, even while repudiating the local consensus in Kansas and Arkansas that permitted segregation.[7] Stephen Macedo's observation that "liberal politics invites all citizens to participate in the process of making, testing, and refining law" is relevant here (1990: 79); but in federations, or states with complex sub-national identity politics or cultural divisions between regions, different groups may reach different conclusions about the law and concomitant social values. Thus, while the *Brown* decision formalised and reinforced the value change in the national majority regarding civil rights and the unacceptability of segregation, it also served a pedagogic function in seeking to inculcate the new norm in the whole of society, but especially those parts that were resistant to it. When the Supreme Court prevents the majority of the community, the political branches, or a group in society from carrying out a policy or some desired civic practice—as it did in *Barnette* by banning the requirement that all children must salute the flag—the Court's decision served to reinforce and inculcate the principle of free speech against the state's desire to inculcate the value of nation during a time of war. Because of the difference between national majority and local majority sentiment in the US, *Brown* represented something of an anomaly in the way that it both formalised a value change among a national majority or (near) national majority, while it also sought to inculcate the decision among those groups that would be resistant to it.[8]

While the formalisation of value changes already in progress in society is more common to American constitutionalism, the inculcation of values also occurs in cases involving what I term *heightened constitutionalism*. Such cases include decisions such as *Barnette* where the Supreme Court blocks or compels an action of another branch of government, even where that action would generally be supported by a majority of the people. The essence of value inculcation, then, is that it involves a court enunciating and applying norms as law which a clear majority of the population and their elected representatives may disagree with. Value inculcation is moot if a majority of the population has already accepted the idea, to use *Brown* again, that 'separate but equal' schooling was morally unacceptable; the question is then just one of formalising the general mood in the national community. However, this value inculcation in the local majority which rejects the new norm will likely be seen by that local majority as undemocratic. Although the decision in *Barnette* can be seen in terms of inculcation of an important right of freedom of expression against a community, those in *Brown* and *Baker* more closely fit the Tocquevillean idea (see De Tocqueville and Renshaw, 1998: 103) that the Court was actually speaking for an emerging or distinct majority, albeit a national one.

Germany in the early 1950s represented a much clearer example of *heightened constitutionalism* as its society was certainly not in tune with the liberal democratic values of its new constitutional order. The *Bundesverfassungsgericht*'s role was therefore significantly one of entrenching the norms of the Basic Law into all of the political and legal institutions of the constitutional order. Then, following the Court's important *Lüth Case* decision (1958), the entire German legal system including private law became subject to the Basic Law. Inculcating the Basic Law's values in society was a much longer-term process involving the *BVerfG*, different state institutions and, from the mid-1960s onwards, became conjoined with the wider Holocaust consciousness that developed in Germany. In fact, for the first decade of the Federal Republic there were probably few values in German society that the *BVerfG* would have wanted to formalise.[9] As Gitta Sereny observed:

> The Nazi trials are being held because the best in Germany feel that the integrity of society depends on the integrity of its laws. Unhappily here we have also learned that the law depends for its integrity on the integrity of society.[10]
>
> (Gitta Sereny, 2000: 85)

The most direct pedagogic effect that the Court has had on German society has been through the constitutional complaint mechanism, examined in Chapter 6. More than 130,000 citizens have petitioned the Court since 1951, which has been credited with developing a broad democratic understanding among the German people (see Collings, 2015: xxxvi). However, as will be assessed in Chapter 6, the emergence of the Green Party as a political force in the 1980s represented a dramatic change in the political scene, one that the *BVerfG* was generally more accepting of than the established political parties.

Whose Values?

The American and German acts of constitution forming each represented an attempt to create a new state and a new constitutional identity from a tabula rasa moment. These parallels, though, do not disguise the significant differences between these acts of constitution making. Justice Oliver Wendell Holmes observed in his famous dissent in *Lochner v New York* that a constitution is "made for people of fundamentally different views" (1905: 76). Although undoubtedly true of the United States, it seems less true of Germany, for reasons that will become clear. Holmes might well have said 'peoples', for while there was certainly a common culture in the colonies, Americans had distinct state, regional, and local identities. Sharp differences existed within states and between the propertied and moneyed elites of the northern states and the farm and plantation owners of the South. Even by the time of the Civil War, almost 75 years after the Constitution was established, Robert E Lee and Jefferson Davis still considered themselves citizens of their states first, of the South second, and of the United States last (Murphy, 2007: 351).

During the Virginia Ratifying Convention, Patrick Henry's indignation at the words in the Constitution's preamble illustrated the fragmented reality of the American colonies.

> What right had they to say, 'We, the people'? ... Who authorized them to speak the language of, 'We, the people', instead of, 'We, the states'? States are the characteristics and the soul of a confederation. If the states be not the agents of this compact, it must be one great, consolidated, national government, of the people of all the states.
>
> (Henry, 1986: 21–22)

The United States as a nation did not exist and would not be forged without the struggle and shedding of blood that Justice Holmes referred to in *State of Missouri v Holland* (1920).

As various groups and interests clashed over their differing conceptions of the constitutional narrative, so the Supreme Court's interpretations became more important as orientation points for the developing nation. Sometimes, however, the divergence in constitutional meaning between the social practices that are permitted in the civic space and those that the state is prepared to accept as law become too wide. In the United States, the Civil War was the end result of the divisions over slavery. As Robert Dahl observed

> Given the extreme polarisation in interests, values, and ways of life between the citizens of the slave states and those of the free states, I cannot imagine any democratic constitution under which the two sections could have continued to coexist peacefully in one country.
>
> (Dahl, 2003: 95)

After the defeat of the South and the passage of the Reconstruction Amendments, the law of the United States and the constitutional interpretation of the North regarding the abhorrence of slavery prevailed. Yet, the Union had won this constitutional argument by force. In terms of the Böckenförde Dilemma, the Union had sacrificed its liberalness and resorted to war in order to restore a constitutional interpretation that would have to be recognised as law in the South.[11] However, recognition of law did not mean that the South had accepted the values and norms embodied in that law. Utilising a historical institutionalist approach, Orren and Skowronek's idea of 'multiple orders' highlights how, during Reconstruction, "Congress had no civilian apparatus of its own to carry out its will in the South and the administration of its laws through local courts, juries, and lawyers promised to stymie the desired outcome" (2004: 138).

Under normal circumstances, though, differences in constitutional meaning between the interpretation of a national majority and that of local majorities need not result in bloodshed. Justice Stephen Breyer noted recently that

> It is not the Supreme Court that tells people what to do. This document [the Constitution] sets boundaries. We are in a sense a boundary commission. … Sometimes those boundary questions are very tough. … The document leaves vast space in between the boundaries for people themselves, through the ballot box, to decide what city, state, or nation they want. That's what [the Constitution] foresees, and if you do not participate, it will not work.
>
> (Breyer, 2016)

The Court's role as "the boundary commission" of the Constitution is, says Breyer, to police only those difficult questions on the edges of the document which people can and will differ on. Invoking Constant's notion of the 'liberty of the ancients' and his view on the people's right to "an active and constant participation in collective power", Justice Breyer has also argued separately that judges interpreting the Constitution should place more emphasis upon the idea of active liberty based on participatory self-governance (2002: 246). This view of a constitution establishing a civic space where political and social life can occur—and the role of any court in policing that space—is very important and will be returned to in this chapter and later ones.

Andreas Voßkuhle, President of the *Bundesverfassungsgericht* from 2010 to 2020, said in a 2013 interview that the role of a court—particularly in the German sense—is defining parameters within which politics can unfold (see Chapter 6, and also Voßkuhle and Von Rahden, 2013). Breyer's and Voßkuhle's remarks may sound similar, but they are essentially describing two different constitutional universes, one broadly conditioned by liberty and one by dignity. More significantly, Breyer is describing, however decorously, a civic space where individuals volunteer, engage in their communities, and live their lives within those spaces. Voßkuhle, though, seems to be describing a purely political space where representative democracy can be permitted to play out, but only if it respects the higher law norms and fundamental rights of the Constitution. This difference sets up the fundamental problem which will be engaged with in this and later chapters, and which Böckenförde and other thinkers have wrestled with: the balance between the state giving citizens the discretion to live their lives free from its interference, while depending on those same citizens to preserve the state, and those very freedoms that the state's existence guarantees.

If the US Constitution was a framework for argument among people of different views (see, for example, Ellis, 2007: 87–126), Germany's Basic Law

(*Grundgesetz*) represented a clear attempt to create a liberal democratic constitutional order based on fundamental rights that the state would be duty bound to protect. Although more homogenous than eighteenth-century America, Germany also contained people of different views, and in the early 1950s many of these people seemed to be aligned against the new Federal Republic and its values (see Chapter 5, and also Kermani, 2014). Whereas the US Constitution had to be general enough to draw together those disparate societal threads within a workable framework of governance, the Basic Law was an unambiguously normative constitution, which was intended not to reconcile the values of discordant parts *of* society, but rather to inculcate its fundamental values *in* society. While the liberal values of the Basic Law represented some of the fruits of the country's two previous liberal constitutions—the Frankfurt Constitution of 1849, which survived less than a day, and the Weimar Constitution of 1919, which lasted 14 years—these values were not rooted deeply in German society.[12]

It is also important to recognise that Germany's post-war constitutional institutions were seen as only one part of the equation. Finding a value system or sense of identification that would resonate with the German people in 1949 and reinforce rather than undermine the values of the Basic Law was every bit as much of a challenge. One widely discussed idea in Germany for decades has been constitutional patriotism (*Verfassungspatriotismus*), which has been developed in the very different work of Dolf Sternberger and Jürgen Habermas (see, for example, Sternberger, 1990; Habermas, 2001). For Sternberger, who had experienced the fall of Weimar, the *Verfassungspatriotismus* was one of 'militancy' and making the state and its institutions strong enough against its enemies, while for Habermas it was about 'memory' and recognising that after the Holocaust the only possible national identity for Germans was one based on a shared public adherence to democratic rights and values. Both of these ideas—of militant democracy and resistant institutions, and public adherence to democratic values—are embodied in important ways within the Basic Law.

Germany's founding fathers, like America's, recognised the tentative nature of their creation. Given the fate of the country's previous attempts at constitution making, the new constitutional document was deliberately not called a constitution (*Verfassung*), but the Basic Law or (*Grundgesetz*). In a country which, despite the Nazi period, still had a profound respect for the law (see Schlink, 1994: 210–211) and the notion of the *Rechtsstaat*, designating the new constitution as 'fundamental law' was a sagacious move. Moreover, the word *Grundgesetz* indicated that the Basic Law was intended to be a temporary and transitional document, which, according to the terms of its preamble, would apply during a "transitional period" until the "entire German people" could "complete the unity and freedom of Germany in free self-determination" (see Friedrich, 1949: 706). The opportunity to create a new Constitution for a reunified Germany came in 1991, but it was one that most Germans showed little interest in taking advantage of.

Böckenförde and the Survival of the Liberal State

There is generally little that unites the outlooks, philosophical or otherwise, of Jürgen Habermas and Carl Schmitt. Both, however, saw that in its first decade the *Bundesverfassungsgericht* had become too powerful (Collings, 2015: 61). For Schmitt, the Court's existence fractured the state's ability to decide, while for Habermas its central role in politics impaired the ability of the people to deliberate (Collings, 2015: 61). As Collings puts it (2015: 61), "Policy came from Bonn; values from Karlsruhe; but what came from the people?" This, of course, was the problem. By the late 1950s, the Federal Republic had gained majority acceptance in Germany, aided in large part by spectacular economic growth and a sense of stability (Collings, 2015: 57). However, the uninvited guest at the German dinner party remained the Nazi period and the willingness of so many Germans to support Hitler, actively or tacitly.[13] While the Basic Law derived its authority and legitimacy from the people (see, for example, Article 20, Clause 2), incorporating their agency into the new body politic was effectively done by migrating the constitutional populism of the Reich President under the Weimar Republic to the *BVerfG* under the Basic Law (Möllers, 2007: 96). Meanwhile, the ability of Germany to maintain a liberal democracy and a sense of societal cohesion and identity purely on the basis of economic growth—and, implicitly, the liberal values being enunciated by the *BVerfG*—was questioned from the left and right.

These questions revealed doubts as to whether the values of Germany's Karlsruhe-inspired constitutionalism—human dignity and democracy itself—resonated strongly enough to keep liberal democracy alive in a country where democratic institutions had fared so dismally. Schmitt referred to the Court's value order as a "tyranny of values" and railed against it (2011). For Schmitt (a Catholic), all significant political concepts were traceable to Christian theology or religious tradition, compared to which the insipid but still menacing Karlsruhe-inspired 'objective value order' was a poor substitute (Gordon, 2013: 180). Schmitt's view was broadly shared by Adenauer's Christian Democrats that "without the moral nourishment or value-orientations provided by Christianity, liberal democracy would suffer a normative deficit and might not long survive" (Gordon, 2013: 184).

This emphasis on religion was on one level a concerted strategy on the part of Christian Democrats to exculpate themselves from the secular materialism of the Third Reich, and to blame the secular left (i.e. the Social Democrats) for facilitating the Nazis. On any objective level this was absurd as the Social Democrats had generally been among the most vociferous opponents of the Nazis. Despite the political motives and advantage the CDU gained by presenting itself as an alternative to National Socialist secularism, an identity crisis was undoubtedly brewing in the FRG, one which became an open wound after the 1960s with the public debate over how Germany came to terms with its Nazi past (*Die Vergangenheitsbewältigung*). Consequently, neither nationalism nor even a milder form of patriotism were seen as viable sources of either constitutional values or societal cohesion in post-war Germany.

It was ironic, then, that it was the value-assertive doctrine of the judicial seers of the *BVerfG* which has become such an unmistakable part of Germany's post-1949 constitutional topography. In this respect, the Court's role has been nothing less than defining the very *telos* of the Basic Law. The impact of the *BVerfG*'s influence was seen, first, through its inculcation of the Basic Law's emerging values and processes in political institutions, and, second, through a growing awareness on the part of ordinary Germans—particularly as a result of the constitutional complaint mechanism—that the Court was there to protect their fundamental and democratic rights. Writing in 1971, Wilhelm Geck argued that "the jurisprudence of the [*Bundesverfassungsgericht*] has, as we all know, fostered the development of true democratic understanding in the Federal Republic" (quoted in Collings, 2015: xxxvi). The Court's role in shaping Germans' expectations and understandings of democracy has been repeatedly manifested through the constitutional complaints of citizens and political parties. As will be shown in Chapter 6, the constitutional complaint mechanism provided the vehicle through which German citizens and political parties could challenge the retention of the statutory 5 percent hurdle for electoral success at the European Parliament level.

A further irony is that it was Ernst-Wolfgang Böckenförde, a political theorist and protégée of Schmitt, who became one of the Court's most influential justices during the 1980s and 1990s. Although their value orientations are fundamentally opposed, both Schmitt and Böckenförde were of the view that to understand a given legal order one must look below the surface of positive law and recognise the power mechanisms, social belief systems, and fundamental norms that structure and stabilise it (see Editor's note, Böckenförde, 2017: 370). One central concern of Böckenförde in postulating his dilemma was to understand the state as it had evolved to the present and to better grasp "the fundamental problems of political organisation that face the present-day state" (1991: 27).

As noted, the key liberal separation between the public and private realms, which Böckenförde saw the French Revolution as ushering in, is important as we proceed. Liberalism, as Shklar notes, is not necessarily linked to any specific religious or scientific doctrine, but is "psychologically more compatible with some rather than with others" (1989: 24). Due to the "primacy of toleration as the irreducible limit on public agents", Shklar argues that liberalism "must reject only those political doctrines that do not recognise any difference between the spheres of the personal and the public" (1989: 24). Although this was true of the US and Germany, the configuration of these spheres, their permissible purposes, and the role of the individual within them was very different in each country. Public freedom in the United States permitted public and private injustice such as segregation and slavery, while in the Federal Republic, public freedom, private autonomy, and the primacy of human dignity in German constitutionalism after 1949 depended on an almost Aristotelian inter-relationship between the individual and their society.

In 1967, Böckenförde wrote an essay, at the heart of which was the question of which values can bind and hold a state and society together in a secular age, and in the absence of the old certainty of religion or the homogeneity provided by nation (1991: 44–45). "Can the state be built on a 'natural ethics'?", he asked, and, "how far can nations united in states live by the guaranteed provision of individual liberty alone, without a unifying bond antecedent to that liberty?" (Böckenförde, 1991: 44). In the aftermath of the collapse of the Nazi secular state and in the first decades of the Federal Republic these questions were seen as existentially significant. After all, nothing in Germany's three previous constitutions of 1849, 1871, and 1919 had done anything to entrench liberal values in German society and its state institutions. From the politically unstable vantage point of the early 1950s, there was no axiomatic or logical reason why it should be 'fourth time lucky'.

When Böckenförde originally posed these questions in the 1960s, Western liberal democratic societies were again in a growing state of flux due to social changes and movements demanding civil rights and greater equality. These factors were also relevant in Germany where student protests and the prospect of change from the CDU government (which had led the country since the establishment of the FRG) to Willy Brandt's Social Democrats, were cause for alarm in some quarters. Böckenförde feared that the reliance of the FRG since its establishment on the "moral values" of the Basic Law as a basis of shared convictions was replete with dangers, potentially opening the door "to subjectivism and positivism in current assessments of values that, each laying claim to objective validity, tend to destroy rather than foster liberty" (1991: 45). In times of changing value orientations and a possibly dissolving social contract, can a normative constitution alone hold a society together if citizens are sceptical or hostile to its values? Böckenförde's question speaks as much to American debates over hyper-individualism and the decline of civil association, and recent Western debates over migration and the rise of populist forces, as it does to German debates over societal change in the 1960s and today.

Böckenförde's argument lies at the heart of the stability versus renewal dichotomy assessed thus far. Can the liberal democratic state successfully preserve its own existence on the basis of its constitutional values without indoctrinating those values in society, and thus, according to Böckenförde, sacrificing its fundamental liberal character? Böckenförde's main point, coming around 20 years before he joined the *BVerfG*, was both a question and a warning.

> The question of bonding forces [in society] is posed afresh and reduced to its actual core: *the liberal, secularised state is nourished by presuppositions that it cannot itself guarantee.* That is the great gamble it has made for liberty's sake. On the one hand, it can only survive as a liberal state if the liberty it allows its citizens regulates itself from within on the basis of the moral substance of the individual and the homogeneity of society. On the other hand, it cannot attempt to guarantee those inner regulatory forces by its own efforts—that is to say, with the instruments of legal coercion and authoritative command—without abandoning its liberalness.
>
> (Böckenförde, 1991: 45; emphasis in original)

Böckenförde then takes aim at the extent to which, in inculcating its value system, the state acting through the *BVerfG* had, at once, sacrificed some of the liberalness of the Federal Republic in the interests of its preservation, *and* eroded the wall between the public and private spheres essential to liberty.

> The prescribed state ideology, the revival of the Aristotelian polis tradition, and the proclamation of an 'objective system of values' all do away with the very split out of which public liberty is constituted. There is no way back across the threshold of 1789 that does not destroy the state as the order of liberty.
>
> (Böckenförde, 1991: 45)

The 'split' of course, was that between state and society, between the public and the private, which the French Revolution and, indeed, the American Revolution, had ushered in (see, for example, Arendt, 1973: 123–8). His 'dilemma' posed in 1964 and his later complaints about ossification among the established parties while he was on the Court can be seen not as an attack on the liberal values of the Basic Law, but as a warning that the inculcation of values, even liberal ones, can end up negating liberalism itself.

While Friedman's view that the notion of "in authority" may be the more appropriate form of authority for a modern society that has lost the sense of a common framework of substantive moral beliefs, the reduction of authority to an institutional mechanism devoid of historical, cultural, or societal linkages or ties is surely far more susceptible to disintegration than authority structures based on such bonds. One of the key points that makes Friedman's argument about authority germane to the relationship between citizen and state, and to Böckenförde's concern, is the question of whether liberalism thrives as a set of values that binds a society together, or whether it succeeds as part of "a common framework of rules of conduct, within which … individuals can then pursue their own ends" (Friedman, 1990: 58)? Friedman's point is that in the modern state, the latter version—what he terms "legal authority"—has effectively eclipsed the previous conception—"a system of authoritative belief" (1990: 58–59). This development of the "elimination of any element of authoritative belief" from present conceptions of political and legal authority, Friedman argues, must be seen as "a historical achievement profoundly tied up with the work of certain modern political philosophers" (1990: 59). For Böckenförde, a "legal authority" devoid of norms would undoubtedly be an unstable basis for societal cohesion and civil peace. Modifying Hobbes, Böckenförde observed that

> a state is not all about power, but about the order of the state as an order of peace. It is not the state that must prescribe and make obligatory a way of life; on the contrary, the state must be sustained by basic attitudes within society.
>
> (Böckenförde, 2017: 384)

It is also undoubtedly the case that over 50 years after Böckenförde penned his dilemma that the values of the Basic Law have become, à la Habermasian constitutional patriotism, a reliable constitutional anchor and identification point for German society as a whole, helping to sustain those 'basic attitudes' that Böckenförde deems so vital. This context of modern liberal Germany is the basis for the analysis of the European Parliament electoral threshold cases in Chapter 6. These cases highlight the question of whether threats to stability still constitute a sufficient justification for restricting the popular sovereignty of certain German voters. However, a larger question posed by the cases is whether the roots of German liberal democracy are now strong enough to sustain a normal political identity again?

Fragmentation and Cohesion

The American framers tried to prevent either legislative or executive tyranny emerging, first, by dividing and limiting power and, second, by placing faith in the people to uphold the Constitution because it protected their own liberties. *Democracy in America* was, says Wolin, less a paean to democracy than a warning about the dangers of what Tocqueville called "democratic despotism" (1989: 68). Americans had developed a political society in which the state was practically invisible (Wolin, 1989: 68). Though invisible at the local level, the state became increasingly complex as the nineteenth century wore on in response, first, to the Civil War, and then the co-development of America's industrial society and the movement of people from the countryside to the growing cities. The fear that the state would become invisible in the lives of the people was one that motivated Jefferson. Attempting to reconcile Jefferson's notoriously contradictory ideas can be challenging, but one can perhaps see in his 'sovereignty of the living generation' a concern that without regular renewal the civic space might ossify or disintegrate due to a lack of citizen participation in their republic.

Addressing this concern, Dana Villa writes that the civic republican and liberal tradition have been competing with one another for two centuries, but the former is much older (2008: 2).

> Whereas the liberal tradition has emphasised constitutional limits on governmental power and the priority of individual rights, the civic republican tradition has focussed far more on active citizenship and the preconditions of public liberty.
>
> (Villa, 2008: 2)

The traditional concern with liberalism among political theorists, as found in the work of Tocqueville, Mill, and Arendt, is that utility maximising individuals abandon any attempt to defend political freedom in the public sphere and instead concentrate on the pursuit of their interests and family life, focussing primarily on exploiting the zone of individual freedom that constitutionalism theoretically protects from the state. The danger with civil republicanism is that in attempting to defend political, or public freedom—what Benjamin Constant called the 'liberty of the ancients'—the individual is subsumed within a potentially repressive public sphere which prioritises the public good over the needs and rights of the individual. Thinkers such as Hegel, Tocqueville, Mill, and Arendt have been motivated by the desire to discover new avenues through which "a sense of agency and public power" could be generated among dispersed and atomised individuals, and to better understand how subjects can become citizens (Villa, 2008: 11). Critically, as Villa notes, all of these theorists view modern political freedom as "a distinctive synthesis of liberal and republican elements" (2008: 11). The fusion between the two is a necessary corollary of Constant's distinction between the liberty of the moderns and the liberty of the ancients. The pursuit of private interests and pleasures leads to a sharp divide between the public and private spheres and the individual retreats into the purely personal zone of autonomy that constitutionalism creates for them to live their life as they wish. It is only 'theoretically' because if individuals disengage completely from the public sphere, participating only as voters and taxpayers, then there is always the risk, as we have seen since September 11th 2001, that the powers of public authority can start to intrude on that zone of freedom in order to allay public fears about terrorism, or to combat whatever particular issue is captivating the attention of the media and politicians for 24 or 48 hours.

However, there is an inescapable connection between public and private freedom, as Constant acknowledged. If the citizen completely abandons the public sphere to become merely a subject, their personal freedom is at risk from whatever laws government enacts in the public sphere. Thus, individual freedom depends on the defence of public freedom. Villa sees in Hegel, Tocqueville, Mill, and Arendt an effort "to create and expand a place for difference within the (previously homogenising and repressive) civic public" (2008: 12). While their efforts, as Villa sees it, "fail to strike a convincing balance between the 'universal' and the 'particular', the common good and the (enlightened) individual or group interest, ... striking or at least articulating that balance is indeed their joint project" (2008: 12). Political theory, however, has a habit of neglecting the extent to which associational activities with family, friends, neighbours, colleagues creates a bridge between the 'isolated individual' and the homogenised public realm. This does not mean that the problems of political disengagement go away, but simply that the differentiation and transition between the public and private sphere is less an abrupt black and white divide, and rather more transitioning shades of grey.

According to Hannah Arendt, Jefferson's fear was that the Constitution had divided the public and private spheres in such a way that all power had been given to the citizens "without giving them the opportunity of *being* republicans and of *acting* as citizens" (1973: 253). Jefferson's realisation, says Arendt, was that "unless the country was a living presence in the midst of its citizens" rather than materialising only every two years in the form of elections, then the necessary bonds to maintain representative government would be insufficient

(1973: 253). Arendt's insight into Jefferson's thought is, in the post-Trump and post-Brexit world, an important one. Jefferson, she said, had

> a foreboding of how dangerous it might be to allow the people a share in public power without providing them at the same time with more public space than the ballot box and with more opportunity to make their voices heard in public than election day.
>
> (Arendt, 1973: 253)

Jefferson's concern about how to sustain representative government and the crucial bond between citizen and state endures.

For Jefferson, the optimal way for the citizens to maintain republican government was for the citizen to play an active role in the state, or for the state to be a living presence in the life of the citizen. If maintaining the precious bond between citizen and state was challenging enough in 1826 when Jefferson died, it became even more so with the development of complex modern industrial states in the late nineteenth and early twentieth centuries where the opportunity for citizens to participate in their government at any time other than at elections was becoming unpractical. 'Voter' and 'taxpayer' may in fact be the principal roles through which citizens in modern states will participate in their governments during peacetime (Eisgruber, 2000: 2139).

It is certainly true that in the United States, as Tocqueville observed, the prevalence of voluntary and religious associations cemented civic loyalties, even though such bonds were at the local rather than national level. For Tocqueville, religion in America was "the first of their political institutions; for if it does not impart a taste for freedom, it facilitates the use of it" (1998: 120). Liberty for Americans in Tocqueville's era was first and foremost about religious freedom, which was seen as indistinguishable from their status as citizens. The linkage between freedom and religion predated the First Amendment rights of freedom of speech and religion, with one important document being Jefferson's 'Virginia Statute for Religious Freedom' (see Note 1). While the migration of large numbers of people to the cities weakened many of those civic and religious bonds—and provided the fodder for electoral malapportionment as the maintenance of naked political power trumped civic engagement—American religion continued to provide an additional source of civic identity well into the second half of the twentieth century (see, for example, Bellah, 1991).

Tocqueville equally saw that the place where republican government ends and despotism begins is when all relationships and associations between people have broken down except with their immediate families. In such a society, "each of them, living apart is a stranger to the fate of the rest" (De Tocqueville and Renshaw, 1998: 358). Such atomisation, the natural end result of the individualist ethos of liberalism, was the product of the division between the public and private spheres which occurred at the end of the eighteenth century. An appreciation of this division is important to our understanding of what the Supreme Court could and could not achieve in its decisions regarding malapportionment.

In terms of constitutionalism, malapportionment was the result of a failure of state legislatures to keep faith with their own constitutional requirements. The Supreme Court's solution to malapportionment involved an invocation and reminder of the values generated from the struggles for equality in American society. These included the Civil War, the end of slavery, Reconstruction, as well as the progressively expanding suffrage for African-Americans, non-property-owning whites, and women.[14] The Supreme Court's narrative in the malapportionment cases was about the right to vote but it had limited longer-term effects. The decision could not address the participation of citizens in their government, or the question of how a society can cohere without shared values, a common identity, or a shared sense of purpose.

The root causes of malapportionment were rapid social change, mass immigration, the growing influence of cities, and a fear in rural areas that the values of god, country, neighbour, community, and civic loyalty—which had held society together up to that point—were fracturing (Smith, 2014: 14–16). The response of the rural areas in states was to try and hold onto power illegitimately by not reapportioning. The *constitutional* solution the Supreme Court provided in the reapportionment cases spoke to the realisation of the county's original principles of equality, and paralleled the liberal values and human rights principles developing in the post-1945 period. However, the decisions could not address the question of individuals playing a participatory role in the civic space, in Arendt's words, *as* citizens, merely as voters. According to Waldron, Arendt de-emphasised the negative liberty aspect of the American Constitution which provided the individual with security against the state, instead focussing on the freedom derived from participation in public affairs (2016: 296).

What the reapportionment decisions did not and could not address was how to reconcile the disparate values in the civic space. Robert Cover's view that "a legal interpretation cannot be valid if no one is prepared to live by it" (1983: 44) is relevant here, identifying as it does the potential distinction and discordance between a legal interpretation of a constitutional principle and a civic interpretation. The values of urban and rural voters, and their interpretations of the Constitution, were simply too far apart for constitutionalism or law to provide a shared vocabulary in the civic space.[15] The danger was that, absent this shared vocabulary and social glue, the values of human dignity and equality as lynchpins of liberal democratic government would be left perilously exposed if they were accepted by only half of a society. The danger of equality without religious belief, said Tocqueville, is it tends to "isolate [men] from one another, to concentrate every man's attention on himself, and it lays open the soul to an inordinate love of material gratification" (1998: 183).

One can have social cohesion in a state without it being a liberal democracy. In the absence of religion, the *Volksgemeinschaftsprinzip* in Germany or 'the dictatorship of the proletariat' can also create a degree of social cohesion. But it would mean a great deal of control of the public sphere over the private sphere so liberal values would be extinguished. The emergence of secular liberal democracy out of the French Revolution split the public and private spheres asunder, establishing a tenuous link between citizen and state. Once the Declaration of the Rights of Man had "stood the individual on his own two feet and handed him his liberty", the problem for government became "how to integrate the emancipated individual into the state" (Böckenförde, 1991: 44). Individuals increasingly concerned themselves with emancipation in the private sphere and their only activity in the public sphere, if at all, was voting at election times every few years. The fundamental values of equality and human dignity in constitutionalism since 1945 are essentially private values in the sense that the state has a duty to provide a sphere for the citizen to live their life where they have equality and human dignity, and, as Hobbes reminds us, security. Within this constitutional constellation the citizen's sole role is, as Arendt suggests, that they vote every two, four, or five years. As Jefferson noted, that constitutes a fragile basis for maintaining republican government.

This was the crux of Böckenförde's essay in 1967, and while it was an especially pertinent warning to Germany, it is equally prescient with respect to the United States and indeed most modern societies. The "split" between the public and private that Böckenförde refers to when he says "there is no way back across the threshold of 1789 that does not destroy the state as the order of liberty" (1991: 45) is exactly the same division between the public and private that Arendt describes Jefferson as being fearful of. That division creates a zone of liberty for the citizens, but the preservation of that zone relies on the collective agency of the citizens to maintain their constitutional order. Böckenförde's key concern was how, in the absence of religion, the vast majority of individuals can maintain the necessary bonds of social cohesion to preserve the peace of their society, and ultimately their liberal democratic polity. In a clear sense, then, Böckenförde and Jefferson are attempting to address the same problem of how to sustain representative government, albeit from different perspectives; Böckenförde, in terms of whether the liberal state—and, implicitly, its constitutional values—can be sustained without internal bonding forces; Jefferson, through the participation of the citizen in government, or the presence of government in the life of the citizen. For Germany after 1949, the constitutional order and its political system had liberal values, but they were not deeply rooted in society. The growing, if unenthusiastic, acceptance of the Federal Republic among German citizens in its first two decades was based more on impressive economic growth and its ability to maintain stability.

One *sui generis* explanation for what eventually provided Germany with the sort of Böckenfördean bonding force of social cohesion to reinforce the values of liberal constitutionalism was the growing Holocaust consciousness in Germany, and the acrimonious debate over coming to terms with the Nazi past (*die Vergangenheitsbewältigung*). That it was acrimonious does not sound like a recipe for social cohesion, and it was not at first as younger Germans asked difficult questions about what their parents and grandparents had done during the Nazi period. In the longer term, younger Germans who came of age after the 1960s and who had been inculcated in the history of the Nazi period and the Holocaust were better able to understand how the liberal democratic values of the Basic Law were a response to events of that period. The decades-long angst caused by the debate over the Nazi period that many Germans at the time would rather have left buried (see Sereny, 2000: 58–59), would in time provide a surer foundation for Germany's liberal democracy.[16]

The initial fragility of Germany's liberal democracy after 1949 was mainly due to the absence of a deep constitutional and political culture which might have allowed democratic values to take root. What initially proved fundamental to the recovery of German constitutionalism in 1949 was Germany's respect for the law, which will be assessed in Chapter 5. The longer-term question regarding the success of the Basic Law was whether the *Bundesverfassungsgericht*'s objective value order that so offended Schmitt, and its 'image of man' conception of the German *polis*, could succeed in binding Germans to their liberal democratic constitution in the absence of god, nation, or civil associational pursuits.

The 'image of man' is a choice of words which the *BVerfG* has repeatedly invoked as representing the central idea of the relationship between the individual and community lying at the heart of the Basic Law.[17] According to this logic, rights could only be realised in a civic space which recognised the relationships between individuals. Pure equality on the basis of individuality rather than community would be dangerous because once "deprived of the internal bonding forces" upon which it relies, the secular liberal state, says Böckenförde, is forced down the social utopian path of attempting to do ever more for its citizens and even fulfil their "eudaemonistic expectations" (1991: 45–46).

The dichotomy between constitutional values and the bonds of social cohesion highlighted by Böckenförde's dilemma is one that will be returned to. Given Böckenförde's theoretical and historical concerns in 1967 on how Germany's liberal constitutional democracy could maintain its bonds with the German people, it is perhaps no surprise that as a justice on the *Bundesverfassungsgericht* from 1983 to 1996 he emerged as a defender of emerging smaller parties like the Greens, while criticising the established parties for their "oligarchical"[18] tendency. As important as stability is and was in the German context, Böckenförde recognised when he was on the Court that constitutional representative democracy had to remain representative in order to maintain its connection with the citizens.

Conclusion

For a concerned German social democrat like Böckenförde, the fear in 1964 would have been that Germany's increasingly strong liberal constitutionalism, as embodied in its powerful new constitutional court, had only been superficially accepted by Germans as a result of international institutions, the country's economic miracle, and the exogenous imperatives imposed by the Cold War. As will be illustrated in Chapters 5 and 6, Germany and its people ultimately answered Böckenförde's concerns about whether the country could sustain liberal democracy. However, the willingness of some Germans to confront their country's traumatic past after the 1960s perhaps played as significant a role in reinforcing the stability of the constitutional order as either internal bonding forces such as religion, or the objective value order of the *Bundesverfassungsgericht*. What remained unanswered was a broader question Böckenförde posed that applied to all liberal secular states wanting to maintain social cohesion and their constitutional institutions: "On what will that state base itself in time of crisis?" (1991: 46). As will be addressed in later chapters, this question is of ongoing relevance within and beyond Germany's borders.

Böckenförde's argument was that the liberal secular state rested on values which it could not guarantee. The state's options were to use its coercive authority to sustain those values, but sacrifice its liberalness, or that it rely on other internal bonding forces such as religion or nation (Böckenförde, 1991: 46). Böckenförde stated more recently that his essay in 1967 was an appeal to his fellow Catholics to see the liberal secular state not as a threat to their religion but as an important means of guaranteeing the liberty which was essential to religious belief (quoted in Rath, 2009). By integrating into the Federal Republic, Böckenförde believed, Catholics would further strengthen the state through the addition of their "ethical imprint" (quoted in Rath, 2009). Tocqueville saw in the United States that religion supports democracy by teaching Americans "the art of being free" (2003: 241), yet it would be unwise to assume that the interrelationship between religion and democracy would always be mutually supportive. Böckenförde's dilemma can perhaps be best seen today as emphasising the practical, ethical, dialectical, and associational tools which religion, and other forms of social bonding or civic associational activity provide as a means of supporting liberal democracy, its institutions, and its values.

The key concern which we return to in the remaining chapters is whether the constitutional values which the respective courts have enunciated in their reapportionment and electoral threshold decisions are ones which can maintain the relationship between the state and citizens, absent other sources of social cohesion such as nation or religion? The context within which this question is asked is the liberty and dignity-oriented paradigms of constitutionalism outlined thus far. What I called 'heightened' constitutionalism in *Barnette* (1943) was an example of the Court defying the will of an unambiguous local and national majority during a time of war. *Barnette* was heard around five years after *Carolene Products*, and—with its protection of a religious minority, Jehovah's Witnesses—entirely ticks the boxes of footnote four, and fits the expanding scope of equality assessed in the next chapter. Having examined how values are mediated in the civic space, we turn now to the question of how the Supreme Court has interpreted values institutionally.

Notes

1 Jefferson's belief in renewal and the promise of new beginnings was encapsulated in the opening words of the 'Virginia Statute for Religious Freedom' which he drafted: "Whereas Almighty God hath created the mind free."

2 Jefferson wrote that "The earth belongs in usufruct to the living" and "the dead have neither powers nor rights over it" (Jefferson, Madison, and Smith, 1995: 632).
3 Böckenförde's statement comes from a series of interviews conducted in 2009/10 by Dieter Gosewinkel (2017: 369–409). Böckenförde's important argument here is also relevant to the Radicals Decree, and is discussed further in Chapter 5.
4 *Barnette* was the second of the Flag Salute Cases. In *Barnette*, the Court reversed its decision in *Minersville School District v Gobitis*. As Wasserman notes, *Barnette* sits at the intersection of the First Amendment's speech and religion clauses and "established a First Amendment liberty against compelled expression, protecting individuals against being compelled to utter government-mandated, -approved, or -certified messages" (2018: 586).
5 In its protection of certain minorities, *Barnette* can be viewed as one of the key decisions following on from footnote four of *US v Carolene Products*, assessed in Chapter 3.
6 Interview with Judge David Edward, October 2013.
7 When it made the decision in *Brown*, the Warren Court recognised the emerging post-war consensus on human rights, and even cited Gunnar Myrdal's seminal book on human dignity (see 1944).
8 On the differences of opinion between national and local majorities, see (Friedman, 2002: 173–174).
9 See Chapter 5 on the lack of popular support for the Federal Republic when it was established.
10 Originally published in March 1967, Sereny was referring to the trials of German civilians (and former Nazis) in the 1960s for the civilian murders of other Germans (mainly Jews) during the Nazi period.
11 The utilisation of emergency powers in order to restore constitutional government—the state of exception—was notably addressed by Carl Schmitt (2005).
12 Bismarck's constitution of 1871, while notionally establishing a parliamentary democracy, was more an extension of the Prussian military state.
13 The German expression for those people (including bureaucrats, intellectuals, and ordinary Germans) who passively followed the Nazis, even while not necessarily sharing their goals is *Mitläufer* (see, for example, Hauer, 2013).
14 See *Reynolds v Sims* (1964: 587) and the analysis in Chapter 5.
15 For example, the shared "respect for constitutionalism and legality" which Orwell described (1986: 397).
16 See Sereny (2000: 59–86) for a contemporary account of the fear of authority among younger Germans and their questions over the Holocaust.
17 See *Life Imprisonment Case* (1977).
18 See Böckenförde's opinion in *Party Finance V Case* (1986).

References

McCulloch v Maryland 17 US 316, 1819
Lochner v New York 198 US 45, 1905
State of Missouri v Holland, 252 US 416, 1920
West Virginia State Board of Education v Barnette, 319 US 624, 1943
Brown v Board of Education of Topeka, 347 US 483, 1954
Lüth Case, 7 BVerfGE 198, 1958
Baker v Carr, 396 US 186, 1962
Reynolds v Sims 377 US 533, 1964
Life Imprisonment Case 45 BVerfGE 187, 1977
Party Finance V Case, 73 BVerfG 40, 1986
Obergefell v Hodges 14–556, 2015

Arendt, H., *On Revolution* (Harmondsworth: Penguin, 1973).

Bellah, R. N., "Civil Religion in America", in *Beyond Belief: Essays on Religion in a Post-Traditional World* (Berkeley: University of California Press, 1991).

Böckenförde, E. W., *Constitutional and Political Theory: Selected Writings*. Vol. 1 (Oxford: Oxford University Press, 2017).

Böckenförde, E. W., "The Rise of the State as a Process of Secularisation", in *State, Society, and Liberty: Studies in Political Theory and Constitutional Law* (New York: Berg Pub Ltd, 1991).

Brennan Jr, W. J., "The Constitution of the United States: Contemporary Ratification", in *Interpreting the Constitution: The Debate over Original Intent*, ed. by Jack N. Rakove (Boston, MA: Northeastern University Press, 1990).

Breyer, S., "Our Democratic Constitution", *New York University Law Review*, 77 (2002), 245.

Breyer, S. "Interview with Justice Stephen Breyer—With Charlie Rose (Transcript)", (2016), available at: https://charlierose.com/episodes/29278 [last accessed 6 October 2016].

Collings, J., *Democracy's Guardians: A History of the German Federal Constitutional Court, 1951–2001* (Oxford: Oxford University Press, 2015).

Cover, R. M., "The Supreme Court 1982 Term Foreword: Nomos and Narrative", *Harvard Law Review*, 97(1) (1983), 4.

Dahl, R. A., *How Democratic is the American Constitution?* 2nd edn (New Haven, CT: Yale University Press, 2003).

De Tocqueville, A., *Democracy in America*. Vol. 10 (Washington, DC: Regnery Publishing, 2003).

De Tocqueville, A. and P. Renshaw, *Democracy in America* (Herts: Wordsworth Editions Limited, 1998).

Deneen, P. J., *Why Liberalism Failed* (New Haven, CT: Yale University Press, 2019).

Eisenhower, D. D. "Press Release, Containing Speech on Radio and Television by President Eisenhower", Eisenhower Presidential Library, 24 September (1957), available at: www.eisenhower.archives.gov/research/online_documents/civil_rights_little_rock/1957_09_24_Press_Release.pdf [last accessed 26 September 2015].

Eizsgruber, C. L., "Civic Virtue and the Limits of Constitutionalism", *Fordham Law Review*, 69 (2000), 2131.

Ellis, J. J., "The Argument", in *American Creation: Triumphs and Tragedies at the Founding of the Republic* (New York: Vintage Books, 2007).

Finn, J. E., *Peopling the Constitution* (Lawrence: University Press of Kansas, 2014).

Friedman, B., "The Birth of an Academic Obsession: The History of the Countermajoritarian Difficulty, Part Five", *Yale Law Journal* (2002), 153–259.

Friedman, R. B., "On the Concept of Authority in Political Philosophy", in *Authority*, ed. by Josephy Raz (Oxford: Basil Blackwell, 1990).

Friedmann, W., *Law in a Changing Society*. 2nd edn (Berkeley: University of California Press, 1972).

Friedrich, C. J., "Rebuilding the German Constitution, II", *The American Political Science Review*, 43(4) (1949), 704–720.

Gordon, P. E., "Between Christian Democracy and Critical Theory: Habermas, Böckenförde, and the Dialectics of Secularization in Postwar Germany", *Social Research: An International Quarterly*, 80(1) (2013), 173–202.

Griswold, E. N., "Right to be Let Alone", *Northwestern University Law Review*, 55 (1960), 216.

Habermas, J., *The Postnational Constellation: Political Essays* (Cambridge: Polity Press, 2001).

Hamilton, A. "Federalist Number 78", in *The Federalist Papers*, ed. by Isaac Kramnick (Harmondsworth: Penguin, 1987).

Hauer, N., *Die Mitläufer oder die Unfähigkeit zu Fragen: Auswirkungen des Nationalsozialismus auf die Demokratie von Heute* (Wiesbaden: Springer-Verlag, 2013).

Henry, P. "Patrick Henry, Virginia Ratifying Convention, 4 June 1788" [Speech] The University of Chicago (1986), available at: http://press-pubs.uchicago.edu/founders/documents/preambles14.html [last accessed 3 November 2019].

Huntington, S. P., *American Politics: The Promise of Disharmony* (Cambridge, MA: Harvard University Press, 1981).

Jefferson, T., J. Madison, and J. M. Smith, "Letter from Jefferson to Madison, 6 September 1789", in *The Republic of Letters: The Correspondence Between Thomas Jefferson and James Madison, 1776–1826*, ed. by James Morton Smith (New York: W.W. Norton and Company, 1995).

Johnson, J. W., *Historic US Court Cases: An Encyclopedia* Vol. 2 (New York: Routledge, 2003).

Kautz, S., "Introduction", in *The Supreme Court and the Idea of Constitutionalism*, ed. by Steven Kautz, Arthur Melzer, Jerry Weinberger, and M. Richard Zinman (Philadelphia: University of Pennsylvania Press, 2011).

Kermani, N., "Rede von Dr. Navid Kermani zur Feierstunde 65 Jahre Grundgesetz" (Berlin: Deutscher Bundestag, 2014).

Koopmans, T., *Courts and Political Institutions: A Comparative View* (Cambridge: Cambridge University Press, 2003).

Macedo, S., *Liberal Virtues: Citizenship, Virtue, and Community in Liberal Constitutionalism* (Oxford: Clarendon Press, 1990).

Möllers, C., "'We Are (Afraid of) the People': Constituent Power in German Constitutionalism", in *The Paradox of Constitutionalism: Constituent Power and Constitutional Form*, ed. by Martin Loughlin and Neil Walker (Oxford: Oxford University Press, 2007).

Murphy, W. F., *Constitutional Democracy: Creating and Maintaining a Just Political Order*. The Johns Hopkins Series in Constitutional Thought (Baltimore, MD: Johns Hopkins University Press, 2007).

Myrdal, G., *An American Dilemma, Volume 2: The Negro Problem and Modern Democracy*. Vol. 2 (New Brunswick: Transaction Publishers, 1944).

Orren, K. and S. Skowronek, *The Search for American Political Development* (Cambridge: Cambridge University Press, 2004).

Orwell, G. and P. H. Davison, *The Complete Works of George Orwell*. Vol. 12 (London: Secker & Warburg, 1986).

Rath, C. "Freiheit ist Ansteckend" (2009), available at: https://taz.de/!576006/ [last accessed 23 August 2018].

Schlink, B., "German Constitutional Culture in Transition", in *Constitutionalism, Identity, Difference, and Legitimacy: Theoretical Perspectives*, ed. by Michel Rosenfeld (Durham, NC: Duke University Press, 1994).

Schmitt, C., *Political Theology: Four Chapters on the Concept of Sovereignty* (Chicago, IL: University of Chicago Press, 2005).

Schmitt, C., *Die Tyrannei der Werte* (Berlin: Duncker & Humblot, 2011).

Sereny, G., "Generation Without a Past", in *The German Trauma: Experiences and Reflections, 1938–2001* (London: Penguin, 2000).

Shklar, J. N., "The Liberalism of Fear", in *Liberalism and the Moral Life*, ed. by Nancy L Rosenblum (Cambridge, MA: Harvard University Press 1989).
Smith, J. D., *On Democracy's Doorstep: The Inside Story of How the Supreme Court Brought "One Person, One Vote" to the United States* (New York: Hill and Wang, 2014).
Sternberger, D., *Verfassungspatriotismus* (Frankfurt: Insel Verlag, 1990).
Villa, D., *Public Freedom* (Princeton, NJ: Princeton University Press, 2008).
Voßkuhle, A. and W. Von Rahden, "Die Rolle des Bundesverfassungsgerichts in Europa: Ein Gespräch", *Gegenworte* (30) (2013).
Waldron, J., "Political Political Theory", in *Political Political Theory: Essays on Institutions* (Cambridge: MA: Harvard University Press, 2016).
Wasserman, H. M., "Introduction: Barnette at 75", *Florida International University Law Review*, 13 (2018), 585.
Whittington, K. E., "Constitutional Constraints in Politics", in *The Supreme Court and the Idea of Constitutionalism*, ed. by Steven Kautz, Arthur Melzer, Jerry Weinberger, and M. Richard Zinman (Philadelphia: University of Pennsylvania Press, 2011).
Wolin, S. S., *The Presence of the Past: Essays on the State and the Constitution* (Baltimore: Johns Hopkins University Press, 1989).

3 People of Different Views

The previous chapter examined alternative sources of values, identity, and association in the civic space which undermine or reinforce the constitutional values of the liberal state. This chapter switches to assess the legal institutional space within which constitutional values emerge and are interpreted by the US federal courts. Chapters 3 and 4 are concerned with the crisis in American representative democracy in the early 1960s due to the widespread practice of malapportionment. This involved the effective exclusion of non-rural voters from the political process by local majorities in many US states through the debasement of citizens' votes. This chapter examines the development of American constitutionalism and the evolving understanding of equality and rights in the Supreme Court's jurisprudence, as well as the theoretical, historical, and jurisprudential roots which shaped the relationship between the Supreme Court, the federal government, and national and local majorities.

Prior to and after the Civil War it did not particularly matter if local majorities subscribed to different constitutional interpretations and values in their lives and social practices provided that the interpretation did not clash with the law of the state on a vital issue for the federal government. To paraphrase Justice Holmes and Justice Breyer, the Constitution was intended to allow for this flexibility in meaning among people of different views. The Civil War, Reconstruction, and the gradual incorporation of the Bill of Rights against the states all incrementally eroded this flexibility. The Civil War effectively broke the Constitution by sacrificing its liberalness, real or pretended, in order to save the state itself.[1] Segregation and civil rights were, likewise, two issues which stretched constitutional meaning to breaking point. With the gradual incorporation of the Bill of Rights, the theoretical possibility of flexibility and divergence between national and local interpretations of the federal constitution began to disappear.

The important distinction here is between the civic space of constitutional meaning and interpretation examined in the previous chapter and the legal institutional space of interpretation examined in the chapter ahead. What the victory of North over South could not do was make the values of equality and emancipation more important to the citizens in the South than their own bonds of homogeneity which rejected Lincoln's emancipatory vision. The Supreme Court and the federal government could impose force and federal law on the states in the legal institutional space, but the constitutional values embodied in those laws were rejected in the lives and social practices of those local majorities. As seen in the last chapter in the ideas of Böckenförde, where differences exist between the authoritative values of the state which sustain constitutional meaning and the values or internal bonding forces which hold individuals, groups, and majorities together, then the survival of the state can be at risk.

While Alexander Bickel looked at the role of the Supreme Court through the prism of the countermajoritarian difficulty, this chapter assesses the Court's interpretive role and emerging doctrine of equality through evolving understandings of constitutionalism itself. One of the blind spots of the countermajoritarian difficulty is that it does not specify 'which majority' is the relevant one. As addressed in the previous chapter, differences between national and local majority views on fundamental constitutional issues started the Civil War, and are deeply implicated in the malapportionment problem examined in Chapter 4. The question of majoritarianism, however, is a useful springboard to assess the Court's role in supporting emerging national majority sentiment, its relationship with the federal government, and its emerging role after 1937 as a defender of minority rights. The Court's institutional role in steering American constitutionalism towards a more emancipatory vision of equality and human dignity was often done by overruling state laws or practices, and was often supported by the federal government (see, for example, Whittington, 2005). The picture of constitutionalism which emerges has been driven largely by political action, and legislative and constitutional initiatives in response to social struggles and conflicts, but also through judicial interpretations. As Walter Murphy notes

> The adoption of the Thirteenth and Fourteenth Amendments, passage of legislation authorising the federal courts to interpret these provisions, and judicial interpretations of them, and the Bill of Rights, have solidified constitutionalism as part of the larger political system, though one should not underestimate legislative and executive action, or the synergistic effects of political institutions and culture.
>
> (Murphy, 1993: 177–178)

This passage by Murphy reflects the content of Chapter 3 and Chapter 4 and more broadly reflects the dichotomy between the legal institutional space, characterised by legislative and judicial initiatives solidifying constitutionalism, and the civic space, where cultural, religious, and nationalist bonding forces can support or undermine constitutional values.

In the chapter ahead, I will begin by explaining the significance of the 'countermajoritarian difficulty' before then addressing the question of 'which majority is relevant?' The chapter then addresses the concerns of Madison over the dangers of majority tyranny at the local level as exemplified by state legislatures, and how Madison's unsuccessful proposal for a veto on unconstitutional state laws eventually came to reside in the legal institutional space through the role of the federal courts in applying the Fourteenth Amendment to the states. The chapter then considers the development of the modern court, its essentially *majoritarian* character, and how administrative and personnel changes in the 1920s and 1930s laid the groundwork for the emergence of a constitutionalism which would prioritise minority rights and the access of voters to democratic processes. The chapter then proceeds to the Holmesian idea that a constitution is "for people of different views" which conceptually bridges the concerns of Chapters 2, 3, and 4. This chapter addresses the key tension inherent in America's liberty-orientated constitutionalism between a constitution designed to liberate its citizens from government power, but is cohesive enough to hold a people together, a constitution general enough to allow people to live their lives without restraint, but which must nevertheless resolve legal questions. The chapter then considers the gradual incorporation of the Bill of Rights against the states, and the recognition of many lawyers that state governments were the quintessential threat to individual rights. To close, the chapter considers the importance of footnote four of *United States v Carolene Products* and, drawing on Robert Cover's important analysis of footnote four, assesses the extent to which it was a catalyst for an increased focus on equality and human dignity after 1938.

Which Majority?

As argued in Chapter 1, one of the main concerns of constitutionalism has been mitigating threats to the state from too much of the wrong kind of participation in the democratic process, or too little of the right kind. The stability renewal dichotomy also frames some of the questions in this chapter and the next in order to understand how developments in American constitutionalism since the founding period help explain the Court's intervention in the malapportionment issue and its eventual 'one person, one vote' decisions. The 'one person, one vote' decision cannot simply be seen through the prism of an expanding franchise, but also as part of a developing understanding of how notions of equality and human dignity have come to be reflected in the Court's conception of the values of a maturing society. As Justice William Douglas put it in *Gray v Sanders*, "the right to have one's vote counted has the same dignity as the right to put a ballot in a box" (1963: 380).

Much like the actions of the *BVerfG* assessed in Chapter 6, which sought to remedy ossification in the German political system, the irony was that it was the Supreme Court rather than elected politicians breathing life into democratic politics and the principle of political equality. For the Supreme Court, this reinvigoration of democratic politics meant equal representation for equal numbers of people. One aspect of this constitutional evolution was the Court's own interpretive journey of renewal. After the Court's intensely countermajoritarian 'Lochner period' (c.1890–1937),[2] where it interpreted the Fourteenth Amendment as protecting economic interests and private property rather than individual rights (Grossman and Epp, 2002: 107), it dramatically changed course in the late 1930s. This change resulted in a belated acceptance of previously stymied progressive legislation, a truce with Franklin Roosevelt over the New Deal legislation, and the enunciation of the famous footnote four in *United States v Carolene Products* (1938). *Carolene* effectively signalled that the Court would only consider checking laws which contravened federally protected rights or which targeted the participation of minorities in the political process.

For Friedman, the puzzle with the 'countermajoritarian difficulty' is that it encompasses very different examples of Supreme Court decision-making across decades, even when it was clear that decisions such as *Brown v Board of Education* in 1954 and the reapportionment decisions of the 1960s carried broad popular support either at the national or local level, and sometimes both. Friedman differentiates between two different types of criticism that the Court faced:

> Even popular dissenters from Court decisions did not claim that the Court was interfering with popular will, as much as that the Court was rushing ahead of legislative (and perhaps) popular decision-making. The claims, though easily confused, are different. The countermajoritarian criticism applies to courts striking down laws that had been enacted by popular legislative bodies, at least theoretically with broad popular support. This was precisely the case during the Progressive Era, with relatively fresh legislation in constant jeopardy. During the Warren era, however, the Court's decisions typically did not invalidate newly enacted legislation. Rather, the Court moved to address social problems that were already of concern to the public.
>
> (Friedman, 2002: 222)

The countermajoritarian difficulty does not address, then, which majority is the relevant one and, as discussed in Chapter 2, whose values are to be preferred? Majority opinions vary from state to state and region to region, and a Supreme Court decision that might be enthusiastically received in northern states might be vilified in the South. Thus, Friedman asks: "is the ruling 'countermajoritarian' because it thwarts a majority in the state, or majoritarian as reflecting a national consensus?" (2002: 173–174). This regional differentiation exactly reflected public attitudes to the Court's unanimous decision in *Brown v Board of Education* in 1954, where polling indicated strong approval of the decision in the East (72 percent approved), West (65 percent approved), and Midwest (57 percent approved), and strong disapproval in the South (71 percent disapproved) (cited in Friedman, 2002: 186). National public opinion was "strongly supportive" of the decision in *Brown*, while the outraged Southerners who attacked the decision did not do so on countermajoritarian grounds (Friedman, 2002: 175). Instead, the arguments those in the South used attacking the *Brown* decision were primarily "grounded in respect for minority viewpoints and states' rights" (Friedman, 2002: 175). This picture was also reflected in the very different value systems that were clashing in the reapportionment cases. The emphasis of the aggrieved Southerners on the idea that their minority rights were being violated in the *Brown* decision exactly mirrored the response of rural areas across the country to reapportionment proposals going back to the 1940s (Smith, 2014: 26).

For our present purposes, the question of national versus local majorities is important for highlighting the potential for state fragmentation from the essential 'value' differences between a national and local majority on an issue of vital importance for the state. What this division between local and national majorities indicated was that an essential value or identity difference existed between constitutional values as interpreted by the Supreme Court and accepted by a national majority, on the one hand, and the values and interpretations of different communities who disagreed with the Supreme Court's and national majority's interpretation, on the other (see, for example, Cover, 1983: 44).

To understand how this value and identity schism between nation and local majorities became so central to the development of American constitutionalism it is first necessary to understand the fears of James Madison over the dangers of local majority tyranny. Although Madison's proposal for a national legislative veto on state laws was defeated at the Constitutional Convention in Philadelphia, this power effectively became vested with the judiciary, with the Supreme Court assuming a key role in supporting federal power and formalising the emerging values of the national majority.

A Legal Check on Local Majorities

For many of the founders the necessity for a new republican government of the United States was precisely because the popularly elected state legislatures had been guilty of pandering to mob tendencies and passing retroactive laws which often stripped property-holders of rights. Summarising the "calamitous" effects of the "mutable policy" of state legislatures, Madison wrote in *Federalist 62* that

> it poisons the blessings of liberty itself. It will be of little avail to the people that the laws are made by men of their own choice if the laws be so voluminous that they cannot be read, or so incoherent that they cannot be understood; if they be repealed or revised before they are promulgated, or undergo such incessant changes that no man, who knows what the law is today, can guess what it will be tomorrow.[3]
>
> (Madison, *Federalist 62*, 1987: 368)

From the outset, and even before the addition of the Bill of Rights, through their emphasis on representative democracy over direct democracy with only the House of Representatives directly elected, the framers appear to have expressed their concerns over the dangers of popular majorities. In an era when the franchise was limited, Madison's main concern was less people's ability to participate in the democratic process and more the protection of private rights from what he viewed as the principal threat: the state legislatures. Preserving rights for the minority would be achieved, Madison believed, both through a balance between social forces in the much larger society created by union, and also through an additional check at the federal level. The first part of Madison's equation worked, writes John Hart Ely, till about the fiftieth anniversary of the republic, when it became clear that the greater plurality of interests in a larger republic was no impediment to the oppression of one group by another (1980: 81). Madison and the other framers failed to foresee the crystallising effect that parties would have on previously disaggregated interests within the political system. Although Madison's proposal to give the new federal legislature a "negative", or veto, over the laws of the states was defeated during the Constitutional Convention, the majority at Philadelphia came to believe that the judiciary was better suited to the task of controlling the states (see Hobson, 1979: 228–229). This view ultimately came to be embodied in the 'Supremacy Clause' of Article VI which declared the Constitution, laws, and treaties of the United States to be the "supreme law of the land" (Hobson, 1979: 228). The power to check state laws at odds with the Constitution consequently fell logically into the hands of the federal judiciary.

The much greater challenge for Madison and the other founders, as Bellah noted, was the particular problem of developing "public virtues in democratic citizens" (1991: 254). The Constitution was designed to bring this about through the instrumentality of checks and balances to offset "the centrifugal and anarchic tendency of competitive individual and local self-interest", and so foster what Madison called the "permanent and aggregate interests of the community" (Bellah, 1991: 255). Madison certainly hoped that a bill of rights could have an educational value in a republic and might over time "become incorporated within the national sentiment" and acquire "the character of fundamental maxims of free government" (quoted in Rakove, 1992: 674). However, the expansion of the franchise and the growing significance of democracy within the republican system provided states—through their control over the machinery of state and federal elections—with additional means to oppress minority groups. Moreover, malapportionment was a classic local problem of precisely the type Madison had identified as exemplifying the iniquity of state politics. These flaws in Madison's republican theory lay at the heart of the malapportionment problem, but they were ones which constitutionalism provided a 'legal' solution for in the form of the federal courts.

Madison had seen first-hand the effects of invidious state laws under the Articles of Confederation where populist majorities ran roughshod over the rights of the minority. By 1787 even initially ardent republicans had become disenchanted by what they viewed as the near tragic experience under popularly responsive state governments (Murphy, 1993: 176). In October 1788 Madison told Jefferson that he had come to believe that

> Wherever the real power in a Government lies, there is the danger of oppression. In our Governments the real power lies in the majority of the Community, and the invasion of private rights is *chiefly* to be apprehended, not from acts of Government contrary to the sense of its constituents, but from acts in which the Government is the mere instrument of the major number of the constituents.
>
> ("Letter, From James Madison to Thomas Jefferson, 17 October 1788"; emphasis in original—underlined by JM)

Madison's concern here resonates with the view of constitutionalism outlined thus far: that the people can be an unpredictable force, sometimes requiring restraint, at other times in need of protection and representation, but sometimes also driving constitutional change. This role of the people in bringing about constitutional change from the founding period onwards through ordinary politics has certainly attracted the attention of scholars (see Ackerman, 2000). However, the specific nature of the people's involvement, the forms it is manifested in, and what it achieves is often harder to pin down. Kramer is right to say that popular pressure from the people was indispensable in bringing "an unruly authority to heel" (2004: 91). However, his claim that the founders had a uniform position in expecting that constitutional limits would be enforced through politics and by the people rather than in the courts is at odds with the views of Madison and Jefferson (below), and the majority gathered at Philadelphia (see also Hobson, 1979: 228–229). As the exchange between the Virginians makes clear, they came to recognise that the federal courts would sometimes be an indispensable check on tyrannical government, whether at the state or federal level, when all other avenues failed.

Given twentieth-century Bickelian debates on the countermajoritarian difficulty, it is easy to overlook the clear view during the American founding period that there needed to be a countermajoritarian institution as a check on odious state laws and to enforce rights provisions.[4] Fundamental to the very idea of a written constitution and Bill of Rights was the non-mutability of certain principles. Jefferson was a key advocate[5] for the adoption of the Bill of Rights, even while recognising and approving of the key check it would give to the judiciary.[6] In March 1789, at the time when Congress was convening for the first time, he wrote to Madison:

> In the arguments in favour of a declaration of rights, you omit one which has great weight with me; the legal check which it puts into the hands of the judiciary. This is a body, which if rendered independent, and kept strictly to their own department merits great confidence.
>
> (Jefferson, Madison, and Smith, 1995)

Still, for Madison, judicial review was an imperfect substitute for his legislative "negative", which would have stopped poor legislation from being enacted in the first place. However, with the defeat of his veto, and the inclusion of the Supremacy Clause in the Constitution, so the Bill of Rights and the judiciary now assumed much greater importance. Addressing Congress in June 1789 to introduce the proposal for a declaration of rights, Madison said:

> If they are incorporated into the constitution, independent tribunals of justice will consider themselves in a peculiar manner the guardians of those rights; they will be an impenetrable bulwark against every assumption of power in the legislative or executive; they will be naturally led to resist every encroachment upon rights expressly stipulated for in the constitution by the declaration of rights.
>
> (Madison, 1986)

These relatively early views of Madison gradually embracing the principle of judicially enforced rights, with the judiciary functioning as a bulwark against extra-legal accumulations of power, illustrate that the founders believed that neither a balance between social forces nor the enforcement of constitutional limits through politics alone would be sufficient to protect rights and hold those in power to account. Ely notes that even in a system where a sufficient mass is able to exert an influence on representatives, that does not provide for "the effective protection of minorities whose interests differ from the interests of most of the rest of us" (1980: 78).

Despite eulogising the proposed Constitution in his *Federalist* essays to ensure ratification, the eventual outcome of shared and divided sovereignty between the federal government and the individual states was one that profoundly dismayed Madison. He saw that the outcome at Philadelphia could be a recipe for conflict because of its generality and the way that the Constitution blurred the lines of sovereignty between the national and state governments, and indirectly gave the states a key role in the federation through their power to appoint senators. Ultimately, Madison believed that the periphery had too much power over the centre and that the Federal Republic of the United States would dance to a tune set by the states. At this stage, Madison believed the generality of the Constitution could be a cause for problems. Later he came to see the ambiguity in the document was its great advantage. One reason that constitutionalism functions as a framework for constitutional renewal, and perhaps debate,[7] is the general nature of the compact agreed to originally. However, as we shall see, this generality causes problems of its own. It is the implications of the relationship between the Court, the federal government and the people for the development of American constitutionalism that will be explored further in the next section.

The Supreme Court and Majoritarian Politics

In the key reapportionment case, *Baker v Carr*, Justice Tom Clark noted in his opinion that the role of the Supreme Court as a defender of federal rights was anticipated as early as 1787.

> As John Rutledge (later Chief Justice) said 175 years ago in the course of the Constitutional Convention, a chief function of the Court is to secure national rights.
>
> (Justice Tom Clark, *Baker v Carr*, 1962: 261)

However, for much of its history, even when it had the Fourteenth Amendment at its disposal, the Court chose to protect economic interests and private property rights rather than individual rights. A key to understanding the Court's evolving jurisprudence on democratic rights in the twentieth century is recognising its position within the national majoritarian system. Of particular significance is how some administrative changes in its docket in the mid-1920s gave it a unique vantage point from which to endorse changing policies such as the New Deal, and later to anticipate and formalise emerging societal norms into law.

The immediate catalyst for footnote four of *Carolene Products* and the Court's change of emphasis was the appointment of two justices which put the normally dissenting Harlan Stone into the unusual position of being in the majority. This personnel shift heralded a return to business as usual in the sense that after an unusually long wait of four years for Roosevelt to get the opportunity to nominate his first justices, his New Deal policy agenda would no longer be at odds with the Court's decisions. As Robert Dahl noted in the 1950s, such personnel shifts and the obvious political orientation of most justices meant that "the policy views dominant on the Court are never for long out of line with the policy views dominant among the lawmaking majorities of the United States" (1957: 285). The Court could on rare occasions block the application of a policy by up to 25 years. However, such outlier cases could not disguise the reality that "Congress and the president do generally succeed in overcoming a hostile court on major policy issues" (Dahl, 1957: 288).

The often close relationship between the federal courts and the federal government has been prominent in the work of Dahl and others (Dahl, 1957; Whittington, 2005). In his 1957 study of the Court's role as a policy-making institution, what was significant for Dahl was not that courts *made* policy, but the extent to which policy decisions were made "by going outside established 'legal' criteria found in precedent, statute, and constitution" (1957: 279–280). Central to his enquiry was understanding the Court's role in either blocking the will of the ruling majority or lending legitimacy to it. The Court is not merely an agent of the governing alliance, wrote Dahl:

> It is an essential part of the political leadership and possesses some bases of power of its own, the most important of which is the unique legitimacy attributed to its interpretations of the Constitution. This legitimacy the Court jeopardizes if it flagrantly opposes the major policies of the dominant alliance.
>
> (Dahl, 1957: 293)

As the sentiment of the dominant national alliance shifted in response to political activity in society, so too did that of the Court.

From 1938 onwards the Court enunciated a changed conception of rights that placed more emphasis on the protection of federally protected rights, and the rights of minorities—particularly their right to participate in the political process. During the Progressive Era from the end of the nineteenth century to the 1930s, the Court dragged its feet while the democratic political institutions of the federal government and the states were passing legislation to ameliorate the conditions of workers and the urban poor. By the late 1930s it had begun to accept the changing political context, after which the gap between the Court's and the federal government's interpretation of the Constitution narrowed considerably. Two parallel trends emerge. As seen in Chapter 2, on the one hand, the Court's decisions have over time come to endorse, or 'formalise', values emerging from ongoing struggles within civil society. On the other hand, the Court became an agent of federal power almost by default. It was less a proactive decision by any particular court or justices than it represented a conjunction between the Court's commitment to uphold an emerging equality-based conception of constitutional rights—which national majorities and the federal government had come to support *first*—and the greater propensity of the states to violate those rights.

Following the passage of the Judiciary Act of 1925, the range and number of cases falling within the Court's mandatory appellate jurisdiction was dramatically reduced, giving the justices far more discretion over which cases the Court heard, most of which would henceforth come by way of petitions for *certiorari* (Grossman and Epp, 2002: 110). This ostensibly simple administrative change had a profound impact on how the Court perceived its emerging role. It was now no longer responsible for correcting 'errors' in the decisions of the lower federal courts. The Court's "primary responsibility now was to focus on those cases which presented issues of general importance—those which 'transcended' the interests of the parties to the case" (Grossman and Epp, 2002: 110).[8] According to Grossman and Epp, this enhanced control over the cases that it heard resulted in a "much broadened judicial vision" and a radically changed agenda "responsive to emerging theories of 'rights consciousness' and expectations of legal redress" (2002: 110).

The Court's increased control over its docket, combined with its vantage point in the American system of government, put it in a strong position to formalise emerging norms, and to recognise the expanded scope of norms. Neither the Court's decision in *Carolene Products* nor its later decisions in *Brown v Board of Education* or the reapportionment cases were ones where it was imposing its will on a reluctant population as the countermajoritarian difficulty implies. Indeed, the complaint could be made that given the Court's role, as Dahl saw it, as part of the ruling coalition, that it has sometimes been overly conscious of what national majority sentiment would tolerate. The sense that the Court does not stick its neck out before there is already a groundswell of national opinion on a given issue fits Tocqueville's view of how attitudes shift from minority to majority acceptance in the United States (see De Tocqueville and Renshaw, 1998: 103). As Klarman puts it:

> The Court identifies and protects minority rights only when a majority or near majority of the community has come to deem those rights worthy of protection.
>
> (Klarman, 1996: 17–18)

The role of the Supreme Court is therefore very much that of a passive arbiter that does not create values but which must sometimes decide between conflicting constitutional values and interpretations arising from already significant social struggles (see, for example, Cover, 1983: 40–42). To this extent, it has been said that the Court has "seldom lagged far behind or forged far ahead of America" (McCloskey and Levinson, 2016: 292). This certainly represents a reasonable assessment of the Warren Court, which sometimes got ahead of the political branches on issues like desegregation and reapportionment, but was largely in step with the emerging value orientations of civil society on those issues.

One example is the Court's evolving interpretation of equality and human dignity. Maxine Goodman notes that in *Brown v Board of Education* the Court cited the Swedish sociologist Gunner Myrdal (1944), who had defined the American Creed as including dignity as an essential ideal (Goodman, 2006: 745). The Court used Myrdal's work as authority for the idea that segregation negatively impacts African-American school children. Perhaps just as significantly, in *Trop v Dulles*, the Court recognised that "the basic concept underlying the Eight Amendment is nothing less than the dignity of man" and that the Amendment must "draw its meaning from the evolving standards of decency that mark the progress of a maturing society" (1958: 100–101). The irony of the Court citing a Swedish study to illustrate that dignity was an essential American ideal does not diminish, to paraphrase Murphy (1993: 177–178), the important role of the Court in 'solidifying constitutionalism' and its values.

Though the Court's role as a legal check on dangerous local majority sentiment became increasingly important as its authority and prestige grew, its writ was still primarily felt in the legal institutional space. It could support and encourage political action in the civic space where the underlying values were aligned with its priorities and national ones. As indicated in previous chapters, however, the Court's capacity to shape the value orientations of either the civic spaces in former slave states, or those of other local majorities, remained limited.

A Janus-Faced Constitution

In the United States the Böckenförde Dilemma also has relevance. Here, the dilemma was addressed partly through the emerging national ideology, and partly through the plethora of voluntary associations which through the nineteenth century allowed community, civic, and religious loyalties to sustain themselves in parallel with, and not in opposition to, American identity. The liberty guaranteed by the Constitution also sustained these voluntary associations. However, the strength of these local bonds has gradually weakened, particularly as church attendance declined.

Jefferson's belief in constitutional renewal left a powerful resonance in American political thought. It is of a country which commits itself to a set of precepts on parchment, but which has had to constantly fight and struggle over the meaning and implications of those ideas. This point was put most strikingly by Walton Hamilton:

> The Bible of verbal inspiration begat the constitution of unquestioned authority. ... As the Bible wanted exegesis, the Constitution demanded

> exposition. Its catholic clauses yielded to deduction precepts suitable to the cause and the occasion; it became the great storehouse of verbal conflict, and rival truths were derived by the same inexorable logic from the same infallible source. The Civil War was waged for a Union which it had created; the object of secession was to secure rights guaranteed by the Constitution.
>
> (Hamilton, 1930: 256)

At the basis of constitutional interpretation, then, there is not merely the possibility, but the probability, of conflict over meaning and values.[9] Given such a range of diametrically opposing interpretations in American history from one relatively short text, the role of the Supreme Court in deciding those tough questions which Justice Breyer identified on the boundary becomes highly significant. Constitutionalism therefore requires not only the enunciation of certain values such as equality and human dignity, but also a reinterpretation of the scope, potential, and applicability of those values over time. That progress is also dependent on the balance between the forces of stability and renewal within a country's constitutional and institutional culture.

As we have seen in earlier chapters, constitutionalism can function as a restraint on democracy, so that adherence to constitutionalism may involve a limitation to democratic preferences. The malapportionment cases illustrate how this view of constitutionalism neglects the extent to which constitutionalism *protects* democratic rights and majority preferences. The crisis for representative democracy manifested in the malapportionment cases did not arise because state legislators were acting in *conformity* with constitutionalism, but because they were manifestly acting in *opposition* to it. By ignoring the equal protection principle of the federal constitution and contravening the terms of their own state constitutions requiring decennial reapportionment, legislative majorities in all but a handful of states had been elected by only a minority of the state's population (see Smith, 2014: 287–288). While this could easily be dismissed as purely a desire to hang onto political power—and it was certainly that—malapportionment also reflected deeper value schisms.

Each malapportioned state was itself split into different value systems. In northern states, the divide was principally between urban and rural, and between the wealthy white business class and urban poor. In the South, segregation added a regressive complexion to these competing values systems. The urban-rural split was replicated across the country: between poorer urban and blue-collar workers demanding better conditions, and those in rural areas who claimed that numerically equal reapportionment would see their liberties and rights trampled over by unprincipled urban majorities (Smith, 2014: 26). Of course, the constitutional rights and liberties which wealthy white rural populations invoked as a reason for *not* reapportioning were found in the same constitutions with decennial reapportionment requirements that those rural interests were disregarding.

Only a system of government based on general principles could bridge the divide between the groups assembled at Philadelphia in 1787. Such principles had to be flexible enough to mean one thing to defenders of states' rights and something quite different to those favouring energetic national government. Justice Holmes' dissent in *Lochner* that a constitution "is made for people of fundamentally different views" (1905: 76) was a message to his colleagues on the majority that attempts to straightjacket the country into a plutocratic reading of the Fourteenth Amendment ignored what constitutions are about. Perhaps just as significantly in terms of stability and renewal, in articulating a 'rational man' conception of liberty in his dissent, Holmes was also setting forth his view that majority understandings of constitutionalism in the present should generally prevail over static definitions from the past.

> I think that the word liberty in the Fourteenth Amendment is perverted when it is held to prevent the natural outcome of a dominant opinion, unless it can be said that a rational and fair man necessarily would admit that the statute proposed would infringe fundamental principles as they have been understood by the traditions of our people and our law. It does not need research to show that no such sweeping condemnation can be passed upon the statute before us.
>
> (1905: 76)

A constitution can be seen as much as a tool for mediating disagreement politically as a final and definitive instrument of governance. This is partly why claims about identifying original intent are problematic if a constitution is a compromise between different groups or interests within 13 sovereign states.[10] Yet as a legal tool, the constitution has to represent the final word of authority, even if it cannot be the final word in interpretation or meaning. Since a constitution acts as both the source of ultimate authority and is also a general instrument of law and governance, this means that its authority may greatly exceed its capacity to provide definitive answers. In other words, constitutions have authority precisely because they are general enough to unite an otherwise disaggregated people around a set of political and societal principles.

Justice Robert Jackson argued that the judicial burden involves "translating the majestic generalities of the Bill of Rights, conceived as part of the pattern of liberal government in the eighteenth century, into concrete restraints on officials dealing with the problems of the twentieth century" (1943: 639). Brenner's point that "only a fragmentary constitution is unstrained, only it can permit a constitutional consensus over the long run" (1999: 136) is relevant here. Such a constitution permits the courts to interpret flexibly to meet the changing needs of a society and reconcile conflicts which could not have been foreseen by the constitutional enactors. Generalities in the text may create or perpetuate debate, arguments, and conflict, but can also provide a basis for consensus. This flexibility was just as well with slavery being the elephant in the room for the first eight decades of America's existence.

Without that generality (and flexibility) in the constitutional text—which still has the force to unite Americans of such disparate political persuasions as can be found in so-called 'red states' and 'blue states'—it seems unlikely that the United States would have even made it intact to fight the Civil War, let alone survived it. In the post-Civil War period, constitutional amendments and Reconstruction seemingly entrenched the logic and value of equality in the constitutional text. However, this was a victory in the legal institutional space; it was not a decisive victory in the 'local' civic space in the former slave states. The emancipated African-Americans living in the former slave states were still not accepted as citizens in those places because the value system in the South rejected the constitutional values which triumphed at the end of the Civil War.

The Supreme Court's part in incorporating the protections of the Fourteenth Amendment against the states would be crushingly slow for the emancipation of African-Americans and other minority groups, as the Court turned towards the protection of economic rights. This reflects and reinforces the point made in the Introduction that the development of American democracy and the expanding suffrage have paralleled, and also driven, the expansion of rights.[11] This is perhaps what Robert Bellah meant when he called slavery "the second time of trial" (1991: 182). Slavery was, said Bellah, "the most salient aspect of the more general problem of the full institutionalisation of democracy within our country" (1991: 182). How and why the incorporation of the Bill of Rights—and especially democratic rights—eventually made headway is the question we now turn to.

Incorporation of the Bill of Rights

By the 1920s the US was still grappling with the thorny question of how, and to what extent, the Bill of Rights of 1791 would be incorporated within the scope of the Equal Protection and Due Process clauses of the Fourteenth Amendment (1868). Incorporation represented a significant evolution in American constitutional jurisprudence towards the idea that the Bill of Rights protected individuals as much against abuses of power by their own states as by the federal government (for more on incorporation, see Amar, 1992).

The Fourteenth Amendment is by some margin the Constitution's most litigated provision. Although passed in 1868 as the United States pushed ahead with Reconstruction, its impact did not really begin to be felt until the 1920s when the Supreme Court began to slowly and selectively hold that its Due Process and Equal Protection clauses applied to the states (see Grossman and Epp, 2002: 107). The evolution of American constitutionalism from a charter of enumerated powers designed to limit government to a value-centric orientation focussed on protecting individual rights parallels the incorporation of the Bill of Rights against the states. Whittington observes that the states have occupied far more of the Supreme Court's constitutional attention than has the federal government, and the states have been the main target of the power of judicial review (2005: 586). This is both because of the Court's role as an agent of national policy since the first decades of the republic examined already (see Dahl, 1957; Whittington, 2005), and the more frequent violations of federally protected rights by the states. It is this second point I wish to concentrate on.

The Bill of Rights was ostensibly enacted as a defence of the people against federal power. By the twentieth century, though, it was becoming clear that some citizens needed to be protected from their own states (see Amar, 1991). The Fourteenth Amendment contains within it the idea that neither federal nor state laws may negate or diminish the constitutional rights of citizens of the United States. The Amendment contains five sections but it is Section 1 which provides some of the Constitution's most significant constitutional rights guarantees, which also makes it the section around which the vast majority of Supreme Court cases are fought over. Still, even as the power of the federal government increased after the Civil War, the innately conservative federal judiciary did not rush to incorporate the protections of the Fourteenth and Fifteenth Amendments against the states. By the beginning of the New Deal period (c.1933) there were as yet few cases dealing with civil liberties, and the constitutional concept of equality in the Equal Protection Clause was generally underdeveloped and "offered little protection against discrimination" (Grossman and Epp, 2002: 107–108).

During the 1960s, the expansion of the suffrage to women was no more than two generations old, but the fulfilment of its extension to African-Americans promised in the post-Civil War amendments was woefully incomplete. After *Brown v Board of Education*, many lawyers felt that the emancipatory promise of the Fourteenth Amendment was finally being fulfilled almost 90 years after its adoption. In decisions including *Brown* and *Gomillion v Lightfoot* (1960) the Supreme Court found itself engaged in what some called the second great period of reconstruction (see Amar, 1991: 1133). Lending credence to the idea of the judiciary as a bulwark against ossification, Martin Shapiro observes that "[the Court] rather than the congress or presidency has been the principal agent of domestic reform in post-World War II American politics" (1972: v). One explanation for this was the recognition by many American politicians, lawyers, and judges that while slavery had been abolished after the Civil War, many of the states were still a regressive and anti-liberal force within the country. To such lawyers, state governments were "the quintessential threat to individual and minority rights", while federal officials, particularly federal courts, were the special guardians of the rights promised in the Fourteenth Amendment (Amar, 1991: 1133). The idea that the biggest threat to liberty and the Union came from the states rather than the federal government was by no means novel. In 1913, Justice Oliver Wendell Holmes Jr observed:

> I do not think the United States would come to an end if we lost our power to declare an Act of Congress void. I do think the Union would be imperiled if we could not make that declaration as to the laws of the several States.
>
> (Holmes, 2007: 295–296)

Holmes was, in fact, merely restating what had been a perennial fear of the framers that the chief threat to minority interests came from the states rather than the incipient federal government. One ironic caveat was that due to the widespread practice of reapportionment, one minority that the states were sublime at protecting was the white rural minority.

The Reconstruction Period after the Civil War created a constitutional and societal architecture which was closer to the twentieth century than to the eighteenth century. However, it took almost a century for some of the promises of the Fourteenth and Fifteenth Amendments to begin to be realised. The catalyst for this much delayed recognition of basic rights was not the civil rights movements of the 1950s and 1960s, but the social and economic crisis of the Great Depression, and a quiet revolution in the Supreme Court's jurisprudence. Out of the defeat of Roosevelt's court packing plan and the Court's belated approval of the hitherto blocked legislation came a new jurisprudence which would take the constitutionality of economic statutes almost as axiomatic, while declaring that legislation which curtails the processes that protect minorities and political participation would be subject to stricter judicial scrutiny.

Footnote Four and the Rise of the Individual

Case summary—*United States v Carolene Products*

United States v Carolene Products (1938), an otherwise mundane case relating to the shipping of milk products across state lines, contains what is regarded as the most famous footnote in Supreme Court history. A 1923 act had banned the interstate shipment of 'filled' milk products (with skimmed milk and vegetable oil added). A manufacturer indicted for shipping filled milk challenged the statute. At issue was whether the statute violated the Commerce Power granted to Congress and the Due Process Clause of the Fifth Amendment. Since the late nineteenth century such cases had normally been decided in favour of the business interest concerned, with the offending statute being struck down. *Carolene* marked a turning point, signifying a shift on the Court from its decades-old defence of business interests dating from the Lochner era which had blocked progressive legislation. Written by Harlan Stone, footnote four signalled that the Court would presume the constitutionality of economic legislation, but would undertake more searching judicial scrutiny with legislation that was prohibited by the Bill of Rights, which affected access to political processes, or which targeted minorities. Apart from speaking to the threats to democratic processes, opposition forces, and minority interests from either oligarchical factions or majoritarian processes, the text can also be read as emphasising the importance of a vibrant public space in the Greek sense (see Cover, 1982: 1293), within which the preferences of citizens can be effectively reflected and implemented through the legislative process, but without injury to the rights of either minority interests, or minority groups.

During the period when the intellectual debate about the nature of judicial review began to gain ground in the 1950s, the US and its allies had just successfully fought fascism in Europe. Many liberal academics who agreed with the leftward policy shift on the Supreme Court following the multiple appointments made by Roosevelt felt a particular intellectual need to find a justification for judicial review given their opposition to it during the Progressive Era. There was, moreover, an intellectual need "to imagine a countermajoritarian Court, even if one did not exist" (Friedman, 2002: 161). Beyond the academy, "for a public that had seen the ugly face of totalitarianism" there was, notes Friedman, "broad support for an institution in a democracy dedicated to protecting minority rights" (2002: 161).

By the end of World War II, humanity had "learned some indelible lessons about the need to find effective constraints for governmental abuse of power" (Durham, 1993: 43). Despite the risks of government by judges, writes Durham, the post-World War II era "witnessed a pronounced convergence towards reliance on 'the least dangerous branch' to control such abuses through judicial review" (1993: 43). Although America had no Holocaust, it had "a history of racism that courts began to dismantle at the beginning of the 1950s" (Durham, 1993: 44). The roots of that process to dismantle racism can be traced to footnote four. Robert Cover refers to the footnote as "the text" for the generation of *Brown v Board of Education* (1954) and the civil rights movement (1982: 1316). The greater willingness of the Supreme Court to intervene on behalf of representative democracy and the individual in the 1960s has its origins in the New Deal period. Roosevelt strongly promoted the idea of a second Bill of Rights that would include a duty to provide for 'welfare rights' (West, 2009: 66). The reapportionment decisions examined in Chapter 4, which were concerned with restoring the integrity of democratic representation, can be seen through the prism of footnote four's statement of the conditions under which the Court would undertake judicial review and intervene in democratic processes (see *US v Carolene Products Co.*, 1938: 152–154 n.4).

The emphasis on group affiliations had remained dominant in the US since the Civil War. This suited the idea of a country where majority rule prevailed, but it seemed ill-suited to changes in society wrought by industrialisation and the migration of huge numbers to the cities. Bobbitt notes that changes were also afoot within American law that would move its orientation away from the interests of groups to a greater focus on the individual (2015: 125). This transition had more significant implications, though, since the greater focus on the individual implied a weakening of the communal bonds, associational activities, and political activity of the civic space through which rights had previously been realised. By the 1930s, economic crisis meant that the old order would no longer hold. Franklin Roosevelt's New Deal programme sought to provide for a new and invigorated relationship between the federal government and the people, but it was one that the Supreme Court was initially resistant to.

David Strauss argues that footnote four was "the Court's first—and maybe only—attempt to say, systematically, when the courts should declare laws unconstitutional" (2010: 1254).[12] Although footnote four signalled a retreat from judicial review of economic regulations and suggested a general inclination towards judicial inertia, it also gave notice that the Court would take a keener interest in cases where federal rights, rights of political participation, or the rights of certain minorities were under threat. *Carolene* served to enshrine the incorporation process within a formula, which while not universally admired, provided some evidence of a logical framework for the use of judicial review rather than the arbitrariness of discretion. *Carolene* can be seen as a clear statement of judicial deference to majority rule, but it was one which came with a significant caveat: the circumstances under which the Court would act to protect individual rights against the will of the majority were made clearer than they had ever been before, or since (Cover, 1982: 1316). Summarising the reasoning behind the footnote, Cover writes:

> The footnote acknowledges that those representatives enjoying office, its power, and its perquisites may conspire to entrench themselves and to defeat the very majoritarian processes that render the acts of legislatures presumptively more legitimate than the acts of judges.
>
> (Cover, 1982: 1292)

However, this change in the Court's jurisprudence and the additional scrutiny it offered to combat efforts intended to pervert the majoritarian process cannot be divorced from the changing political context of the time. In 1937–1938, that context was "the New Deal at home and totalitarianism abroad" (Cover, 1982: 1289). The Court was announcing its intention to withdraw almost totally from its decades-long oversight of economic regulations which had culminated in the confrontation with Franklin Roosevelt. Yet this withdrawal did not mean that "in the age of Hitler, majoritarianism itself would not require more in the way of justification than its professedly democratic nature" (Cover, 1982: 1289). According to Robert Cover, the central danger that footnote four was addressing was the possibility that incumbency of elected officials might "degenerate into 'apparatus', manipulating the formal machinery of choice in elections, districting, and control of public benefits" (1982: 1293).

Stone signalled in footnote four that civil liberties would still be subject to judicial protection when specific wires were tripped. These tripwires—one for each paragraph of the footnote—can be summarised as 'federal rights', 'political participation', and 'representation'. Second, the decision established a principle of closer judicial scrutiny for the protection of the rights of "discrete and insular minorities" (1938: 155). Third, it articulated a principle which linked the proper functioning of political processes with a system that protected minority rights. Provided the political processes are working normally and are not excluding any groups then the courts will not normally intervene. Particularly relevant to the reapportionment decisions is the second paragraph of footnote four since it links the legitimacy of democratic processes with the ability of citizens to participate fully in the political processes without hindrance from their elected representatives.

> It is unnecessary to consider now whether legislation which restricts those political processes which can ordinarily be expected to bring about repeal of undesirable legislation, is to be subjected to more exacting judicial scrutiny under the general prohibitions of the Fourteenth Amendment than are most other types of legislation.
>
> ('Footnote four' of *US v Carolene Products* 1938: 155)

Footnote four created a legitimacy test for legislative acts against which civil liberties claims could be measured. Taking each paragraph in turn, legislative actions attracting judicial scrutiny might be 1) ones prohibited by the Bill of Rights as incorporated by the Fourteenth Amendment; 2) ones which disadvantage citizens generally by restricting their participation in the political process, or which sabotage the process by prioritising the interests of certain groups or legislators themselves; and 3) ones which discriminate against specific minorities, thereby damaging the political processes which protect them and affect the quality of their representation within those processes. Cover writes that the scope for extending judicial review is determined not by "the special value of certain rights" but by "their vulnerability to perversions by the majoritarian process" (Cover, 1982: 1291–1292). Footnote four's intent in subjecting certain legislative actions to more searching judicial inquiry also speaks to the importance of ensuring that a vibrant and unrestricted public space is maintained to ensure that the opinions and democratic preferences of citizens at election time translated into representation. The footnote suggests, writes Cover, that "the space for politics in the Greek sense must be ample and unencumbered" for if the state through its manifestation in party structures was able to orchestrate mass politics, "even honest elections would not avail" (Cover, 1982: 1293).

The paradox in the reapportionment cases was that while they were ostensibly a problem of illegitimate minority rule as a result of decades-old malapportionment, they were fundamentally about the denial of individual rights to the majority of the population located in urban and suburban areas. So while 'the minority' was in charge of state legislatures, many of the groups which collectively constituted the numerical majority were the very minorities that footnote four alluded to: African-Americans, Catholics, Jews, immigrants, and other minority groups. The 'minority' who were responsible for malapportionment refers to groups which may be losers in the political process sometimes, but may be successful at other times. However, sometimes the losing 'minority' in a political battle may also belong to a racial, religious, or other minority; these were the 'discrete and insular minorities' that footnote four referred to. As Robert Cover notes, "they are not simply losers in the political arena, they are perpetual losers" who may become "scapegoats in the real political struggles between other groups" (1982: 1296).

Due to changes in personnel on the Court in the 1940s a period of intense judicial deference to federal and state legislatures began, but there were exceptions such as *West Virginia v Barnette*, which illustrated the influence of *Carolene*. Eventually, the deference to majorities went too far, with a divided court led by Justice Felix Frankfurter upholding many McCarthyite anti-civil liberties laws in the 1950s (see Horwitz, 1997: 26).[13] However, three appointments to the Court in the 1950s by Dwight Eisenhower—Earl Warren, William Brennan, and Potter Stewart—laid the basis for *Baker v Carr*, the other reapportionment decisions, and a succession of landmark rulings which heralded a new emphasis on the protection of the rights of minorities.

Conclusion

A renewal-oriented development in constitutional values can be seen in the evolving understanding of equality and human dignity represented by the incorporation of the Bill of Rights against the states, the expanding franchise, and the important consequences of the Court's changed jurisprudence after its decision in *Carolene Products*. Characterising the Court's shift from its pre-New Deal jurisprudence to its post-footnote four jurisprudential orientation, Lietzmann argues that after it lost the economic fight with Franklin Roosevelt over the New Deal, the Supreme Court "withdrew to the sidelines of political morality" (2002: 94).

I would rather characterise this, though, as an emerging national liberal morality, based on the constitutional development of equality highlighted above. It was one that drew particular political sustenance from urban, suburban, and northern parts of the US, rather than rural areas, the American heartland, or the South. The second paragraph of footnote four, which provided a judicial standard for stricter scrutiny of cases involving the functioning of the political process and its ability to provide relief from undesirable legislation, anticipated precisely the sort of problem presented by the reapportionment cases. James Madison believed that the multiplicity of interests in a continent-sized republic would make it more difficult for tyrannical factions to form as they could at the local level. Although Madison was partially correct, the intractable difficulty with malapportionment was that electoral districting at the state and federal level was still run by the states, and the state legislatures refused to reapportion. Civil society groups such as the League of Women Voters were hugely important in highlighting the issue of malapportionment with the public, but their efforts to shame legislators into reapportioning and so solve the issue politically ran into legislative roadblocks. Resolving the problem would eventually require the intervention of the federal courts. The reapportionment decisions were ones which brought the constitutional order back into alignment with majority sentiment and, as Barry Friedman argues, anticipated issues that were becoming a concern to the public (see 2002: 222). Overall, the effects of the reapportionment cases were more significant in the legal institutional space because they altered the political system through which laws are made. The next chapter examines the factors that brought the Supreme Court to pronounce on the proper form of representative government in the United States, as well as the longer-term developments in American constitutionalism which led to this political transformation.

Notes

1 As Lincoln put it at the time, "Must a government of necessity be too strong for the liberties of its people, or too weak to maintain its own existence?" (Paludan, 1977: 12).
2 *Lochner v New York*, which struck down a New York State statute aimed at preventing bakery workers having to work over 60 hours a week, has received more criticism than perhaps any other Supreme Court decision in the twentieth century.
3 Here, one is reminded of Tacitus' observation that "when the state was most corrupt, laws were most abundant" (Tacitus, 1931, Book III, Section 27).
4 In fact, the only clearly majoritarian institution in the federal government was the House of Representatives, and that was on the basis of a distinctly countermajoritarian franchise.
5 Jefferson had urged the adoption of the Bill of Rights while minister in Paris, and persuaded Madison to support them (see Labunski, 2006: 51).
6 Later, Jefferson came to view the federal judiciary as a threat to republicanism.
7 This resonates with the point made in Chapter 2 about the Constitution as a framework for argument (see Ellis, 2007: 87–126).
8 To the present day, litigation involving redistricting, the Voting Rights Act, and aspects of campaign finance remain within the Court's mandatory jurisdiction (see Douglas, 2011).
9 This is also a theme in the work of Robert Cover.
10 The *BVerfG*'s rigid application of its coherence doctrine to legislation is another example of where courts are sometimes insufficiently sensitive to the type of compromises necessary to forge political agreements.
11 By contrast, post-1949 German constitutionalism has seen fundamental rights as a precondition for democracy.
12 Justice Stone's former law clerk, Louis Lusky, writes that the footnote was being offered not as a Court-approved standard of judicial review, but "as a starting point for debate" (1982: 1098).
13 Horwitz noted that "under Justice Frankfurter's influence, the Court had rubber-stamped a wide variety of repressive McCarthyite laws" (1997: 26).

References

Lochner v New York 198 US 45, 1905
United States v Carolene Products Company, 304 US 144, 1938
West Virginia State Board of Education v Barnette, 319 US 624, 1943
Brown v Board of Education of Topeka, 347 US 483, 1954
Trop v Dulles, 356 US 86, 1958
Gomillion v Lightfoot, 364 US 339, 1960
Baker v Carr, 396 US 186, 1962
Gray v Sanders, 372 US 368, 1963

Ackerman, B., *We the People, Volume 2: Transformations* (Cambridge, MA: Harvard University Press, 2000).
Amar, A. R., "The Bill of Rights as a Constitution", *Yale Law Journal* (1991), 1131–1210.

Amar, A. R., "The Bill of Rights and the Fourteenth Amendment", *Yale Law Journal* (1992), 1193–1284.

Bellah, R. N., "Civil Religion in America", in *Beyond Belief: Essays on Religion in a Post-Traditional World* (Berkeley, CA: University of California Press, 1991).

Bobbitt, P., "The Age of Consent", in *The Ages of American Law*, ed. by Grant Gilmore and Philip Bobbitt (New Haven, CT: Yale University Press, 2015).

Brenner, M., "The Constitutional Framework of Democratic Representation", in *Constitutionalism, Universalism and Democracy: A Comparative Analysis*, ed. by Christian Starck (Baden-Baden: Nomos-Verlag-Ges., 1999).

Cover, R. M., "The Origins of Judicial Activism in The Protection of Minorities", *The Yale Law Journal*, 91 (7) (1982), 1287–1316.

Cover, R. M., "The Supreme Court 1982 Term Foreword: Nomos and Narrative", *Harvard Law Review*, 97 (1) (1983), 4.

Dahl, R. A., "Decision-Making in a Democracy: The Supreme Court as a National Policy-Maker", *Journal of Public Law*, 6 (1957), 279.

De Tocqueville, A. and P. Renshaw, *Democracy in America* (Herts: Wordsworth Editions Limited, 1998).

Douglas, J. A., "The Procedure of Election Law in Federal Courts", *Utah Law Review* (2011), 433.

Durham, C., "General Asseessment of the Basic Law—An American View", in *Germany and its Basic Law: Past, Present, and Future: A German-American Symposium*, ed. by Paul Kirchhof and Donald P. Kommers (Baden-Baden: Nomos, 1993).

Ellis, J. J., "The Argument", in *American Creation: Triumphs and Tragedies at the Founding of the Republic* (New York: Vintage Books, 2007).

Ely, J. H., *Democracy and Distrust: A Theory of Judicial Review* (Cambridge: Harvard University Press, 1980).

Friedman, B., "The Birth of an Academic Obsession: The History of the Countermajoritarian Difficulty, Part Five", *Yale Law Journal* (2002), 153–259.

Goodman, M., "Human Dignity in Supreme Court Constitutional Jurisprudence", *Nebraska Law Review*, 84 (2006).

Grossman, J. B. and C. R. Epp, "Agenda Formation on the Policy Active U.S. Supreme Court", in *Constitutional Courts in Comparison: The U.S. Supreme Court and The German Federal Constitutional Court*, ed. by Ralf Rogowski and Thomas Gawron (New York: Berghahn Books, 2002).

Hamilton, W. H., "Constitutionalism", in *Encyclopaedia of the Social Sciences*, ed. by Edwin R. A. Seligman and Alvin Johnson (New York: Macmillan, 1930).

Hobson, C. F., "The Negative on State Laws: James Madison, the Constitution, and the Crisis of Republican Government", *The William and Mary Quarterly: A Magazine of Early American History* (1979), 215–235.

Holmes, O. W., "Speech at a Dinner of the Harvard Law School Association of New York, 15 Feb 1913", in *The Collected Legal Papers* (New York: Dover Publications, 2007).

Horwitz, M. J., "In Memoriam: William J. Brennan, Jr", *Harvard Law Review* (1997), 1–50.

Jefferson, T., J. Madison, and J. M. Smith, "Letter From Jefferson to Madison, 15 March 1789", in *The Republic of Letters: The Correspondence Between Thomas Jefferson and James Madison, 1776–1826*, ed. by James Morton Smith (New York: W.W. Norton and Company, 1995).

Klarman, M. J., "Rethinking the Civil Rights and Civil Liberties Revolutions", *Virginia Law Review* (1996), 1–67.

Kramer, L., *The People Themselves: Popular Constitutionalism and Judicial Review* (Oxford: Oxford University Press, 2004).

Labunski, R. E., *James Madison and the Struggle for the Bill of Rights* (Oxford: Oxford University Press, 2006).

Lietzmann, H., "Constitutional Courts in Changing Political Systems", in *Constitutional Courts in Comparison: The US Supreme Court and the German Federal Constitutional Court*, ed. by Ralf Rogowski and Thomas Gawron (New York: Berghahn Books, 2002).

Lusky, L., "Footnote Redux: A 'Carolene Products' Reminiscence", *Columbia Law Review*, 82 (6) (1982), 1093–1109.

Madison, J. "From James Madison to Thomas Jefferson, 17 October 1788", National Archives, (1788), available at: https://founders.archives.gov/documents/Madison/01-11-02-0218 [last accessed 28 July 2019].

Madison, J., "Speech, House of Representatives, 8 June 1789", in *The Founders' Constitution* (Chicago: University of Chicago Press, 1986), available at: http://press-pubs.uchicago.edu/founders/documents/v1ch14s50.html [last accessed 30 June 2020].

Madison, J., "Federalist Number 62", in *The Federalist Papers*, ed. by Isaac Kramnick (Harmondsworth: Penguin, 1987).

McCloskey, R. G. and S. Levinson, *The American Supreme Court*. 6th edn (Chicago: University of Chicago Press, 2016).

Murphy, W. F., "Excluding Political Parties: Problems for Democratic and Constitutional Theory", in *Germany and its Basic Law: Past, Present, and Future: A German–American Symposium*, ed. by Paul Kirchhof and Donald P Kommers (Baden-Baden: Nomos, 1993).

Myrdal, G., *An American Dilemma, Volume 2: The Negro Problem and Modern Democracy*. Vol. 2 (New Brunswick: Transaction Publishers, 1944).

Paludan, P. S., "Lincoln, the Rule of Law, and the American Revolution", *Journal of the Illinois State Historical Society (1908–1984)*, 70 (1) (1977), 10–17.

Rakove, J. N., "James Madison and the Bill Of Rights: A Broader Context", *Presidential Studies Quarterly*, 22 (4) (1992), 667–677.

Shapiro, M., "Foreword", in *The Modern Supreme Court*, ed. by Robert Green McCloskey (Cambridge, MA: Harvard University Press, 1972).

Smith, J. D., *On Democracy's Doorstep: The Inside Story of How the Supreme Court Brought "One Person, One Vote" to the United States* (New York: Hill and Wang, 2014).

Strauss, D. A., "Is Carolene Products Obsolete", *University of Illinois Law Review* (2010), 1251.

Tacitus, C., "The Annals", in Loeb Classical Library (Cambridge, MA: Harvard University Press, 1931).

West, R., "Ennobling Politics", in *Law and Democracy in the Empire of Force*, ed. by James Boyd White and Jefferson Powell (Ann Arbor: University of Michigan Press, 2009).

Whittington, K. E., "'Interpose Your Friendly Hand': Political Supports for the Exercise of Judicial Review by the United States Supreme Court", *American Political Science Review*, 99 (4) (2005), 583–596.

4 A Changing Concept of Equality

> I think generally in our society change is incremental, and real change, enduring change, happens one step at a time.
>
> (Justice Ruth Bader Ginsburg, Senate Confirmation Hearing, 1993)

> Our constitutional system amply provides for the protection of minorities by means other than giving them majority control of state legislatures.
>
> (Chief Justice Earl Warren in *Reynolds v Sims*, 1964: 566)

The widespread practice of malapportionment effectively represented a decades-old countermajoritarian power grab at the heart of American constitutional government by pro-segregationists in the South, and wealthy rural and business interests across the country (see Smith, 2014: 15). The abuse of civil and democratic rights in state legislatures which had endured intermittently since America's founding provided the political imperative and moral impetus for the stronger judicial defence of representative democracy which was seen in the reapportionment cases. However, in the United States this scrutiny took the form of intense corrective intervention over a period of three years rather than the more permanent role of the *Bundesverfassungsgericht* in Germany.

As seen in previous chapters the division between the civic space and legal institutional space was a significant factor in how the reapportionment cases reached the Court and were eventually dealt with. Civil society actors played an important role in bringing the problem of malapportionment to the public's attention. The reapportionment cases dealt with issues addressed in previous chapters, particularly the growing schism between constitutional values as enunciated by the Supreme Court which matched national majority sentiment, and the competing value systems and interpretations of local majorities who were refusing to reapportion. The record of the reapportionment cases suggests that in the absence of an agreement on values, and when the dogged and persistent activity of civil society actors fails to persuade legislators to reapportion, there must as a last resort be an institution with the authority and legitimacy to provide a remedy (see Shapiro, 1972: vi).

Malapportionment illustrated the extent to which the preservation of human dignity relies on functional representative democracy, and ultimately relies, as the Supreme Court cases showed, on constitutionalism itself. By leaping into the "mathematical quagmire" of reapportionment which Justice Felix Frankfurter's dissent in *Baker v Carr* (1962a: 268) warned about, the Court found itself eventually having to decide upon the fundamental principle of representative government in the United States; one which was based on the clear idea of majority rule, or one which took geographic, historical, or community factors into account. In its decision, first, to enter the reapportionment fray in *Baker*, and then later to declare 'one person, one vote' as the constitutional standard for representative government in *Reynolds v Sims*, the Court grounded its reasoning squarely in the Equal Protection Clause of the Fourteenth Amendment. Since the Constitution did not specify a form of republican government, the idea that it had to be based on equal representation was certainly not self-evident. Yet as Bruce Terris, an assistant to the Solicitor General noted, this development towards a 'one person, one vote' standard was inevitable seen in the light of the steadily expanding franchise and a changed understanding of equality (see Smith, 2014: 161).

Baker v Carr highlighted not merely the general question of the permissibility of judicial review in a democratic society as more mundane cases have. The case also raised questions of fundamental constitutional importance such as the nature of republican government, the separation of powers, and the tension between state sovereignty and the rights of United States citizens, all of which were understood and deliberated upon by the justices. The reapportionment cases illustrate the stability versus renewal paradigm of constitutionalism addressed in previous chapters in the form of a complex political and legal dilemma. The focus of this chapter is on the development in the Court's reasoning from its initial ruling in *Baker v Carr*, which avoided pronouncing on principle, to the later rulings which declared 'one person, one vote' to be the standard of representation in the United States.

In what follows I will first explain how malapportionment entrenched political ossification and minority rule in most of the state legislatures in the Union, before addressing the Supreme Court's dilemma over whether to wade into Justice Felix Frankfurter's "political thicket", as civil society actors and (some) political actors were urging the justices to. The image of constitutionalism offered in the reapportionment cases is of the Court responding to the demands of civil society by formalising an understanding of equality—'one person, one vote'—that polling showed a large majority of Americans approved of (see Smith, 2014: 233). The reapportionment cases also evidence a Supreme Court formalising value changes that are already occurring in civil society. The chapter then proceeds to assess the Supreme Court's shift from a standard of republican government that merely avoids arbitrariness in *Baker v Carr* to its eventual destination of 'one person, one vote' in *Reynolds v Sims*. The evolution in jurisprudence that was seen in the reapportionment opinions of Justice Douglas in *Gray v Sanders* and Chief Justice Warren in *Reynold v Sims* reflected fundamental struggles between different interests, regions, and groups in American history, resulting in a gradual expansion of the groups to whom the protections of the Bill of Rights applied. Although this shift towards human dignity and political equality mirrored some constitutional developments in Europe as a result of the increased focus on human rights after World War II, it was predominantly based on the uniquely American factors of the Incorporation of the Bill of Rights and footnote four of *US v Carolene Products* addressed in the last chapter.[1] To conclude, the chapter evaluates the success and permanence of the Supreme Court's restoration of majority rule and individual rights in the reapportionment cases, amid the continued problem of gerrymandering.

The reapportionment decisions had a dramatic political effect at the time, forcing almost every state legislature to reapportion. Overall, however, the reapportionment cases reveal the limitations of the Supreme Court in being able to influence the mores of the civic space and the processes of representative democracy in the same way that the *Bundesverfassungsgericht* is able to in Germany. The decisions are a testament to the progressive role that courts can have in a country committed to the idea of government under law. Yet they also illustrate that such progress may be limited if the values underlying those legal decisions are not embraced within the civic space and wider political system as well.

Overview

Case summary—*Baker v Carr and Reynolds v Sims*

Baker v Carr (1962a) arose from a federal court action filed against the State of Tennessee by a number of officials from across the state on behalf of qualified voters in underrepresented areas. The case against Tennessee hinged on the failure of legislatures since the turn of the century to meet their constitutional requirement to reapportion. The attorneys sought to show that this failure to reapportion constituted a violation of the Equal Protection and Due Process Clauses of the Fourteenth Amendment, and that the maldistribution of state revenues arising out of the malapportionment demonstrated a pattern of discrimination against urban voters. The case was dismissed by the three judge district federal court, who noted that the state legislature was "guilty of a clear violation of the state constitution", but that on the basis of the precedent set by *Colegrove v Green* (1946) the remedy did not lie with the courts. The case was then appealed directly to the Supreme Court (see Smith, 2014: 57–67).

Reynolds v Sims (1964) was one of dozens of lawsuits initiated in the aftermath of the Supreme Court's ruling in *Baker* that malapportionment *was* a justiciable issue. On July 21 1962, the three judge district court unanimously declared Alabama's system of apportionment a violation of the Equal Protection Clause of the Fourteenth Amendment. The Court increased the representation of under-represented urban counties, changing Jefferson Country's delegation from seven to seventeen and Mobile County's from three to eight (Smith, 2014: 131). Bernard Reynolds, a probate judge in Dallas County, an overwhelmingly white rural county that feared being lumped into a district with Lowndes County and its overwhelming African-American majority, filed an appeal against the district court's ruling with the US Supreme Court, with the case being heard as *Reynolds v Sims* (Smith, 2014: 124–137). The eventual 8–1 decision in *Reynolds* declared 'one person, one vote' to be the required standard of apportionment in the United States, based on the principle of numerically equal districts.

Asked after his retirement what the most significant cases had been during his 15 years on the Supreme Court, Chief Justice Earl Warren identified the legislative reapportionment cases, *Baker v Carr*, *Reynolds v Sims*, and a number of parallel cases. (Smith, 2014: 3). The decision in *Baker* (1962a) was controversial in the academy and divisive within the Court, although it met with broad public approval across the United States. The inability of the justices to reach a decision in *Baker* at the end of the 1961 term following oral arguments in April 1961 led to it being carried over to the following term, with a second series of oral arguments in October 1961. Over seven hours of oral arguments took place in *Baker*, a highly unusual occurrence.[2] *Baker* was constitutionally significant for many reasons, not least because of the acrimonious nature of the debate between some of the justices over the standard of republican government, differences which ultimately destroyed the health of Justice Felix Frankfurter and Justice Charles E. Whittaker, forcing them off the Court. Two years after *Baker*, the Court made its famous 'one person, one vote' decision in *Reynolds v Sims*. It is a testament to how far the Court travelled in two years that in *Reynolds* it eventually embraced the population-based apportionment for both houses of a bicameral legislature that Solicitor General Archibald Cox believed was an unachievable outcome in *Baker*. The Supreme Court's odyssey from holding in *Baker* that the question of reapportionment was merely 'justiciable' to its sweeping decision in *Reynolds* (see 1964: 534) that "The Equal Protection Clause requires substantially equal legislative representation for all citizens in a State regardless of where they reside" was completed in two years rather than the two to three decades Cox originally envisaged (Smith, 2014: 204).

Political and Civil Rights Context

New life was breathed into the civil rights movement in the post-war period, helped in part by the conviction that African-Americans who had fought for the United States overseas must be protected at home. As John F. Kennedy put it: "when Americans are sent to Vietnam or West Berlin, we do not ask for whites only" (Kennedy, 1963). The Cold War context was a particular problem for the US with the Soviet Union making capital out of the treatment of African-Americans as early as 1949 (Dudziak, 2000: 38). Progress in the area of equality for African-Americans had been slow, with decisions such as *Brown v Board of Education* (1954) and *Gomillion v Lightfoot* (1960) being rare examples of improvement in a country where McCarthyism tore down many constitutional protections for the individual.

When President Lyndon Johnson introduced the Voting Rights Act in a speech before Congress in March 1965, his opening words reflected the fundamental linkage between equal voting rights and the future of American self-government: "I speak tonight for the dignity of man and the destiny of democracy" (Johnson, 1965). Malapportionment and the denial of voting rights were separate but symbiotic issues, neither of which could be completely resolved while the other persisted. Rectifying the malapportionment issue would have somewhat rebalanced power towards urban areas in the South and across the country, but as long as voting rights were being denied to African-Americans then the victory would be incomplete. The passing of the voting rights legislation without the Supreme Court's action to end malapportionment would have effectively made the Voting Rights Act meaningless since, even if urban-dwelling African-Americans had the vote, it would make little difference if it was still worth only about 10 percent that of a rural white voter.

For American liberals, the rulings of the Warren Court are viewed as a halcyon moment in American history when the traditionally conservative judiciary acted to remedy racial, social, political, and constitutional injustices, some of which were as old as America itself. By contrast, American conservatives tend to see a period of judicial activism when the Court strayed far outside its brief in imposing its own prescription for social and political change. What the latter view neglects is the rapidly changing civil rights context within which the Court was operating. Even during the Eisenhower Administration, civil rights were on the agenda. By the 1960s under Kennedy, and even more so under Johnson, civil rights was joined on the White House's legislative agenda by voting rights, the Great Society, education, and Medicare. This was the true revolution in the 1960s, and it was being orchestrated in precisely the place seismic political progress ought to occur—democratic institutions. As with its rulings on segregation, the Warren Court's decisions on reapportionment did not usurp legislative and political prerogatives, but largely anticipated them.

American Constitutionalism and Malapportionment

The Supreme Court's emergence as a defender of rights in American constitutionalism can be traced to footnote four of *Carolene Products* (1938). However, this progress did not become evident until the 1950s at the earliest. Although this progress has been far from linear, and the Court's role often far from exemplary, one notable trend has been the steady expansion of the groups in American society to whom equality applies. However, as seen in the previous chapter, the struggles which have characterised the development of constitutionalism have not only come about as a result of a clash in interpretations between different groups in society, but also because of the competing value systems and "internal bonding forces" (1991: 46) that Böckenförde noted.

At the heart of the reapportionment issue were a number of deep, underlying social and political changes. These changes include the emerging conflict between the interests of wealthy white rural areas, on one side, and, on the other, poorer urban areas with faster growing populations of immigrants, African-Americans and blue-collar workers. Malapportionment was also a manifestation of a proxy conflict between big business interests, which strongly supported the rural legislators, and organised labour unions which supported the efforts of civil society and urban areas to receive more representation.

Although no standard of republican government was explicitly defined in the federal constitution, this would not have been a problem had state legislatures complied with the terms of their own constitutions for decennial reapportionment. Malapportionment can therefore be regarded both as a failure of normal politics and an unconstitutional effort by legislators to remain in power, requiring a constitutional solution that only the Supreme Court seemed capable of providing. In resolving the cases and the broader malapportionment problem, the Supreme Court made reference to both the progressive understanding of political equality that had emerged in the United States with the expansion of the right to suffrage, and invoked texts and moments from the Declaration of Independence onwards.[3] Collectively, the reapportionment decisions can be seen as enunciating a conception of political equality based on an ever-widening arc of social and political relationships, which was reflected in the incorporation of the Bill of Rights, footnote four of *US v Carolene Products*, and the equality-based decisions in *Gomillion v Lightfoot* (1960) and *Brown v Board of Education* (1954).

Germany had learned the hard way from the National Socialist period what could happen when an elected government began to dismantle democracy and rights protections from within using unscrupulous legislative methods. In the United States, it took the McCarthyite assault on individual rights in the 1950s to make many Americans conscious of the dangers that can emerge from legislatures, as indeed Jefferson had warned of.[4] *Baker v Carr* (1962a) and the subsequent reapportionment cases which enshrined the principle of 'one person, one vote' still resonate today because malapportionment disproportionately impacted on poorer and less powerful urban voters, many of whom were African-Americans. J Douglas Smith writes that "In the American South ... malapportionment served as a cornerstone of white supremacy ensuring the overrepresentation of the most ardent segregationists and thus further delaying the realisation of civil and voting rights for African-Americans" (2014: 5).

Many state legislatures had so corrupted the principle of republican government through their practice of malapportionment that by the time *Baker* came before the Court in the early 1960s there were no political avenues available to urban-dwelling citizens in Tennessee or other states to seek redress for their underrepresentation in state legislatures. *Baker* represented a paradox because the widespread practice of malapportionment, which was found in almost every state of the Union, was in fact a problem of minority rule by mainly rural voters who were overrepresented in the legislatures. Malapportionment represented not so much the tyranny of the majority that the founders warned of, but rather the tyranny of a minority controlling a legislative majority. However, the urban majority was comprised of various minority groups, while the rural minority was predominantly white. This demographic aspect highlighted how malapportionment directly attacked the political processes marked out for special judicial protection in paragraph two of *US v Carolene Products*' footnote four.

By the early twentieth century, social change, immigration to the United States, and mass migration from rural areas to the cities had turned wealthy white rural majorities into minorities in almost every state. The gross iniquity of malapportionment in Tennessee and almost all other states in the Union was manifested in voting districts with population variances of tens of thousands or even hundreds of thousands of people which, as the Supreme Court noted, meant rural citizens' votes were worth many times that of urban citizens. Such disparities meant that majority control of both houses of state legislatures could be achieved by legislators representing less than 40 percent of the population and, in some of the worst cases, less than 25 percent of the population.[5] The smallest district in Tennessee's lower house in 1962 had 3,454 inhabitants, while the largest district had 79,301 (see Smith, 2014: 288). The reapportionment cases were fundamentally about the quality and quantity of representation, and the power balance between, on one side, wealthy white rural voters and business interests, and, on the other, the interests and rights of groups in faster growing urban areas including blue-collar workers, immigrants, African-Americans, Catholics, and Jews.

Although the worst excesses of malapportionment were in state legislatures, congressional districts were also affected because the states were primarily responsible for federal redistricting.[6] Thirty-five percent of congressional districts were said to be malapportioned by 1960 (Smith, 2014: 18). Congressional districts in Michigan drawn by the Republican-controlled legislature ranged in population from 117,431 to 802,994.[7] Malapportionment of congressional districts thus compounded the underrepresentation of urban residents in state legislatures. In the House of Representatives, eight of the 20 powerful committee chairs came from overrepresented districts, highlighting the pervasive effect of malapportionment on politics at the state and national level.

In a 1960s America where the questions of civil rights and political equality were becoming incendiary issues, malapportionment seemingly constituted a further injustice preventing the adequate representation of certain groups in American society if they happened to live in urban rather than rural areas. James Madison's observation that "the censorial power is in the people over the government, and not in the government over the people" (Madison, "Letter to James Monroe", 1794) illustrates the extent to which malapportionment had usurped and overturned fundamental principles of American government as understood by the framers. Aside from the damage to the integrity of state and national politics that flowed from malapportionment, the effects of this unconstitutional perpetuation of minority rule on the civil, social, and economic rights of citizens were even more serious.

The Tyranny of the Local Minority

Malapportionment was also present in the state legislatures of the eighteenth century. James Madison recognised that tyranny was most likely at the local level, but he also feared that malapportionment would contaminate representation at the federal level unless Congress had the power to override state control of federal elections. Jefferson deplored the situation in Virginia where the tidewater counties continued to insist on the older territorial principle of two representatives per county to offset the growing influence of Western counties in the state assembly (Adams, 2001: 234). During the Constitutional Convention, Madison observed that

> The inequality of the Representation in the Legislatures of particular States, would produce a like inequality in their representation in the Natl. Legislature, as it was presumable that the Counties having the power in the former case would secure it to themselves in the latter.
>
> (Madison, 1986b)

Madison also anticipated the late nineteenth- and twentieth-century practice of many states to award their counties one senator each to create one chamber based on a non-population basis in order to counterbalance the power shift to urban areas. Madison argued in *Federalist 51* that a natural balance between the large number of interests in a continental-sized republic would render "an unjust combination of a majority of the whole very improbable, if not impracticable" (1987b: 321). The Virginian's faith in a balance between social forces to prevent tyranny across the country as a whole was partially correct. However, politics remained local and the same self-interest that Madison identified in state legislatures in the eighteenth century frustrated political attempts to solve the malapportionment issue in the twentieth century.

Appearing before the justices, Charles Rhyne, attorney for the appellants seeking judicial relief in *Baker,* noted that in Tennessee

> every bill for reapportionment since 1901 has [been] voted down in the Senate; no such bill has ever received more than 13 of the 33 votes; and in the House, no bill has ever received more than 36 of the 99 votes.
>
> (Oral Arguments, *Baker v Carr*, 1962b)

With the vote of a rural inhabitant of Tennessee worth up to 20 times that of an urban dweller in some cases, the result was that in state and federal elections legislators would be elected who would represent the interests and rights of a minority of (mainly) white voters and not the majority who dwelt in the cities. James Cummings, one of the most prominent rural legislators, unabashedly highlighted the consequences of this electoral imbalance to a reporter when he said: "I believe in collecting the taxes where the money is—in the cities—and spending it where it's needed—in the country" (Smith, 2014: 54).

Malapportionment showed that when representative democracy did not represent certain groups, they were more likely to have their individual rights infringed as well. One example was how malapportionment exacerbated the effects of segregation and allowed state legislatures to resist the Court's integration ruling in *Brown v Board of Education.* In 1956, when the Virginia legislature voted to close public schools rather than integrate, the 17 senators who opposed the measure represented more Virginians than the 21 state senators who voted in favour.[8]

Malapportionment was therefore not merely a problem for democratic legitimacy. It affected citizens' individual, economic, civil, and social rights. Minority control of legislatures across the United States impacted on the ability of civil society groups and others seeking progressive reform to improve working conditions, increase funding for health and education programmes, and advance civil rights protections (Smith, 2014: 19). As Justice William Brennan's majority opinion in *Baker* put it, "if present representation has a policy at all, it is to maintain the status quo of invidious discrimination at any cost" (1962a: 258). Urban areas with larger populations suffered from chronic underfunding of community infrastructure and educational provision. City and municipal officials across Tennessee joined the court action in *Baker* including Nashville mayor, Ben West, whose office provided crucial statistical evidence of the discriminatory effects of malapportionment, information which made a significant impression on the Court when the case was reargued in October 1961 (Smith, 2014: 61).

The involvement of civil society actors such as the League of Women Voters (LWV), state municipal officials, and the executive branches of the federal government in highlighting the iniquity of malapportionment gave the issue a profile which proved indispensable to its eventual resolution. This public awareness proved important in initiating the litigation in *Baker* and in bringing on board the *amicus curae* support from both the Eisenhower and Kennedy administrations for the Supreme Court challenge. Equally clear, however, was that years of concerted civil society action against malapportionment had failed to shame legislators into reapportioning or secure change through political channels. In 1962, only five states—Massachusetts, New Hampshire, Oregon, West Virginia, and Wisconsin—apportioned, "so that majorities in both chambers of the legislature represented at least 40 percent of the population" (Smith, 2014: 17).[9] Individual voters and even active civil society groups such as the LWV lacked the means to resist due to the political institutions of the state having been captured by legislators who had manifestly subverted the law, their state constitutions, and the US Constitution to secure their office. The reapportionment cases are paradigmatic examples of political issues that could *not* have been solved without judicial intervention since it was too much to expect legislators to willingly vote themselves out of office and a job.

Appearing before the Court during oral arguments in *Baker*, Archibald Cox, the US Solicitor General, highlighted the unequal nature of the standoff between legislative usurpation and the frustrated resistance of the citizens, a problem which he argued could only be resolved in the federal courts:

> We've often been reminded and quite right that the ultimate safeguard of constitutional rights is a vigilant electorate. But where the wrong goes to the existence or distribution of the franchise, then the electorate can do nothing

> to protect itself. No matter how vigilant the majority of the people of Tennessee are, there is nothing that they can do under these circumstances to assert their constitutional rights. … The short of this case is, as Judge Miller pointed out in his opinion convening the three-judge court, that either there is a remedy in the federal courts or there is no remedy at all.
>
> (Oral Arguments, *Baker v Carr*, 1962b)

As will be seen in the next section, the arguments presented before the Court in *Baker* and the other reapportionment cases represented a tension within the Constitution, regarding whether the federal courts could compel the state legislatures to reapportion and the demands of citizens to have their constitutional rights upheld.

A Political Necessity

Theoretically at least, respect for the principle of separation of powers requires that the courts only rule on cases which are 'justiciable' in order to preserve the distinctions between the 'political' and 'judicial' functions (see Stone Sweet, 2003: 2777). The idea behind this demarcation is simply but importantly to preserve the principle of representative government which is clearly established by the Constitution. That the threat *to* representative government was originating *from* citizens' legislative representatives was an irony lost on none of those involved in the battle against malapportionment.

As noted in the previous section, *Baker v Carr* arose partly as a consequence of long-term concerns among civil society groups in the US over malapportionment by state legislatures. Groups like the LWV and other civil society groups were acutely aware of the constitutional requirements of their own states and wanted their state representatives to uphold the oaths they had taken (Smith, 2014: 52). Individuals and municipal officials repeatedly sought relief through political channels but were thwarted by what Smith called "a conspiracy of inaction" (2014: 5). The case standing in the way of federal support to end the iniquity of malapportionment was *Colegrove v Green* (1946) in which Justice Felix Frankfurter had written the majority opinion calling for judicial abstention.[10] Almost 16 years later and Frankfurter was still adamantly opposed to the Court getting involved in reapportionment. However, six new justices had joined the Court in the intervening years and malapportionment by the states was now on the agenda of the executive branch.

The publication of the Kestnbaum Report in 1955 on the relationship between the federal government and the states had highlighted the issue of malapportionment. Senator John F. Kennedy referred to the issue of malapportionment as "The Shame of the States" in an article he wrote for *New York Times Magazine* (Kennedy, 1958). Support for those fighting malapportionment in the states also came from the federal government. J. Lee Rankin, the Solicitor General in the Eisenhower Administration, saw malapportionment as an invidious practice which required judicial relief. During the transition period to the incoming

Kennedy Administration Rankin arranged for the Justice Department to file an *amicus* brief in support of the Tennessee appellants, of whom Baker was the first named on the appeal (Smith, 2014). Such *amicus* support from the executive branch of the federal government for an appellant is quite unusual, and possibly convinced two of the justices, Potter Stewart and Tom Clark, that only the federal courts could resolve malapportionment (see Clayton, 2015: 134). In total, seven amicus briefs were filed in support of Baker, much higher than the mean average for the period 1955–1965 of 1.90, and indicating a large degree of support from the executive branch of the federal government, and from civil society groups including trade unions and the League of Women Voters (Kearney and Merrill, 2000: 754). Overall, the *amicus* support highlighted how malapportionment had created an unspoken alliance between the federal government and civil society against the states.

The reapportionment cases showed how existing American values, particularly *equality*, were recapitulated in the context of a period where, for once, civil society and the federal government were equally active in driving the rights agenda. Sheldon Wolin puts this slightly differently, noting that the democratic gains from the mid-twentieth century onwards were "mainly initiated, not by the state, but by an increasingly politicised civil society" (1989: 78). Still, constitutionalism itself requires a higher principle—political processes which are logical and not arbitrary, and a set of statutory and policy outcomes that do not infringe a citizen's fundamental rights. Indeed, as Murphy notes, constitutionalism is predominantly concerned with value outcomes (1979: 729). Equality *was* such a higher principle and its providence in American political theory back to the Declaration of Independence is clear. While equality would be central to the Court's reasoning in its later 'one person, one vote' ruling in *Reynolds v Sims*, it did not fundamentally figure in *Baker* as a justification for the decision. Rather, the main question at issue was *justiciability* and whether malapportionment was a ripe topic for judicial oversight.

To some, the involvement of a court in managing the processes of representative democracy raised the spectre of the countermajoritarian difficulty. With the reapportionment cases, the Supreme Court acted to support majority rule and the demands of civil society by ensuring that representative government functioned properly. A key point that arises in the reapportionment cases, though, was that representative government need not mean perfect equality in terms of 'one person, one vote'; the American framers, for whom "pure democracy" was a danger to be avoided (see Madison's concerns in *Federalist 10*, 1987a), never defined republican government in such democratic terms.[11] One irony was that neither did Solicitor General Archibald Cox, who appeared in *Baker* as *amicus curae* to support the appellants' case against the State of Tennessee. During oral arguments, Cox went out of his way to emphasise that population equality was *not required* by the Fourteenth Amendment:

> I am not … intending to suggest that the Fourteenth Amendment requires the apportionment of Representatives in both houses of the Legislature, in

> the ratio to the population. It's quite plain [to me] that that is not the Fourteenth Amendment requirement.
>
> (Oral Arguments, *Baker v Carr*, 1962b)

Cox was deliberately cautious in not seeking a more sweeping ruling from the justices in *Baker* as he felt that might jeopardise his fundamental goal that the Court reverse the precedent in *Colegrove v Green* and declare reapportionment a justiciable issue. Despite calling for the Court to intervene in state redistricting, Cox's position was, like his former law professor, Felix Frankfurter, highly cautious about how judicial power ought to be applied. As much as Cox wanted the Court to grasp the reapportionment nettle, his concern that the Court might sleepwalk into enunciating a mathematical standard too fast likely bolstered the credibility of his argument among the justices whose votes were needed to overturn *Colegrove*. During the re-argument of *Baker*, Cox observed:

> This Court doesn't carry the whole burden of Government and for it to rush in to try and right political wrongs instead of leaving them to the other branches—the political branches of the Government—could impair its usefulness in our constitutional system. But I suggest to you that judicial inaction through excessive caution or through a fancied impotence in the face of crying necessity and very serious wrong may also do damage to our constitutional system.
>
> (Oral Arguments, *Baker v Carr*, 1962b)

Wrapping up his remarks, Cox then reminded the justices of Robert Jackson's thoughts on the relationship between the Court and democracy prior to him being appointed to the Court. In 1941, when he was still Attorney General, Jackson wrote in *The Struggle for Judicial Supremacy*:

> [W]hen the channels of opinion and of peaceful persuasion are corrupted or clogged, these political correctives can no longer be relied on, and the democratic system is threatened at its most vital point. In that event, the Court, by intervening, restores the processes of democratic government; it does not disrupt them. ... [A] court which is governed by a sense of self-restraint does not thereby become paralyzed. It simply conserves its strength to strike more telling blows in the cause of a working democracy.
>
> (Jackson, 1941: 285)

Jackson's view here echoes Madison's speech in Congress introducing the Bill of Rights where he referred to the judiciary as "an impenetrable bulwark against every assumption of power in the legislative or executive" (see Madison, 1986b; see also Chapter 3). It also represents the essence of footnote four of *Carolene Products*.

The majority opinion in *Baker* rejected the idea that granting relief was a violation of separation of powers boundaries, arguing that the individual states were not protected by the political question doctrine, and that the only relevant issue was "the consistency of state action with the Federal Constitution" (1962a: 226). Without deciding on the merits of the claim, the majority opinion of Justice William Brennan held that "the complaint's allegations of a denial of equal protection presented a justiciable constitutional cause of action upon which appellants are entitled to a trial and a decision" (1962a: 237).

Although the eventual result in *Baker* was 6–2, it had been a fairly evenly divided Court for much of the deliberations. While Cox argued that the case looked like a Fourteenth Amendment violation, he did not want to push the justices to make that call, because if they had been forced to decide *Baker* on the merits of the case rather than merely the justiciability question, they would then have had to supply a remedy for which there was probably insufficient votes.[12] Indeed, had the Court felt compelled to decide on the principle at issue, it would also have had to decide whether a principle—such as equality—would have to apply to *both* houses of a bicameral legislature. Justice Tom Clark was also concerned about stepping into the "political thicket" that Frankfurter warned about in *Colegrove v Green* (1946: 556), and began to write an opinion rejecting the complaint of *Baker* and the other Tennessee voters who were seeking relief. After trying to muster arguments against granting relief to the Tennessee voters, Clark changed his mind, accepting Cox's argument that the situation would never resolve itself without the intervention of the federal courts (Smith, 2014: 88–89). Once he recognised this, Clark was keen for the Court to leap in and decide the case on its merits, by stating that the Tennessee malapportionment *was* a clear violation of the Equal Protection Clause (1962a: 251). Clark went on to say in his concurrence opinion that the apportionment picture in Tennessee was "a topsy-turvical of gigantic proportions" and "a crazy quilt without rational basis" (1962a: 254). Once the Court had ruled that reapportionment was justiciable in *Baker*, the question before the justices in future cases was whether they ought to simply restore a modicum of rationality to the process or would have to come up with a constitutional standard of representation.

Struggle, Progress, and Renewal

> Held: The right of suffrage is denied by debasement or dilution of a citizen's vote in a state or federal election. … The seats in both houses of a bicameral legislature must under the Equal Protection Clause be apportioned substantially on a population basis.
>
> (Majority Opinion, Chief Justice Earl Warren, *Reynolds v Sims*, 1964)

With these words, the Supreme Court launched a constitutional and political revolution in the United States. The development in the Court's reasoning from *Baker v Carr* to the later reapportionment cases *Gray v Sanders* and *Reynolds v Sims* presents us with two starkly different visions of representative government. Although the more circumscribed 6–2 majority opinion in *Baker* did not pronounce on the principle at issue in the case, the holding that it *was* a justiciable matter opened a floodgate of litigation[13] against the malapportioning states. Just over one year later in *Gray v Sanders*, Justice Douglas' majority opinion first enunciated the 'one person, one vote' principle, and then in *Reynolds v Sims*, Chief Justice Warren officially declared that 'one person, one vote' would be the new standard for both houses of a bicameral legislature.

This move from a system of apportionment that merely has to avoid being arbitrary and capricious to 'one person, one vote' can be explained through the shift in constitutionalism from a charter of fixed rules intended to, as Kay puts it, "fence out certain subjects from … public regulation" (1998: 19) to a system of values which recognises the gradual realisation of equality and human dignity in American history, and the extension of these principles to ever more citizens. This renewal-oriented development fits the historical understanding of constitutionalism identified by Stanley Katz as a process of struggle (2007). The move to 'one person, one vote' can be seen in this light as reflecting a number of parallel transitions and struggles. The first shift was the change within law from an emphasis on groups (including racial and ethnic groups, unions, political parties, sectarian organisations, the underprivileged, and marginalised) to a greater focus on individuals, which was manifested in the 'rights revolution', "wherein the interests of groups against the state were vindicated through individual lawsuits" (see Bobbitt, 2015: 125). The second shift, seen in Chapter 3, was a parallel change in the jurisprudential stance of the Supreme Court in 1938 from its decades-old defence of economic rights to an equality-centric orientation which would instead give greater protection in law to individuals and minority groups (McCloskey, 1972: 3). Thus, as Goodman argues, since the mid-1940s the Supreme Court has treated human dignity as a constitutional value (2006: 748).

The breakdown of group identifications and associational bonds within society, and the changed focus within law from groups to individuals represented precisely the problem that Böckenförde was concerned about, where the state no longer possessed the necessary glue to hold itself together and maintain its relationship with its citizens. Filiopietistic sentiment surrounding the Constitution in American life could not disguise the deep divisions and conflict that American history had revealed. Many of these divisions were based on a strong differentiation in values between urban and rural areas, and between North and South. These shifts towards individual equality also indicated that the civic space where clashes between interests were previously mediated was not functioning well. This change from individuals as communal beings to isolated ones meant that rights could only be realised through law rather than from cooperation, contestation, and association in the civic space.

Politically, malapportionment was intrinsically about the problem of disproportionate power being wielded in the interests of ever smaller groups of people. Yet the dire implications of this imbalance for the rights of those citizens without power in terms of education, health and welfare, and other areas of social and civic activity illustrated that the principle fundamentally at stake was human dignity itself. As Ely notes, the Fourteenth Amendment and Fifteenth Amendment along with the extension of the franchise to wider groups and constituencies reflects a developing commitment to "equality in the distribution of various goods" (1980: 123). "Valuing a vote thus granted at a fraction of the votes of others obviously undercut the commitment this constitutional development reflects" (Ely, 1980: 123).

In his dissent in *Baker*, Justice Frankfurter wrote that the Court's decision that state legislative apportionment was a justiciable matter amounted to "a massive repudiation of the experience of our whole past in asserting destructively novel judicial power" (1962a: 267). *Baker* reversed the decision in *Colegrove v Green* (1946), which he had authored, that legislative apportionment represented a "political question" that was non-justiciable. In denying the wisdom of the Court intervening in the reapportionment question, Frankfurter's technical argument was that nowhere in the Constitution was equal representation between districts assumed to be the basis of republican government. Frankfurter's advice that Tennessee voters use the political channels to resolve malapportionment seemed equally out of touch with the reality, both of what America had become, and the practical possibility of getting a large number of rural legislators to reapportion themselves out of a job. His dogged embrace of the past in the face of the manifest injustice of malapportionment in the present suggest someone struggling to recognise the merit of his mentor Holmes' view in *Missouri v Holland* that the Constitution needs interpreting "in the light of our whole experience and not merely in that of what was said a hundred years ago" (1920: 433–434). While Frankfurter was passionate about judicial restraint, that philosophy led him, I think, down the intellectual cul-de-sac of the political question doctrine, which ultimately produced inconsistencies in his own thinking about when the Court should intervene in the political system to defend individual rights.[14]

The development in the Court's thinking in overruling its previous decision of non-justiciability in *Colegrove* illustrates the innate tension between stability and renewal in constitutionalism, and reflects a longer-term expansion in the number of individuals and groups to whom the terms 'equality' and 'dignity' could be applied, along with the particular areas of individual activity liable for protection. Hence, the Court should be guided by the understanding of equality in the early 1960s, not 1868, or even 1776. While popular majorities can sometimes lead to the promulgation of laws that can be a threat to equality and human dignity, it is also clear, as Murphy observes, that "allowing all adults to participate in governing the community is a mark of respect for human dignity" (1979: 746). There was, therefore a fundamental inconsistency between Frankfurter's dogged embrace of a philosophy of judicial deference to the will of democratic majorities and his opposition to the Court entering "the political thicket" to restore majority rule.

With six post-*Baker* cases scheduled for oral arguments in November 1963 including the Alabama case, *Reynolds v Sims*, Bruce Terris, an assistant to Archibald Cox, sent the Solicitor General a memo addressing the question of what position the Justice Department should take on the standard of apportionment.

The question that the Supreme Court had ducked in *Baker* was what the standard of apportionment should be. Would the vast majority of states with bicameral legislatures be able to reapportion one house on factors other than population? Crucially, Terris noted that historical precedents for a reapportionment standard based on factors other than population were no longer tenable in the light of changing social circumstances and the evolving understanding of equality. Terris wrote that "the meaning of equal protection is necessarily a changing concept" (Smith, 2014: 161). Citing the assimilation of African-Americans and women into the American body politic, and the Seventeenth Amendment of 1913 providing for the direct election of senators, Terris added that

> the history of this country shows increasing awareness of the requirement that all citizens be permitted to participate equally in our government. … The Equal Protection Clause today requires that both houses of the state legislature be apportioned on the basis of population.
>
> (Quoted in Smith, 2014: 161)

Far more than Cox, who remained cautious in asking the Court to put its reputation on the line—and possibly create a constitutional crisis[15]—by committing to a standard of equality, Terris saw that a majority of justices were moving towards a conception of equality based on 'one person, one vote'. By contrast, Cox's gradualist approach anticipated that the country might be ready for total population equality between electoral districts in perhaps 20 or 30 years; in a memo to Robert Kennedy, Cox wrote that "reading the principle 'one man, one vote' into the Equal Protection Clause" would be "a major blunder today" (Smith, 2014: 204). The narrative of struggle followed by progressive historic development that Terris outlines, anticipates almost exactly Earl Warren's *Reynolds* opinion which notes the "continuing expansion of the scope of the right of suffrage" (1964: 555). More broadly, the memo from Terris reflects the shifting jurisprudence of the Supreme Court towards a more equal conception of representative democracy based on the idea that each person's vote must be weighted the same. Once the Court had decided that the existing system was wrong, 'one person, one vote' had to be the end destination.

If the Court had not announced a 'one person, one vote' standard and had instead left it as 'not capricious or arbitrary', then it would likely have ended up sitting in judgement on every apportionment plan for the 50 states—every bit the mathematical quagmire Felix Frankfurter had warned about.[16] Arbitrariness might lie in the eye of the beholder and "a map that one judge might think was pure hodgepodge might to another judge reflect a permissible balance of historical boundaries and multifactored modern realities" (Amar, 2012: 193). When the Court announced 'one person, one vote', more than 40 state legislatures were apportioned on a basis that did not meet the new standard (Amar, 2012: 194). This was certainly an indication of the bureaucratic level of judicial scrutiny that most of these states would have had to face with a less equitable system and a more administratively burdensome standard than 'one person, one vote'.

The principle of equality in the Equal Protection Clause was the cause of the original complaint in *Baker*. Equality had been one of America's defining values since 1776. The precedent that 'separate' was not 'unequal' which had stood since *Plessy v Ferguson* (1896) was quashed in the *Brown* decision and, along with *Gray*, *Reynolds* and the other reapportionment cases underlined the idea that equality and human dignity had become fundamental principles of American constitutional government. Justice Douglas' majority opinion in *Gray v Sanders* observed that

> The conception of political equality from the Declaration of Independence, to Lincoln's Gettysburg Address, to the Fifteenth, Seventeenth, and Nineteenth Amendments can mean only one thing—one person, one vote.
>
> (*Gray v Sanders*, 1963: 381)

There was no indication in the Constitution or from the founders that 'one person, one vote' was the proper standard of representation for republican government. What was beyond doubt, however, was that the framers had clearly "acknowledged popular consent as the indispensable basis for setting up that process of government in the first place" (McCloskey, 1972: 283). The consent of the governed was the fundamental basis of legitimacy for the entire revolutionary endeavour. This resonates with the German cases where representative government is the primary means through which popular sovereignty is represented, and thus is vital to ensure the legitimacy of political action. As Brenner notes, "the principle of representation effectuates the people's sovereignty in a state governed by a constitution" (1999: 139).

One founding document which did point the way was the Northwest Ordinance of 1787 which established the principle of equality in legislative apportionment for future states beyond the Appalachian Mountains (Smith, 2014: 14). While the Ordinance meant an equality for some white men only, it nevertheless guaranteed "a proportionate representation of the people in the legislature" (see 'The Northwest Ordinance', Sec. 14, Art. 2). As with the Declaration of Independence, the Northwest Ordinance, the Gettysburg Address, and *Brown v Board of Education*, so *Baker v Carr* and *Reynolds v Sims* symbolised the progressive expansion of the individuals and groups to whom equal protection applied. According to Eberle, only around the time of *Brown* did the Court "make equality a premier organising principle of American society" (2002: 50).

As I suggested at the outset, equality or equal protection means little without some sense of the individuals and groups to whom these principles should apply, and who is equal with whom. Constitutionalism therefore requires not just equality but a framework for reimagining its scope and potential over time. 'One person, one vote' represented a progress and renewal-centric view of American constitutionalism which saw the malapportionment problem in the context of the country's emerging constitutional narrative. Through decisions such as *Brown*, *Baker*, and *Reynolds*, the jurisprudence handed down by the Warren Court for 15 years tilted American constitutionalism dramatically towards a conception of human dignity and equality where the emancipated individual was not completely isolated as 'liberty' would suggest.

Restoring Majority Rule and Individual Rights

Baker and the reapportionment cases highlight the extent to which the countermajoritarian critique was based on several rather questionable assumptions. One was the idea that there was even agreement on what the standard of representative government ought to be. Another dubious assumption was the idea that the representatives and officials being overruled by the courts were actually enacting the policies of the majority, rather than representing the interests of a rural minority which was the reality prior to the reapportionment decisions. The 'countermajoritarian' label was merely a more virtuous sounding term for the idea that judges shouldn't meddle in politics, as Frankfurter instinctively felt. Such a lethargic view of the Court's role would probably have surprised John Rutledge, who argued at the Constitutional Convention that one of the Court's chief functions was to "secure national rights" (May and Ides, 2007: 21).

When the political processes had ossified as much as they had in the United States prior to the reapportionment decisions, the potential for crises to develop is just as likely as when change occurs too suddenly. The reapportionment decisions ended the usurpation of the political process by rural minorities and brought about the majority rule that malapportionment had stymied. The decisions in the reapportionment cases illustrate the development towards a conception of constitutionalism centred on the values of human dignity and democracy. As Justice William Brennan put it, "interpretation must account for the transformative purpose of the text" and that purpose was "a sublime oration on the dignity of man" (1990: 28). However, the reapportionment cases also remind us, as some have suggested, that preserving America's constitutional tradition means "unconventional innovation and democratic renewal" (Ackerman and Katyal, 1995: 573). Although there was criticism of the decisions in *Baker* and *Reynolds* from politicians across the South and in the academy, the degree of compliance with them was significant. By the summer of 1966, 46 of the 50 states had "substantially complied with the Supreme Court's mandate" (Smith, 2014: 270) and over half of the new intake to the House of Representatives in 1968 were from newly drawn congressional districts (Hodder-Williams, 1980: 126). The principle of equal representation may well press a button in the American psyche which goes back to the revolutionary cry of 'no taxation without representation'. Indeed, as Ely puts it, "the equal weighting of everyone's vote turned out to be a notion with which most people could sympathise" (1980: 121).

"Every government degenerates", wrote Jefferson in 1781, "when trusted to the rulers of the people alone. The people themselves therefore are its only safe depositories" (2008). Jefferson's instinctive faith in the people was vindicated by the civil society actors that fought malapportionment during the 1950s and 1960s, even though those groups were fighting the wealthy rural interests from which Jefferson himself came. The involvement of newspapers and civil society actors like the League of Women Voters over a prolonged period sustained a vital public dialogue about malapportionment which put the issue on the agenda of parts of the federal government. However, their considerable efforts had met only resistance from state legislatures. When civil society turns to the courts to correct structural defects, inequalities, and corruption in political institutions—which devalue citizens' votes by up to 20 to 1—it could be said that the standard countermajoritarian paradigm of judges overruling democratically elected officials needs revising. Indeed, the reaction among the public and the media to the Court's reapportionment decisions was almost uniformly positive (Friedman, 2002: 207). Opinion polling by Gallup indicated that the public approved of the reapportionment rulings by a margin of two to one, suggesting that the Court had successfully anticipated the national mood (Smith, 2014: 233). Friedman notes that the "the very popularity of the reapportionment decisions belied any perception that legislative bodies were reflecting popular will, and that the courts were not" (Friedman, 2002: 221).

Criticisms of the decision such as that of US Senator Everett Dirksen—that "the will of six men on the Supreme Court" was contrary to the will of the people—were rare, because in Friedman's words "probably they were not true" (2002: 208). Explaining why, Friedman adds

> The judiciary apparently was the only place to go when malapportionment had locked out the will of the people, who could not get politicians, anxious to retain their employment, to solve the problem themselves.
>
> (Friedman, 2002: 208)

Even an initial critic of the decision such as Louis Jaffe conceded that

> At least some of us who shook our heads over *Baker v Carr* are prepared to admit that it has not been futile, that it has not impaired, indeed that it has enhanced, the prestige of the Court. It has been a peculiarly popular opinion.
>
> (Jaffe, 1966: 991)

The malapportionment issue and the Supreme Court's decisions in the reapportionment cases reflect many of the deep tensions between national and local majorities that have been discussed in previous chapters. However, they also demonstrate the counter-intuitive relationship between majority rule and individual rights. The reapportionment cases restored majority rule in the United States in the interests of democracy. Yet that ruling was based on the principle that every individual's vote must count the same as every other person's. Ostensibly the Court proclaimed the value-oriented principle of equal representation; yet the decisions in the reapportionment cases were also fundamentally a corrective intended to instil the principles of equality into the participatory processes of representative government. In this respect the reapportionment decisions also reflected the principles of footnote four. As Dixon eloquently put it in a passage that was included in Justice Ginsburg's 'Madison Lecture':

> The ultimate rationale to be given for *Baker v Carr* and its numerous progeny is that when political avenues for redressing political problems become dead-end streets, some judicial intervention in the politics of the people may be essential in order to *have* any effective politics.
>
> (Dixon, 1968: 8; quoted in Ginsburg, 1992: 1207–1208; emphasis in original)

It is perhaps unsurprising that Justice Ginsburg, whose dissent in the affirmative action case *Fisher v University of Texas at Austin* (2013a) was based on footnote four (Caplan, 2013), would also see the decisions in *Baker* and *Reynolds* through the participatory prism of Harlan Stone's opinion in *US v Carolene Products*.

Running counter to some conventional understandings of constitutionalism that what is good for democracy is bad for rights, in the reapportionment cases the Court instead saw a more symmetrical relationship, where the rights of all citizens were more likely to be undermined when representative democracy was malfunctioning and treating citizens unequally. Crucially, the reapportionment cases illustrate that the standard assumption that constitutionalism and democracy are opposing forces does not reflect the more complex interdependence that exists between them. Democracy has tended to empower rights in America, but local variations in value differences meant that in certain places they were antithetical to one another. Thus, footnote four of *Carolene Products* speaks directly to the dangers of political ossification and the circumstances under which the courts had a role to play in protecting individual rights when normal political channels had become dysfunctional. Constitutionalism, through its manifestation in judicial power, can have a restorative effect on democracy rather than debilitating it. As Issacharoff puts it,

> Judicial intervention against the malapportioned deformities of the electoral process could be justified as an example of solicitude for the 'discrete and insular' outcasts from the broader polity.
>
> (Issacharoff, 2010: 963)

This view was also reflected in Justice Jackson's remarks which were cited by Archibald Cox during oral arguments in *Baker*. Ending that political ossification might, according to Bickel, have been achieved simply through the Court's ruling in *Baker* if it prompted state legislatures to finally take action (1986: 196–197). That was not sufficient, however, for an American constitutionalism where every person's opinion has the potential to become more widely held.

Conclusion

One lesson from the malapportionment cases is that when representative rights are restricted then democracy becomes an empty vessel. The reapportionment cases are important because they highlight how the Supreme Court's writ is all powerful in the legal institutional space and in those limited areas of communal activity that federal law and the Constitution gives it jurisdiction in. While the decisions in *Baker v Carr* and the other reapportionment cases corrected a deep problem with voter exclusion and restored the representative nature of US representative democracy, they did not reconcile the fundamental value differences between rural and urban inhabitants, and between different interest groups, that contributed to malapportionment. One consequence of this failure has been that gerrymandering has been able to reclaim many of the gains made from the striking down of numerical malapportionment. The Warren Court's decisions extended to the political sphere, with state legislatures across the country complying with it. However, its capacity to improve the quality of the civic space—where the relationship between citizen and state matters most—was limited.

The schism between America's broadly idealistic constitutional values and its often unscrupulous political instincts is clearly manifested in the reapportionment cases. The Supreme Court's intervention in the reapportionment of electoral districts had a seismic effect on politics. Theodore Olson, US Solicitor General from 2001–2004, recently commented on the positive legacy of *Baker* and the other reapportionment decisions. "It is hard to imagine what this country would be like, or what political crises we may have had because of the continued exasperation of that system of smaller numbers of people having greater concentrations of power" (Olson, 2015).

Among the writing of the founders, particularly Hamilton and Madison, it is hard to discern any desire for a concept of republican government based on numerical equality. Yet in the United States after *Carolene Products* and *Brown v Board of Education*, and after the beginning of the civil rights era, it seemed unthinkable for representation to be based on anything other than political equality. Grossly unequal representation is now recognised as being unconstitutional. The recent case of *Evenwel v Abbott* (2016), in which the Court unanimously upheld the principle of 'one person, one vote' against a challenge from a Texas voter, illustrates how efforts by some vested interests to skew the principles and structure of representative government against those with less wealth and influence have not abated. Gross inequalities in political representation as existed in the United States before the reapportionment decisions are particularly dangerous in a democracy, potentially leading to a wider crisis of confidence in political institutions, with all the concomitant risks to political stability that implies.

Gerrymandering is today the primary instrument of malapportionment. In the 2012 mid-term elections, Democrats received 1.5 million more votes than Republicans nationally, but gained only eight house seats, leaving the Republican house majority of 33 seats intact.[17] The effects of gerrymandering are pervasive since, by drawing boundaries favourable to one party, the centre-ground of American politics has largely disappeared with incumbents more concerned with primary challengers than attempting to appeal beyond their party base. Solving gerrymandering would require the Supreme Court to leap into the political thicket once again, but without the aid of either a fundamental constitutional value such as equality or a principle such as 'one person, one vote' which most voters can appreciate the rationality of. A solution would more likely require a process-driven approach, perhaps adopting the logic behind reapportionment laws passed by Congress in the nineteenth and early twentieth centuries requiring "compact districts of contiguous territory" (Eagles, 2010: 30). The Roberts Court's myopia in its 5–4 decision in *Rucho v Common Cause* (2019) that "partisan gerrymandering claims present political questions beyond the reach of the federal courts" can be contrasted with the deliberate and judicious approach of the Warren Court in tackling numerical malapportionment—which was also seen as a political question by some at the time. No one today questions the principle of 'one person, one vote' which the Warren Court established with *Reynolds v Sims*. Yet the refusal of a bare majority of justices on the Roberts Court to enforce equal protection provisions and protect the democratic rights of all citizens by tackling gerrymandering is conspiring to make the 'one person, one vote' principle redundant in some states (see, for example, Hayden, 2003: 215). The least controversial solution to gerrymandering might be to take the responsibility for electoral districting out of the hands of state legislatures and political machines altogether as some states have done with the creation of non-partisan commissions.[18]

The role of the Court in upholding the Constitution has generally made it a useful proxy of federal power. As I have argued in this chapter and the previous one, this has often been less about the Court pro-actively acting to advance federal goals and more about a correlation of interests and values, and a higher propensity for malfeasance on the part of the state legislatures, making judicial intervention more likely. The Court's 5–4 decision in 2013 to invalidate key parts of the 1965 Voting Rights Act (VRA) represents both a seismic departure from this support for federal action, and a repudiation of the principles contained in *Carolene Products*' footnote four. The majority opinion in *Shelby* noted that "the conditions that originally justified these measures no longer characterize voting in the covered jurisdictions" (2013c: 2). Unlike the decisions of the *BVerfG* to strike down minimum thresholds for electoral success *because* they prevented all Germans from exercising their vote and participating in a representative democracy, in *Shelby*, the Supreme Court effectively defended the right of certain states to exclude voters from the democratic process. Apart from overruling the considered judgment of congressional lawmakers who had voted overwhelmingly in 2006 to re-authorise the VRA for an additional 25 years,[19] the Court reversed the progressive development towards equality and human dignity that marked the century between the end of the Civil War and the passing of the VRA in 1965. More significantly, the Court broke the link between human dignity and the right of all individuals to participate in the political process which characterised the reapportionment decisions and the VRA itself.

As argued in Chapter 2, America's liberty-oriented constitutionalism has tended to work to formalise existing value changes as a result of political activity in civil society. This was the case with the reapportionment cases, *Brown v Board of Education*, and *Obergefell v Hodges*, the 2015 case which recognised gay marriage. None of these cases are ones where the Court acted counter to existing majority sentiment in the United States. Rather, it declared, to paraphrase Justice William Brennan, what it considered to be "the community's interpretation" (1990: 25). One might say, then, that the Supreme Court's role merely reflects and institutionalises Tocqueville's observation about social change in America, that once the majority has decided to embrace a new social principle, be it desegregation or gay marriage, the minority tends to fall in and accept that new value (De Tocqueville and Renshaw, 1998: 103; see also Rauch, 2013). The Court can play a role then in helping society make the transition from minority to majority acceptance of the new value. In the American reapportionment cases we can discern an account of constitutionalism which shows that social forces were hugely important in driving some political action. However, the self-interest of legislators in keeping their jobs meant that the federal courts were the only possible source of relief.

Given its undisputed powers in the Basic Law, the *Bundesverfassungsgericht* would not have had to justify its role in restoring majority rule the way the Supreme Court had to. The post-war recovery of Germany is widely seen as a political and economic miracle. Yet it was a miracle which was neither pre-ordained nor particularly likely given the assault on constitutional democracy by the Nazis and the distinct lack of affection among Germans for the new Federal Republic in its early years. Few would have predicted in the early 1950s that the institution of the German state which would do most to underpin the country's nascent democracy over the next seven decades would be the *Bundesverfassungsgericht*.

Given Germany's traumatic past, German constitutionalism has been oriented towards the idea of 'less' participation rather than 'more'. In the early 1950s what was perhaps most needed in Germany was political stability and a renewed faith in law. The development in German constitutionalism through which the *BVerfG* restored that faith was controversial for it created exactly the kind of Aristotelian *polis* that Ernst-Wolfgang Böckenförde was concerned about. This value order broke down the barrier between public and private law, and declared that individuals were not isolated human beings but realised their dignity and freedom in relation to their role in the community. Democracy in the German context did not, therefore, arise out of liberty as in the American view, but arose out of fundamental rights including human dignity, which it is the state's duty to protect. The Court's role in stabilising German democracy and restoring the trust of Germans in law will now be assessed.

Notes

1 As seen in Chapter 3, though, Justice Harlan Stone was not oblivious to events outside the United States while he was writing the majority opinion in *US v Carolene Products*.

2 Today, the norm is one hour of oral arguments per case.

3 See *Gray v Sanders* (1963: 381), which captures the idea of the progressive development of equality.

4 "It will be no alleviation that these powers will be exercised by a plurality of hands, and not by a single one. 173 despots would surely be as oppressive as one." Thomas Jefferson, 'Query XIII', in *Notes on the State of Virginia* (New Haven, CT: The Avalon Project, Yale Law School, 1781).

5 In Tennessee, the theoretical minimum percentage of the population capable of electing a majority of the legislature was 28.7 in the lower house and 26.9 in the state's Senate. In Florida, the figure was 12 percent in both houses. In California, the figure was 10.7 percent for the Senate, while in Nevada it was 8 percent (see Smith, 2014: 287–288).
6 Article 1, Section 4 of the Constitution gives Congress the power to legislate and amend any state regulations for the conduct of federal elections.
7 Sam Rayburn, a Democrat from Texas, and House Speaker, came from the fifteenth least populous district in the country, receiving fewer than 16,000 votes when he was re-elected in 1958 (Smith, 2014: 19).
8 These decisions to close public schools rather than allow integration were subsequently overturned in state and federal courts. (See Smith, 2014: 19).
9 In 23 states the theoretical minimum of the population electing a majority of the state Senate was less than 30 percent, and in ten of those the figure did not reach 20 percent. (See Smith, 2014: 17).
10 See Black on the differences between the two cases (1962: 14).
11 Some of the founders required only that a government not be a monarchy to meet the republican test (see Ely, 1980: 123).
12 After the decision came down in *Baker*, Cox wrote in a memorandum to Attorney General, Robert Kennedy: "It is no exaggeration to recognize among ourselves that we played the most important role in *Baker v Carr*, and our brief and argument may even have determined the result" (see Clayton, 2015: 134–135).
13 Within seven weeks of the decision in *Baker*, law suits were commenced in 22 states (see Atleson, 1963: 535).
14 The key inconsistency being his defence of judicial intervention in politics in *Gomillion v Lightfoot* (1960). Frankfurter was prepared to tackle racially motivated malapportionment, but not to tackle malapportionment directed against other groups in society.
15 In fact, a long-running constitutional crisis did unfold. Everett Dirksen, the Senate Minority leader, drove an unsuccessful effort to adopt a constitutional amendment stripping the Court of jurisdiction over reapportionment.
16 Frankfurter wrote in his dissent that the Court was catapulting the lower courts of the country into a "mathematical quagmire … without so much as adumbrating the basis for a legal calculus as a means of extrication" (1962a: 268).
17 In Ohio, 52 percent of the vote went to Republicans in the 2012 election but they carried 12 of the state's 16 house seats, or 75 percent of the seats. (See "REDMAP Summary Report", 2013b).
18 Arizona, California, Colorado, Hawaii, Idaho, Iowa, Michigan, New Jersey, and Washington have created non-partisan commissions to deal with reapportionment.
19 The vote in favour of renewing the VRA was 390 to 33 in the House, and unanimous in the Senate.

References

Plessy v Ferguson, 163 US 537, 1896
State of Missouri v Holland, 252 US 416, 1920
United States v Carolene Products Company, 304 US 144, 1938
Colegrove v Green 328 US 549, 1946
Brown v Board of Education of Topeka, 347 US 483, 1954
Gomillion v Lightfoot, 364 US 339, 1960
Baker v Carr, 396 US 186, 1962a
Baker v Carr (Oral Argument), 396 US 186, 1962b
Gray v Sanders, 372 US 368, 1963

Reynolds v Sims 377 US 533, 1964
Fisher v University of Texas at Austin, No. 11–345, 2013a
Shelby County, Alabama v Holder, Attorney General et al., No. 12–96, 2013c
Obergefell v Hodges 14–556, 2015
Evenwel v Abbott, 14–940 (2016), 2016
Rucho v Common Cause, 18–422, 2019

Ackerman, B. and N. Katyal, "Our Unconventional Founding", *The University of Chicago Law Review*, 62(2) (1995), 475–573.

Adams, W. P., *The First American Constitutions: Republican Ideology and The Making of The State Constitutions in the Revolutionary Era* (Lanham, MD: Rowman & Littlefield Publishers, 2001).

Amar, A. R., *America's Unwritten Constitution: The Precedents and Principles We Live By* (New York: Basic Books, 2012).

Atleson, J. B., "The Aftermath of Baker v. Carr. An Adventure in Judicial Experimentation", *California Law Review* (1963), 535–572.

Bickel, A. M., *The Least Dangerous Branch: The Supreme Court at the Bar of Politics.* 2nd edn (New Haven: Yale University Press, 1986).

Black, C. L., "Inequities in Districting for Congress: Baker v. Carr and Colegrove v. Green", *Yale Law Journal*, 72 (1962), 13.

Bobbitt, P., "The Age of Consent", in *The Ages of American Law*, ed. by Grant Gilmore and Philip Bobbitt (New Haven, CT: Yale University Press, 2015).

Böckenförde, E. W., "The Rise of the State as a Process of Secularisation", in *State, Society, and Liberty: Studies in Political Theory and Constitutional Law* (New York: Berg Pub Ltd, 1991).

Brennan Jr, W. J., "The Constitution of the United States: Contemporary Ratification", in *Interpreting the Constitution: The Debate over Original Intent*, ed. by Jack N. Rakove (Boston, MA: Northeastern University Press, 1990).

Brenner, M., "The Constitutional Framework of Democratic Representation", in *Constitutionalism, Universalism and Democracy: A Comparative Analysis*, ed. by Christian Starck (Baden-Baden: Nomos-Verlag-Ges., 1999).

Caplan, L., "Ruth Bader Ginsburg and Footnote Four", *The New Yorker*, 13 September 2013, available at: www.newyorker.com/news/news-desk/ruth-bader-ginsburg-and-footnote-four [last Accessed 14 October 2016].

Clayton, C. W., *The Politics of Justice: Attorney General and the Making of Government Legal Policy* (New York: Routledge, 2015).

De Tocqueville, A. and P. Renshaw, *Democracy in America* (Herts: Wordsworth Editions Limited, 1998).

Dixon, R. G., *Democratic Representation: Reapportionment in Law and Politics* (New York: Oxford University Press, 1968).

Dudziak, M. L., *Cold War Civil Rights: Race and the Image of American Democracy* (Princeton, NJ: Princeton University Press, 2000).

Eagles, C. W., *Democracy Delayed: Congressional Reapportionment and Urban-Rural Conflict in the 1920s* (Athens: University of Georgia Press, 2010).

Eberle, E. J., *Dignity and Liberty: Constitutional Visions in Germany and the United States* (Westport, CT: Praeger, 2002).

Ely, J. H., *Democracy and Distrust: A Theory of Judicial Review* (Cambridge: Harvard University Press, 1980).

Friedman, B., "The Birth of an Academic Obsession: The History of the Countermajoritarian Difficulty, Part Five", *Yale Law Journal* (2002), 153–259.

Ginsburg, R. B., "Speaking in a Judicial Voice", *New York University Law Review*, 67 (1992), 1185.

Ginsburg, R. B., "Ginsburg Confirmation Hearing Day 1 Part 2" C-Span, 20 July 1993 (1993), available at: www.c-span.org/video/?45747-1/ginsburg-confirmation-hearing-day-1-part-2&start=2039 [last accessed 15 June 2019].

Goodman, M., "Human Dignity in Supreme Court Constitutional Jurisprudence", *Nebraska Law Review*, 84 (2006).

Hayden, G. M., "The False Promise of One Person, One Vote", *Michigan Law Review*, 102 (2003), 213.

Hodder-Williams, R., *The Politics of the U.S. Supreme Court* (London: Allen & Unwin, 1980).

Issacharoff, S., "Constitutional Courts and Democratic Hedging", *Georgetown Law Journal*, 99 (2010), 961.

Jackson, R. H., *The Struggle for Judicial Supremacy: A Study of a Crisis in American Power Politics*. Caravelle edn, Vintage (New York: Vintage Books, 1941).

Jaffe, L. L., "Was Brandeis an Activist-the Search for Intermediate Premises", *Harvard Law Review*, 80 (1966), 986.

Jefferson, T. "Notes on the State of Virginia, 1781", Yale Law School, (2008), available at: http://avalon.law.yale.edu/18th_century/jeffvir.asp [last accessed 30 November 2016].

Johnson, L. B., "President Johnson's Special Message to the Congress: The American Promise" (LBJ Presidential Library, 1965).

Katz, S. "Who's Afraid of Senator Byrd? The Constitution and the Uses of American History" (2007), available at: www.princeton.edu/~snkatz/papers/snkatzConstitution.pdf [last accessed 15 May 2014].

Kay, R. S., "American Constitutionalism", in *Constitutionalism: Philosophical Foundations*, ed. by Lawrence A. Alexander (Cambridge: Cambridge University Press, 1998).

Kearney, J. D. and T. W. Merrill, "The Influence of Amicus Curiae Briefs on the Supreme Court", *University of Pennsylvania Law Review*, 148(3) (2000), 743–855.

Kennedy, J. F., "The Shame of the States", *New York Times Magazine*, 18 May 1958 [last accessed 23 March 2019].

Kennedy, J. F., "Radio and Television Report to the American People on Civil Rights" [Speech] John F Kennedy Presidential Library and Museum, 11 June 1963, available at: www.jfklibrary.org/Research/Research-Aids/JFK-Speeches/Civil-_19630611.aspx [last accessed 1 July 2020].

Madison, J., "Speech, House of Representatives, 8 June 1789", in *The Founders' Constitution* (Chicago, IL: University of Chicago Press, 1986a), available at: http://press-pubs.uchicago.edu/founders/documents/v1ch14s50.html [last accessed 30 June 2020].

Madison, J., "Records of the Federal Convention, 9 August 1787" [Speech] in *The Founders' Constitution* (Chicago: University of Chicago Press, 1986b), available at: http://press-pubs.uchicago.edu/founders/documents/a1_4_1s1.html [last accessed 1 July 2020].

Madison, J., "Federalist Number 10", in *The Federalist Papers*, ed. by Isaac Kramnick (Harmondsworth: Penguin, 1987a).

Madison, J., "Federalist Number 51", in *The Federalist Papers*, ed. by Isaac Kramnick (Harmondsworth: Penguin, 1987b).

Madison, J., "Letter from James Madison to James Monroe, 4 December 1794" (Retrieved from Library of Congress, 1794), available at: www.loc.gov/item/mjm013124/ [last accessed 1 July 2020].

May, C. N. and A. Ides, *Constitutional Law National Power and Federalism: Examples and Explanations* (Aspen Publishers Online, 2007).

McCloskey, R. G., *The Modern Supreme Court* (Cambridge, MA: Harvard University Press, 1972).

Murphy, W. F., "An Ordering of Constitutional Values", *Southern California Law Review*, 53 (1979), 703–760.

"The Northwest Ordinance; July 13, 1787" Lillian Goldman Law Library, Yale Law School, (2008), available at: http://avalon.law.yale.edu/18th_century/nworder.asp [last accessed 27 August 2016].

Olson, T. "Baker v Carr (Supreme Court Landmark Cases)" [Interview] C-Span, 7 December 2015 (2015), available at: www.c-span.org/video/?327719-1/supreme-court-landmark-case-baker-v-carr&start=4363 [last accessed 13 July 2016].

Rauch, J. "A Gay Awakening" (2013), available at: www.jonathanrauch.com/jrauch_articles/2013/10/a-gay-awakening.html [last accessed 7 April 2020].

"REDMAP Summary Report", Republican State Leadership Committee, 4 January 2013 (2013b), available at: www.redistrictingmajorityproject.com/?p=646 [last accessed 1 July 2020].

Shapiro, M., "Foreword", in *The Modern Supreme Court*, ed. by Robert Green McCloskey (Cambridge, MA: Harvard University Press, 1972).

Smith, J. D., *On Democracy's Doorstep: The Inside Story of How the Supreme Court Brought "One Person, One Vote" to the United States* (New York: Hill and Wang, 2014).

Stone Sweet, A., "Why Europe Rejected American Judicial Review: And Why it May Not Matter", *Michigan Law Review*, 101(8) (2003), 2744–2780.

Wolin, S. S., *The Presence of the Past: Essays on the State and the Constitution* (Baltimore, MD: Johns Hopkins University Press, 1989).

5 The Democracy Training Programme

> We got democracy from you, as a gift I would say, in the forties and fifties. But I'm not sure if these democratic attitudes are very well established in my country. We Germans always have to practice democracy—we're still on the training programme.
>
> (Dirk Kurbjuweit, quoted in Packer, 2014)

This statement by the writer Dirk Kurbjuweit encapsulates the challenge to democracy and to constitutionalism that faced the Federal Republic's founders in the late 1940s. It was a challenge that seemed, on the surface, to spring primarily from the malignant effects of National Socialism, and the continued presence of Nazi sympathisers in German politics and society. Yet Kurbjuweit's observation also highlights a concern among the country's post-war founders that democracy needed time and assistance in order to take root among ordinary Germans. While the 'gift' of democracy may have initially stemmed from the destruction of Nazi power by the Allies at the end of World War II, its longevity depended on the success of the Federal Republic's constitutional institutions in inculcating a respect for democracy and constitutionalism among the German people.

In the previous two chapters, the Supreme Court's developing jurisprudence recognised, often belatedly and tentatively, the changing concept of equality within US society. Only after 1938 with *US v Carolene Products* footnote four and the later emancipatory decisions of the Warren Court did its 'formalising' decisions catch up with, and occasionally overtake, the pace of societal change. By contrast, the role of the Federal Constitutional Court or *Bundesverfassungsgericht* (*BVerfG*) in shaping the development of fundamental constitutional values and moving away from the legal positivism of the Weimar Republic has been anything but tentative. The emergence of the Basic Law's 'objective value order' as enunciated by the *BVerfG* can be seen as an attempt both to create a basis for stability by entrenching the fundamental values of human dignity and the free democratic basic order at the centre of the constitutional order, while also allowing a space for political and societal renewal through the gradual inclusion of newer political forces into the party constellation. The balance between stability and renewal in the Court's decisions, I contend in this chapter, has shifted over time from the stability-oriented emphasis on the 'militant democracy' in the Federal Republic's early years to, beginning in the 1970s, a greater emphasis on democratic renewal and a rejection of any sense of a "timeless validity"[1] in constitutional interpretation.

Of particular interest is how the country's constitutional recovery was placed almost entirely in the hands of a small group of constitutional court justices in the small German city of Karlsruhe. Their mandate empowered them to restrict democracy in order to preserve it against the uniquely anti-democratic conditions which it faced at its inception. When the Court began hearing cases in 1951, Nazi sympathisers were again on the political march and in state elections that year far right parties won between 7 and 11 percent of the vote (Collings, 2015: 2). Even as the German Parliament, the *Bundestag*, was appointing the first justices to the *BVerfG*, Konrad Adenauer's new government considered asking it to ban the largest far right party, the Socialist Reich Party (SRP) (Collings, 2015: 2). German constitutionalism as it emerged from the decisions of the *BVerfG* has increasingly exerted huge influence over the interpretation of constitutional values and the power balance between legal and political institutions. This influence ensured that the role of the *BVerfG* in the development of German constitutionalism after 1949 would be one of entrenching the values of democracy and human dignity within the constitutional order, while providing a stable basis for those values to take root among a German populace that needed time and space, as Dick Kurbjuweit suggested, to "practice democracy" (quoted in Packer, 2014).

This chapter will assess the theoretical, historical, and jurisprudential context within which German constitutionalism has mediated the competing imperatives of stability and renewal. Chapter 6 will assess how in practice the *BVerfG* has intervened in Germany's political processes and why, to some, it has become the guardian of German democracy. I will begin by first addressing the constitutional challenges faced by the Federal Republic of Germany (hereafter Germany) after 1949 and the perceived need to forge it into a more resistant constitutional order than the Weimar Republic. The theoretical and jurisprudential underpinnings for German constitutionalism will be considered in this chapter with reference to the higher law basis of the Basic Law as a charter of justice, one which rejected legal positivism in favour of the natural-law thinking of Gustav Radbruch. This created a constitutional tableau in which the Court began to be seen as "a necessary precondition—and not as an institutional threat—to democracy" (Collings, 2015: 1). I will then assess the *BVerfG*'s objective value order which created the idea of the 'image of man' in the Basic Law where the dignity of the individual was bound to their role in the community. Ernst-Wolfgang Böckenförde's theoretical and historical critique of this Aristotelian *polis* view, which was examined in Chapter 2, raised the question of whether the Court's objective value order had sufficient cohesive appeal among ordinary Germans to maintain liberal democracy without some other *internal bonding force*. To conclude, I will assess the crucial role of law as precisely such a bonding force, which both underwrote the *BVerfG*'s authority and provided Germany with a necessary civic space for liberal constitutional values to develop.

Creating a Constitutional Culture

Jeremy Waldron's observation that "it is not conceptually impossible for a democracy to vote itself out of existence" (1998: 272) seems almost ahistorical given the experience of the Weimar Republic. Germany during the 1920s and 1930s remains the classic example of what can go wrong in a democratic system when there are insufficient constitutional safeguards in place. Germany was a constitutional state in the 1920s, and the tradition of the *Rechtsstaat* in German jurisprudence was strong; Germany was also, as Martin Amis argues, "the most highly educated society there had ever been on Earth" (2014). Why this cultured and educated society with its belief in the law-governed state did not translate into a population and lawyer class more willing to challenge the National Socialist assault on constitutional democracy is still the historical and jurisprudential elephant in the room. The National Socialist onslaught on the Weimar Constitution illustrated how prescribed constitutional methods could be used by politically repellent ideologies to dismantle constitutional democracy from within. The German people in 1945 may have become disillusioned with the Nazis after 12 years of a police state and six years of total war, but a plurality of voters had elected the National Socialists freely in July 1932 according to the provisions of the liberal democratic Weimar Constitution.[2] One German writer suggests that even as late as 1939, "Hitler would still have been overwhelmingly re-elected, even in a free and secret poll" (Frei, 2001: 303). This point mattered, both as salutary warning about the dangers of unconstrained majority will and as an orientation point for Germany's emerging post-1949 constitutionalism and its militant democracy (*streitbare Demokratie*).

Count One of the indictment at Nuremberg emphasised how the German people had been repressed by the Nazis.[3] The Allies and Germany's post-war founders saw it as important not to be perceived as blaming the German people for supporting Hitler, so as to give the Federal Republic's political institutions the necessary space to recover and stabilise. However, while many groups and hundreds of thousands of Germans were repressed by the Nazis, there was still broad support for the regime till the end of the war (see, for example, Gellately, 2002). Even after the establishment of the Federal Republic in 1949, polling data indicates a longing for previous regimes. In a speech before the *Bundestag* in 2014 to celebrate the 65th anniversary of the Basic Law, Dr Navid Kermani cited a representative survey of Germans conducted in 1951 (see also Noelle and Neumann, 1967: 195) which asked when Germany had its most prosperous time: 45 percent indicated the *Kaiserreich* prior to 1914, 7 percent indicated the Weimar Republic, 42 percent indicated the Nazi period, but only 2 percent opted for the newly established Federal Republic (see Kermani, 2014). While this poll did not ask about support for Hitler or the National Socialists, the overall picture painted is of a population longing for any constitutional regime but the FRG. The potential challenge this environment posed for democracy and for constitutionalism was clear.

When the details of a new German constitution were being debated and discussed by the Parliamentary Council in 1948 and 1949, some called for the

Weimar Constitution to be revived, leading one member to observe that "a democracy which allows a tyranny to emerge from its midst with so little resistance does not deserve being recreated for a second time" (Hucko, 1987: 68). Correcting these deficiencies in the post-war period emphasised a focus on two areas which were seen as the weak point of the Weimar Republic: 1) bullet-proofing the constitutional structure through the dispersal and limitation of the powers of public authority; 2) placing the fundamental rights of the individual at the heart of the constitutional order so that their rigorous application and protection in law became the *sine qua non* of all organs of power within the West German state.

Following the end of the war, free elections were instituted by the Allies at a local level as early as January 1946 before democratic parliaments were created at the *Land* (state) level a year later (Hucko, 1987: 63). Thus, as with the United States, the formation of the Federal Republic arose from a system of functional democratic accountability at the state level. The importance that the German founders attached to the federal and democratic structure of the state is reflected in Article 79(3) and Article 20, the unamendable articles of the Basic Law which deal with the "division of the Federation into *Länder* [states]", and the "democratic and social" character of the Federal Republic. Under the Basic Law, power is divided horizontally within the federal state itself, and then divided again vertically by giving the individual German states a formal role in the national government,[4] a structural feature which is absent in the American model.

The overwhelming focus on the deficiencies of the Weimar Constitution by the Parliamentary Council could not conceal uncomfortable questions over the role of the German people in failing to support constitutional democracy. As Hucko put it,

> Looking back on the Nazi period, it was the German people who had failed in 1933, rather than the Weimar Constitution, and the concept of failure would appear to be more appropriate in this respect than the notion of guilt.
> (Hucko, 1987: 62)

Blaming Weimar for what may also have been the failings of the German people was possibly the only serious political option in a society attempting to get back on its feet.[5] "Engaged democrats", writes Forner, "rejected a uniform German guilt while exhorting fellow Germans to consider the degrees and modes of their own responsibility" (2014: 62). If it was simply failure rather than guilt, then the question for Germany's founders became a structural one: how might the institutions of the Basic Law be designed more resiliently, and its values disseminated more effectively in German politics and society? Even with an apparently formidable constitutional structure in the form of the Basic Law and the elevation of rights to the summit of the new order, these remained necessary but not sufficient conditions for liberal democratic constitutionalism to take root in German society. Given the failures of Germany's previous liberal constitutions the key questions for the German post-war founders were whether any structural features of those dead constitutions might be safely resurrected within the Basic Law, and if so, upon which values would their legitimacy rest?

Although the impoverished state of the German economy in the immediate post-war period can hardly have helped, the idea that there was a political dimension to the longing among Germans for the *Kaiserreich* and Third Reich periods is also borne out by other sources. The opinion poll data also matches historical accounts of the wide variance between the more liberal democratic views of German elites in politics, the judiciary, and the arts in the immediate post-war period, and the less enlightened views of segments of the German population. According to the historian Gitta Sereny, "the majority of Germans wanted nothing more than that all trials, all writings, films and plays about that period would stop" (2000: 58). It was, she observes

> [the] intense preoccupation with their country's past of leading writers, artists, thinkers, the judiciary and, yes, also of politicians in those early years, and their ability to maintain their convictions against the pressures of large sections of the public, which even more than the Marshall Plan and the resultant Wirtschaftswunder, has been the source of Germany's remarkable moral recovery.
>
> (Sereny, 2000: 58–59)

Sereny's account highlights the crucial division in German society which produced the Basic Law. It was the country's elites rather than the constituent power of the German people that dragged Germany into the post-war constitutional light. However, in 1949 the conditions looked intensely inhospitable for constitutional democracy. The challenge for the Federal Republic's founders, politicians, and judges was how to strengthen the institutions of the new constitutionalism and build the kind of support for them within German society that was absent during Weimar.

In the period after the destruction of the Nazi state, the emergence of liberal democracy faced daunting challenges, reflecting historical ebbs and flows in the acceptance of liberal values and constitutionalism in Germany. These ebbs and flows can be seen in German constitutional history going back to the short-lived liberal constitution of 1849 in which the first ever catalogue of rights of the German people was enacted (see Hucko, 1987). German liberals had been attempting to create a constitutional democracy for a century but had been beaten back by conservatives in 1849, by Bismarck, by Kaiser Wilhelm II and, finally, Hitler.[6] While the tradition of the *Rechtsstaat* ran deep, instilling in Germans a profound respect for law, this did not extend to politics which was generally regarded with a mixture of detachment, if not contempt. This distaste for politics and reverence for law among ordinary Germans, even prior to the Nazi period, partly explains the relatively early respect accorded to the *BVerfG* after 1951 (see, for example, Schlink, 1994: 210–211).

While the threats posed to German constitutionalism in 1949 were probably more acute than those America faced in 1789, both polities had to deal with the challenge of creating a supportive constitutional culture. In 1949, as highlighted by the polling evidence earlier, the Basic Law had nothing to fall back on by way of a public virtue or a supportive culture. Reflecting on the failure of the previous German constitutions, Hucko writes:

> Basic rights, even those which have been enshrined in a constitutional document, require open breathing spaces where political life can organise and express itself. Above all, these must be defended and fought for day after day.
>
> (Hucko, 1987: 21)

Although Hucko's words were inspired by the unfulfilled promise of the German constitution of 1849 and certainly speak to the need for vibrant political processes, they also speak to the need for a civic space where the people can shape and give meaning to constitutional values. Only the untested resilience of the *streitbare Demokratie* offered the possibility of a breathing space for a supportive constitutional culture to develop, and guard Germany from a re-run of its 1932–1945 experience.

The Basic Law as a Charter of Justice

In reaction to the assault on human dignity and democracy by the National Socialists, the founders of the Federal Republic "drew deep upon German tradition to found the legal order on moral and rational idealism, particularly that of Kant and Hegel" (Eberle, 2002: 7). Treating individuals always as an end in themselves and never as a means to an end was the most fundamental Kantian precept to undergird the Basic Law. Perhaps more significantly, the Basic Law includes a provision that makes international law an integral part of German federal law, thus signifying the country's rejection of absolute sovereignty and its embrace of international human rights values, and a desire to play an active role in European integration (Howard, 2009: 17). The fundamentally normative character of the Basic Law is noted by Kommers and Miller.

> Germans no longer understand their constitution as the simple expression of an existential order of power. They commonly agree that the Basic Law is fundamentally a normative constitution embracing values, rights and duties. That the Basic Law is a value-oriented document—indeed, one that establishes a hierarchical value order—is a familiar refrain in German constitutional case law.
>
> (Kommers and Miller, 2012: 45)

The Basic Law was drafted by the Parliamentary Council which met in 1948 while the country was still in flux and going through the process of de-Nazification. Hans Kelsen, seen as the founder of the Austrian Constitutional Court, was also involved in drafting the proposals at the Parliamentary Council for a new constitutional tribunal (Kommers and Miller, 2012: 7). It was the ideas of American and Western constitutional government which "shaped the political ideas of the 70 men and women who produced the Basic Law in Bonn in just under 9 months"

(Stern, 1993: 18). Here, the experience of where democracy can go awry from the 1930s permeates practically every section of the Basic Law. Thornhill notes that "the constitution clearly construed state legitimacy as arising from a modification of classical concepts of the democratic-legal state to include principles of material equality" (2011: 336).

Achieving such a complex balance between individual rights, the collective agency of the people, and the state after the unfulfilled promise of Germany's previous constitutions demanded that the new constitutional order be based on the one institution which might still be able to command the respect of the German people: the law. In this vein, Stern writes:

> Following the American constitutional tradition, the Basic Law provided from the very beginning a state system subject to law. The Constitution was adopted as a law of paramount obligation to which all other law was—and is—subordinate. It has perhaps become more than anywhere else *the* legal rule of legal rules.
>
> (Stern, 1993: 20; emphasis in original)

The emphasis on legal mechanisms and the judicial role in preserving and shaping the post-1949 German constitutional order and its separation of powers system allows individuals, state organs, and political parties to file constitutional complaints with the *BVerfG* when they perceive their rights have been violated by state authority.

As with the Supreme Court's jurisprudence in *Carolene Products*' footnote four, which was designed to ensure more searching judicial scrutiny where democratic processes and the political rights of minority groups were restricted, so the *BVerfG* sees the constitutional complaints process in the German system as particularly crucial for the protection of minority parties in Parliament and to ensure important checks on government power. The constitutional complaint mechanism presented the *BVerfG* with the opportunity to greatly expand its own authority in its famous decision in *Lüth Case* (1958) where it articulated its "objective order of values" which permeates the country's entire constitutional order. This is what Kommers calls "the gloss" that the Court has put on the text of the Basic Law (1991: 858). The enunciation of the Court's value order was a significant development in German constitutionalism, and signified that human dignity and the free democratic basic order represented the most fundamental values of society. As we will see, though, when the values of human dignity and the free democratic basic order have clashed, dignity has not always emerged on top (see Murphy, 1979: 752).

Higher Law and Pre-Constitutional Rights as a Democratic Precondition

The theoretical sources and normative principles which contributed to the framing of the Basic Law continue to play a role in its interpretation, while also helping us understand how the *BVerfG* perceives the role of the individual within the constitutional mix. Partly, these principles are "rooted in the dialectic between the liberal, socialist, and Christian natural-law traditions that shaped the original document", but they are also derived from what the Court calls "supra-positive principles of law" that "bind legislators and other political decision makers" (Kommers and Miller, 2012: 70). Within the German constitutional order these principles contribute to what Kommers and Miller describe as "communitarian values" which are "suggestive of aspects of the Aristotelian polis as well as the early American traditions of civic republicanism" (2012: 46). In signifying the identity of the new order, those who created the Basic Law had "given up on the old positivist idea that law and morality—and justice—are separate domains. Constitutional morality would now govern both law and politics" (Kommers and Miller, 2012: 1). Escaping from legal positivism meant that the Basic Law became a fundamental charter of justice. Legality would now be measured against supra-positive principles of justice. The *Rechtsstaat* of the Basic Law is no longer an end in itself; it is a means which serves the ends of the *Verfassungsstaat* (constitutional state) (Kommers, 1991: 846).

Gustav Radbruch was the German legal thinker most responsible for setting out the distinction between positive law and justice. His article "Statutory Injustice and Suprastatutory Law" (see Radbruch, 1946), in which he provided a formula for dealing with the conflict between positive law and justice, has been described as "one of the most important texts in 20th century legal philosophy" (Mertens, 2003: 277). The importance of Radbruch's formula has been confirmed by a number of judgments of both the *BVerfG* and the German High Court (Mertens, 2003: 293). Most significantly, in the context of the Basic Law, Radbruch's view that certain higher principles of justice trumped positive law has been repeatedly cited by the *BVerfG*. In *Equality Case* (1953), the Court's opinion "quotes with approval Radbruch's affirmation of natural-law theory" (Kommers and Miller, 2012: 746). The 'Radbruch formula' was primarily a response to the abuse of written law by the Nazis in the interest of injustice. As the German legal philosopher, Ralf Dreier, put it, "Radbruch's formula was a reaction to Auschwitz" (quoted in Quint, 1999: 318). Russell Miller has observed that the *BVerfG* "rather self-consciously imagines itself to be Radbruch's heir" and from its earliest decisions the Court "acknowledged its authority to refuse to enforce unjust laws" (2017: 115). The Court's willingness to challenge legislative preferences, including its controversial decisions to strike down statutory electoral thresholds for EU Parliament elections which are assessed in Chapter 6, cannot be fully understood without recognising Radbruch's influence.

The desire to embrace law but to reject positivism is reflective of an older German tradition of fidelity to the *Rechtsstaat* which meant more than simply the robotic adherence to statutory law associated with positivism. The Basic Law "represents a major break from this positivist tradition" by not conceiving of the state "as the source of fundamental rights. The core of individual freedom, like human dignity itself, is regarded as anterior to the state" (Kommers and Miller, 2012: 56). As Kommers and Miller note, "the notion of 'inviolable and inalienable' rights is also sharply at variance with the spirit of earlier German constitutions, for the Basic Law is Germany's first national constitution to recognise the pre-constitutional existence of guaranteed rights" (2012: 44). This post-war German view on the existence of pre-constitutional rights vested in people by nature has become fused with a post-1945 juridical-legal view where principles are often prioritised over written law or constitutional text:

> In Germany, where the courts are by the constitution stated to be "bound to statute and to law" (*Gesetz* and *Recht*), the reference to a body of law wider than the written statute law has been interpreted as requiring courts to expound fundamental principles implicit in the law, sometimes even in preference to the letter of the law.
>
> (MacCormick et al., 1997: 484–485)

Rights are, thus, not derived from the *Rechtsstaat*, but their maintenance and protection requires, in the German legal mind, the presence of the order of legality (which the *Rechtsstaat* represents) at the centre of the constitutional order to maintain the coherence and unity of the system.

There is, however, a paradox in this view of rights as existing prior to the state. Rights are dependent on the state for their protection, but the post-1945 rights mindset emphasised the idea that rights were anterior to the state (in the sense of natural) and that their existence was not derived from the existence of the state. In Germany, the general post-1945 move towards legally recognised rights was fused with an older notion of the *Rechtsstaat* where human dignity and personal freedom were seen as being derived from rights laid down in law. The discontinuity with the pre-constitutional rights view is that the preservation of individual autonomy through the imposition of rules on the state "presupposes that the planning and acting that are to be protected must take place in a social environment" (Kay, 1998: 21). The paradox is, thus, that rights in reality cannot be protected if the constitutional order that supports them collapses—this was one lesson from the Nazi period; but equally, the Nazi period also showed that rights could not just be seen to be derived from, or dependent on, state power.

In the Court's *Elfes* ruling of 1957 it further defined the nature of the value order and the constitutional implications of the move away from a German legal positivism that had automatically equated law with justice. This would mean the Court's interpretations of the Basic Law, and of unwritten higher law principles, and parliamentary statutes represent the final word on constitutional meaning. The Court's First Senate declared that under the Basic Law,

> Laws are not constitutional merely because they have been passed in conformity with procedural provisions. They must be substantively compatible with the highest values of a free and democratic order, and must also conform to unwritten fundamental constitutional principles.
>
> (*Elfes Case*, 1957)

The implications of this new *BVerfG*-shaped understanding—that rights were anterior to the state and to democracy itself—for the new constitutionalism and for representative democracy itself were startling. This was not an American liberty-oriented conception of rights. Rather, rights and democracy were joined at the hip and could only be exercised in the social and political landscape created by the Basic Law, and by the *BVerfG*.

This was, then, the historical, logical, and political imperative which shaped Germany's post-war constitutionalism. Maintaining stability was a key political goal as much as it was a legal one to allow the country's new constitutional institutions to become accepted. However, making democracy contingent on rights also meant defining the individual not as a lone, isolated, and free person—as in the US conception of liberty—but as a person within the community. The Court's decision in the *Lüth Case* of 1958 to declare that the Basic Law governed not only public law, but also private law, automatically brought private relationships within the scope of constitutional protection, while also shaping Germany's evolving conception of democracy.

The Stability Renewal Transition

The gradual transition from a constitutionalism of stability to one of renewal has been embodied in both the Court's interpretational methodology and in its conception of how minority opinions can become a majority.[7] Within German constitutionalism, the 'stability' dynamic is squarely embodied in the concept of the militant democracy which dominated the Court's jurisprudence in its first few decades. This was illustrated in cases which upheld the political status quo, such as when the Court upheld government raids on the offices of *Der Spiegel* magazine.[8] By the 1970s this balance shifted tentatively towards renewal. In *Official Propaganda Case* (1977b) the Court seemed to embrace greater political inclusivity, while in *Life Imprisonment Case* (1977a) it rejected the idea that even architectonic principles such as human dignity could have eternal definitions. Through its decisions in the 1980s favouring the Green Party which accelerated the Greens' integration into the German political system, the Court was seen to have become more unsympathetic to apparent oligarchical tendencies in Germany's established parties and more supportive of the role of opposition parties in the functioning of German democracy.[9]

Accompanying the transition from stability to renewal in German constitutionalism, though, has been a more opaque methodology and a more erratic style of decision-making from the *BVerfG*. While this transition towards renewal has been good for Germany's smaller political parties such as the Greens and opposition groups whose interests the Court has sought to protect, in other areas it has resulted in a weakening of the Basic Law's fundamental rights protections through the use of principles such as proportionality. Proportionality uses a means/ends test to evaluate any piece of legislation to decide the extent to which any subjective right (i.e. fundamental right) can be interfered with to realise an objective principle (i.e. a legitimate end of state power). The effect of the

Court's use of proportionality—which assumes that no right is absolute and has to be circumscribed by duties—has attracted criticism among German legal circles because it gives unlimited discretion to the *BVerfG* to weaken fundamental rights.[10]

The tension between stability and renewal, and the paradoxical character of intrinsic values within German constitutionalism is highlighted by a famous opinion of the Court—*the Life Imprisonment Case*. Much like Justice Holmes' opinion in *State of Missouri v Holland* (1920), this illustrates a fundamental antipathy to any interpretation based on originalist or permanent understandings.

> Any decision defining human dignity in concrete terms must be based on our present understanding of it, and not on any claim to a conception of timeless validity.
>
> (Life Imprisonment Case, 1977)

In the parlance of the *BVerfG* even the architectonic principle of human dignity can never be absolute as a right because it depends on a conception of the individual as part of a social unit. This change is inexorably linked to the development of the Court's objective value order and its Aristotelian *polis* conception of German constitutionalism which effectively erodes the wall separating the private and the public spheres, and that between individual and community.

Yet this poses an ostensible disjuncture between the eternal commitment to human dignity in the Basic Law and the *BVerfG*'s declaration against any conception of a timeless validity when defining human dignity. The only way to bridge this gap is through context, interpretation, and meaning, which for jurists like Bernhard Schlink is the real problem (1994: 199–200). The danger becomes that a fundamental principle like human dignity—that the framers of the Basic Law intended should be a subjective right against state intrusion—can be interpreted out of existence through a judicial balancing exercise. So clear were Germany's framers about the logic and premise of these principles that fundamental rights including human dignity were protected from constitutional amendment through their entrenchment under the 'eternity clause' of Article 79. This reflects the view of the Federal Republic's founders that human dignity was "the right that could 'trump' all other rights" and "was not open to any form of balancing test" (Möllers, 2009: 419). The whole point of the post-1945 codification of human rights and the concept of human dignity is that they were intended to draw a line in the sand; perhaps not so much a Fukuyama-esque end of history moment in terms of the triumph of liberalism, but certainly the idea that respect for the principle of fundamental human rights and human dignity are not negotiable. Given its protection under the eternity clause and its preeminent position atop the Basic Law's value order, there is clearly a problem if the *BVerfG* can interpret human dignity to mean anything.

An Objective Value Order

Philip Allott has called the Basic Law "the *fine fleur*, the *ne plus ultra*, of democratic rationalism, a pure distillation of long centuries of European constitutionalism" (2002: 205). Hucko echoes this when he writes:

> The Basic Law has proved its worth. It is the fruit of a hundred years of German constitutional history, combining with it the merits of the three previous constitutions, and at the same time avoiding their weaknesses.
>
> (Hucko, 1987: 76)

The assertive value orientation of the Basic Law and its interpretation by the *Bundesverfassungsgericht* shapes every aspect of the constitutional order including the structuring of the institutions, the force of basic rights, and the relationship between the individual and society. The Basic Law is not a constitution which only has relevance in a court room when transgressions occur. Institutional and administrative elements of the German state measure official actions against what fidelity to the Basic Law demands. The principle of legality (*Gesetzmäßigkeit*) is important in German administration and helps ensure that government actions conform to the law and the constitution. Carl Friedrich noted that individuals are "notoriously willing" to appeal to the administrative courts (1968: 132–133), indicating the importance that Germans attach to law as the basis of public authority.

The *BVerfG*'s enunciation of the Basic Law's objective value order means that a hierarchy of norms existed, with some more important than others. Thus, the value order is not merely an interpretational or balancing tool for the Court; the concept also imposes obligations on all institutions within the state to ensure that government actions are carried out in accordance with the constitution and law. In analysing this value order and its implications for German representative democracy, of central importance are the principles of *human dignity* and the *free democratic basic order*. The value of human dignity implies a focus on how individual rights can be protected and realised within a context which includes the state, society, and other individuals; the free democratic basic order value implies a focus on how popular sovereignty can be constrained both to protect individual rights and preserve the existence of the constitutional structure itself.

Inevitably, these two values sometimes come into conflict when human dignity and liberty must be balanced against the security and preservation of the free democratic basic order. In interpretational terms, the 'objective order of values' can be seen as a ranking of values in terms of their importance—which the Court then uses as an interpretational framework when adjudicating cases. By identifying which values are at issue in a case and the relative weighting (in importance) of each value, the Court can use balancing principles such as 'proportionality' to come to a decision. The *BVerfG* is the final arbiter on whether any constraints on democratic process may be justified by the state such as when the Court determines the constitutionality of political parties or other threats to the 'free democratic basic order'. In the *NPD Banning Case* (2017) the *BVerfG* decided against banning the far right neo-Nazi party, the *NPD*, on the basis that there were no indications that it will succeed in achieving its unconstitutional aims.

Far from being a value neutral document the Court has used the *objective value order* phraseology that it created to interpret the Basic Law as being based on a particular vision of German society, a vision which the Court seeks to orient its rulings towards. The idea of the Court enunciating the existence of a constitutional value order of its own creation, which it then uses as a basis for further broad interpretations of the Basic Law, may sound like a judicial tautology or constitutional chutzpah depending on one's view on judicial power. As we will also see with some of the electoral threshold cases in Chapter 6 and its decisions in other areas, the *BVerfG* cites itself far more than it cites the Basic Law (Collings, 2015: 302), potentially raising methodological and interpretational concerns. The larger concern is that the Court's rulings become understandable only through its own case law and its value order—and sometimes not even then—rather than through the text of the Basic Law itself.

In the first few years of its existence, the *BVerfG* enunciated a conception of the person where their individual rights were inextricably linked to their role within their community. This idea has been a much repeated phraseology in the Court's case law.

> The image of man in the Basic Law is not that of an isolated, sovereign individual; rather, the Basic Law has decided in favour of a relationship between individual and community in the sense of a person's dependence on and commitment to the community, without infringing upon a person's individual value.
>
> (*Investment Aid I Case*, 1954)

Striking the correct balance between these two poles of 'individual autonomy' and the 'interests of the wider community' will, of course, often come down to judicial interpretation of the written, unwritten, and pre-constitutional principles within the German constitutional order. Although the Court sees human dignity as the preeminent value of the Basic Law, it is a dignity which is realised most through the relationship between the individual and society. The 'image of man' idea has been repeated often in the Court's jurisprudence.[11] Much of the Court's case law, as Kommers and Miller observe, identifies "a polity that reminds Americans of Lincoln's image of a fraternal democracy" (2012: 70).

Most of the *BVerfG*'s jurisprudence and the effects of its pronouncements on German society arise out of the inter-relationship between the fundamental values of human dignity and the free democratic basic order. There is a sense here of an older tradition of rights which is neither uniquely German, nor can it be said to be pre-political in a natural-law sense. In the American political tradition there is a recognition that preserving the liberty of the individual from state intrusion depends not on a full retreat into a private zone of autonomy, but on ongoing engagement in social life. Similarly, "any realisation of dignity implies a fusion of individual rights and social responsibilities" (Kommers, 1991: 856). As indicated in earlier chapters, the significant difference between how autonomy is shaped in the American and German contexts is the complete absence of a role for the state (at least originally) in the former, and the instrumental role of the state in the latter. As important as dignity is for one person, the achievement of this right cannot impinge on the dignity of others. This illustrates the extent to which the constitutionalism of the Karlsruhe justices implies a commitment on the part of individuals to see their own rights within a social and communitarian context which also considers the effect that the exercise of those rights will have on others. The effect of this emphasis on the social and communitarian context is profound, not least in how it reinforces the idea that democracy in the Basic Law can never be an end in itself. Democracy can only be legitimate if it respects fundamental rights.

Guarding the Constitution

Writing in the early 1990s, Steinberger noted that "politicians and political scientists understand representative democracy to be primarily the antithesis of direct democracy" (1993: 121). Despite Germany having a more powerful form of constitutional review than that in the US, democratic values occupy a central position within the Basic Law. This democratic principle is also entrenched in the unamendable Article 20 which states that "The Federal Republic of Germany is a democratic and social federal state" (Basic Law, Art. 20(1)).

More than any other principle in the German constitution, the free democratic basic order is squarely rooted in the idea of the militant democracy. The concept of militant democracy does not speak to equality as much as to the survival of the *possibility* for equality and dignity. Although the free democratic basic order and human dignity are the two supreme principles of the Basic Law, dignity will not always emerge on top in a balancing exercise. In *Der Spiegel Case* (1966), which arose from Gestapo-like raids by the West German security services on the offices of *Der Spiegel* magazine over stolen military documents containing sensitive information, the *BVerfG* was split 4–4 on whether the state actions were invalid. Murphy notes that this case provided "a pair of strong hints that, if squarely presented with a clear clash between dignity and security, the court will not automatically put dignity above survival, but will rationalize that survival is essential to dignity" (1979: 752). In the post-1949 German constitutional framework, the 'free democratic basic order' is decidedly not negotiable. It is what Kommers calls the "architectonic political principle" which informs the Basic Law as a whole; based on the jurisprudence of the *BVerfG*, the preservation of this principle can, crucially, be used to limit all rights, even those cast in absolute terms (1991: 857). In practice, the principle can be used by the Court to declare as unconstitutional any political parties which might threaten the democratic system (Basic Law, Art. 21(2)). Since the establishment of the Basic Law the Court has only exercised this sweeping power twice, in *Socialist Reich Party Case* (1952) and *Communist Party Case* (1956).

Carl Schmitt's question of who guards the constitution against the enemies of democracy[12] dominated post-war legal debates (Müller, 2009: 18–19), and avoiding the pitfalls of the Weimar Republic thus became the *sine qua non* of the 1949 German constitutional project. Possible contenders who could fight the enemies of democracy ranged, notes Müller, from "a strong president (who would have been Schmitt's own choice), to the state bureaucracy and even the trade unions" (2009: 19). For Hans Kelsen, Schmitt's long-time antagonist, the guardian of the constitution had to be a process of constitutional judicial review by a dedicated tribunal.[13] Through its 1958 *Lüth* ruling it was ultimately the *BVerfG* which emerged in this 'enemy-fighting' role in which "judicial review of almost any legal and political decision became legitimate" (Müller, 2009: 19). In *Lüth*, the Court stated:

> The Basic Law is not a value-neutral document. Its section on basic rights establishes an objective order of values, and this order strongly reinforces the effective power of basic rights. This value system, which centres upon the dignity of the human personality developing freely within the social community must be looked upon as a fundamental constitutional decision affecting all spheres of law, both public and private.
>
> (*Lüth Case*, 1958)

Lüth is probably the Court's most important ever case and effectively "constitutionalised the whole of German law" (Collings, 2015: 54). As well as enunciating its objective value order and repeating its 'image of man' vision of the relationship between the individual and the community, it declared that the Basic Law applied to private relationships and contracts, and not just public authority as is the case with the US Constitution. Indeed, the doctrine of Third Party Effect followed logically from the Court's demolition of the border between public and private law, and from its Aristotelian conception of the individual person as part of their community. Böckenförde traces the normative supremacy of the Basic Law within the constitutional and legal order to *Lüth*, which shifted the view of rights as defensive rights against the state to the idea that fundamental rights are also value decisions which radiate into every aspect of law (2017: 399).

Through a string of decisions in the 1950s, including *Lüth*, the *Bundesverfassungsgericht* consolidated its position at the top of the Federal Republic's legal order. It was, above all, through the Court that the 'leave nothing to chance' mantra of Karl Löwenstein's militant democracy was made real (see Loewenstein, 1937a, b). As Teitel puts it, "a militant constitutional order is vigilant not only to the excesses of state power but also to those of popular sovereignty" (2000: 203). Its end result, as Kommers notes, is that the unchangeable principle of democracy enshrined in the Basic Law now "finds itself locked in the permanent embrace of mutual tension with constitutionalism" (1991: 853). This represents a move from the value neutral democracy of Weimar to the constitutional democracy of the Federal Republic and its 'objective order of values' as promulgated by the justices in Karlsruhe. Such a democracy is, as Müller notes, "expressly not neutral about its own principles and values—and puts in place strong checks on those hostile to its principles" (2006: 279). The concept of the militant democracy is perhaps best encapsulated in Popper's observation on the 'paradox of tolerance' where "unlimited tolerance must lead to the disappearance of tolerance" (1962: 265). Following Saint-Just, the Basic Law's mantra, particularly at its establishment, can be said to have been 'no freedom for the enemies of freedom'. Three articles in the Basic Law form the crux of the Federal Republic's militant democracy. Article 9 prohibits associations that are "directed against the constitutional order", Article 18 allows for the "forfeiture" of basic rights for anyone using them "to combat the free democratic basic order", which the *BVerfG* alone can decide, and Article 21 allows the *BVerfG* to declare as unconstitutional any political parties which "seek to undermine or abolish the free democratic basic order" (Basic Law, Art. 9, 18, and 21). Even during a state of emergency the Court retains jurisdiction (Kommers and Miller, 2012: 52). "To avoid the possibility of 'democratic suicide' the constitution of the Federal Republic included an article, the so-called eternity clause, closing off the possibility of abrogating the fundamental principles underlying a liberal democratic order" (Müller, 2003: 65).

Of the 18 articles contained in the Basic Rights section of the Basic Law, several are "word for word reproductions of corresponding articles in the Weimar Constitution of 1919"; the difference being that Weimar viewed the norms as being "aspirational" while in the Basic Law, these are "judicially enforceable norms" (Kommers and Miller, 2012: 44). Unlike the Weimar Constitution, the Basic Law is supreme over the German Parliament and all other organs of the state, and governs the entire German legal order. The judicially enforceable rights provisions included in the Basic Law are declared by Article 1, paragraph 3 "to bind the legislature, the executive and the judiciary as directly applicable law". Article 20 underpins the supremacy of the Basic Law while also underscoring the difference from the legal positivist focus only on *Gesetz*, stating that: "the legislature shall be bound by the constitutional order, the executive and the judiciary by law (*Gesetz*) and justice (*Recht*)". These and other sections of the Basic Law such as the Article 79 eternity clause (*Ewigkeitsklausel*), which forbids amendments to Article 1 or Article 20, conveys the idea of the Basic Law as a protective shield for German democracy and German constitutionalism. Indeed, such is the shadow that the experience of Weimar and the 1930s continues to cast that the German constitution paradoxically imposes certain constraints on democracy in the interests both of constitutionalism and "the free democratic basic order" which is one of the most oft-repeated and significant phrases in the Basic Law.[14] The paradox inherent in curbing democratic processes to preserve the super principle of the free democratic basic order is a palpable feature of German constitutionalism.

Böckenförde's concern over both the Aristotelian *polis* aspects of the Basic Law and the implications of the *BVerfG*'s objective value order for liberalism possibly reached its apotheosis in the controversy over the Radicals Decree of 1972. This decree, aimed principally at communists, sought to prevent leftist radicals entering the civil service (Braunthal, 1990: 28–29). Supporters of the Decree cited the decisions of the *BVerfG* in 1952 and 1956 to outlaw extremist parties as establishing the legal foundation for the free democratic basic order (Braunthal, 1990: 13), and for the militant democracy. Böckenförde felt that as a means of countering extremism the Radicals Decree was "incompatible with the basic structure of the liberal state" (2017: 383). Identifying a similar paradox to the Böckenförde Dilemma itself, Brinkmann notes that

> militant democracy can only find its justification as a principle of a liberal democratic constitution if it remains a liberal democracy. This can only be maintained if it is supported by its citizens, by their commitment to, and their confidence in liberal democracy; its life-force depends on that support and not on repressive measures.
>
> (Brinkmann, 1983: 594)

In other words, if the citizens support liberal democratic values, there should be no need to impose them, and if they are imposed by the state then it can hardly call itself 'liberal'. For Böckenförde, the Radicals Decree highlighted the contradiction between the *Rechtsstaat* and an objective value order that could make activities illegitimate that were not prohibited by law:

> A use of liberty that remains within the boundaries of the law cannot be declared illegitimate because it adheres to values that are rejected. That undercuts and hollows out the structure of the Rechtsstaat.
>
> (Böckenförde, 2017: 376)

Therefore, in restricting the freedom of individuals to profess certain opinions, Böckenförde believed that the Radicals Decree, as well as the militant democracy and objective value order which underpinned it, were acting in a way that was fundamentally counter to liberal principles.

By the early 1980s, after three decades of economic growth and with an apparently stable democracy the people and leaders of the Federal Republic could reasonably point to some success. Yet despite the militant democracy, doubts remained about how resilient a constitutional democracy the 'Bonn republic' had actually become, revealing Böckenförde's concern again. To some there was a suspicion that the stability of the political system was perhaps no more than a temporal illusion created by the increasing distance from 1945, where economic performance masked political commitment (Lepsius, 1982: 116). If the Federal Republic was only a fair-weather democracy, the concern was whether there was "a reliable political culture, a firm value orientation which would safeguard the democratic regime in time of crisis" (Lepsius, 1982: 116).[15]

While the fair-weather democracy argument may have still been faintly plausible in the 1980s, this point still neglects two important aspects of Germany's development after 1949. One was the important domestic debate over the *Vergangenheitsbewältigung* and the coming to terms with the so-called *NS Zeit* which paralleled the growing sense of affinity between the German people and their Basic Law. However, the implications of the 'Böckenförde Dilemma' were that liberal democracies, especially Germany's, lay perilously exposed without the internal bonding forces of religion or country. For the Germany of 1964 'country' was certainly not an option, leaving only Böckenförde's emphasis on religion as an acceptable internal source of cohesion. One other important source of cohesion in Germany, though, was law itself. It was the deep cultural respect for law among Germans (that pre-dated the Federal Republic) which provided the newly established *Bundesverfassungsgericht* with enhanced legitimacy at a time when there was little trust in political institutions.

In Law Germany Trusts

> There is hardly an essential process of constitutional life that cannot become embroiled in a proceeding before the Federal Constitutional Court. ... Thus are the gates thrown open, despite various warnings and terrifying precedents from earlier times, to the double danger of a juridification of politics and a politicisation of justice.
>
> (Werner Weber, 1949: 25; quoted in Collings, 2015: xxvii)

The Basic Law put in place mechanisms to divide and limit political power, and place law at the heart of the constitutional order. Positive law via the application of the German legal code was still relevant, but with the rights articles of the Basic Law and their associated values governing the entire legal order, all aspects of German law have increasingly taken on constitutional significance. Germany's new constitutionalism differed markedly from the Weimar Republic and the previous German constitutions by emphasising, first, that "all state authority is derived from the people" (Basic Law Art. 20(2)) to be exercised through the medium of representative democracy, and second, the central importance of *law* in political and economic matters. "The founders of the Federal Republic, successive legislators and, above all, the justices in the Federal Constitutional Court have relied upon the power of legal provisions to ensure the proper functioning of many important elements in the country's political system" (Schweitzer, 1984: xvi).

To appreciate the special status given to legal mechanisms in binding Germany's post-1949 constitutional system and political system one must recognise the historic affinity for law in Germany. Bernhard Schlink observes that

> Politics had been discredited by the Weimar Republic and the Third Reich, and the old German belief that politics was essentially a dirty business and

> law a clean one reappeared and gained confirmation. … The German belief in the purity of law had always differentiated between law in its original and natural state, and that which lawyers and judges make of it. … Dirty politics suffered from a deficit of legitimacy, while clean law and its representative, the Bundesverfassungsgericht, enjoyed a legitimacy "surplus". These were the conditions that invited and demanded that the BVerfG take on an activist role.
>
> (Schlink, 1994: 210–211)

In 1951, when the Court first began to hear cases, it remained to be seen how effective it would be in protecting the new democratic constitutional order, how authoritative would be its rulings, and whether it could instil in the German people a respect for constitutional government which had been discredited, first, by the shortcomings of Weimar, and then by the assault on the constitution by the Nazis. Constitutional courts of the German variety have fared well, writes Somek, "where the people are traditionally respectful towards, and heedful of, authority" (2014: 96). Of course, it was this same excessive respect for authority in Germany that had made things so easy for the Nazis in the first place. While it may be some comfort that it is the benign justices of the *BVerfG* who are in change constitutionally, Germany would be a weak liberal democracy if its citizens simply respected the authority of judges rather than the substantive values they are enunciating.

Rights, human dignity, and party democracy constitute the centrepiece of constitutionalism in the Basic Law (Stern, 1993: 19). Compared to the American Bill of Rights which was only added to the Constitution as an afterthought through the amendment process, the fundamental and unamendable rights provisions of the German Basic Law are at the very start of the constitutional text. From the outset the framers of the Basic Law recognised that the document had to restore the faith of ordinary Germans in law after the 13-year assault on the *Rechtsstaat* by the National Socialists. Equally important, though, was rooting the new constitutional order in society through an emphasis on *human dignity* and *law*. Stern explains (1993: 22) that in the Germany shaped by the Basic Law

> We do not have a government of judges. What has evolved is that which was expressed by the Parliamentary Council (and which could also be said about the Supreme Court of the United States of America):
>
>> The foundation of the state is at stake here: Law is either recognized as the basis of human society and enforced with the necessary guarantees for its implementation, or political expediency will rule the day, leading once again to the dangerous fundamentalist dogmas of the past where law is reduced simply to what benefits the people or the government or the state.
>>
>> (Parliamentary Council, quoted in Stern, 1993: 22)[16]

As Stern notes, this declaration echoes the choice of words used in the proclamation which the July 20th plotters planned to sign in the event that they had succeeded in killing Hitler:

> Our first task is to re-establish the unimpaired majesty of the law. … No human society can exist without law; no one, not even those who fail to honour the law, can do without it.
>
> (Quoted in Stern, 1993: 33)

This was not mere prose. The continuity between the ideas of some of the plotters and Germany's post-war constitutional order is perhaps best seen in the figure of Fabian von Schlabrendorff, who escaped almost certain execution in February 1945 when a US bomb crashed through the roof of the Nazi People's Court (*Volksgerichtshof*) killing the notorious presiding judge Roland Freisler. In 1967, Von Schlabrendorff became a judge on the *Bundesverfassungsgericht*. It is impossible, as Bruce Ackerman notes, to understand the success of the *BVerfG* without recognising that "the Basic Law has become, in the society at large, a central symbol of the nation's break with its Nazi past" (1997: 778). Thus, the very basis on which the Federal Republic's Constitutional Court was founded was a repudiation of the Nazi period where positivist law became a means to nefarious ends.

To ensure the Court's removal from political pressure the country's founders determined that it should be located in Karlsruhe, far away from the West German institutions of power in Bonn. In the more than 70-year existence of the Federal Republic, the Court's judgements have profoundly influenced German life to such an extent that some speak of the 'Karlsruhe Republic' (Wefing, 2016). As Möllers observes: "since its inception, the *Bundesverfassungsgericht* has been Germany's most popular institution" (2007: 96). The central role of the *BVerfG* in constitutional interpretation and the respect which is afforded to it in modern Germany have had important consequences, such as in the moulding of the country's political system. In the German context, however, some of these effects which the Court's rulings have had on political and social life go beyond even the generally political nature of constitutional decision-making, and are the result of the specific circumstances of twentieth-century German history. Despite the concerns of commentators like Werner Weber about the "juridification of politics" (see Collings, 2015: xxvii), Germany's post-war founders came to the conclusion that confident judicial authority pronouncing on political and social questions was a more acceptable alternative than strident executive or legislative power.

For many modern theorists of constitutionalism, the German model of constitutionalism is correct precisely because it is, as Stern notes, a "legal constitution" based on fundamental normative principles and "legitimized by the ultimate source of state power, namely the people" (1993: 19). The key role of fundamental rights in post-war German constitutionalism and the far more dominant position of the *BVerfG* within Germany's constitutional system relative to the Supreme Court makes the US-centric academic debate over the 'countermajoritarian difficulty' irrelevant. Given the already mentioned contempt that many Germans have traditionally felt for politics, legitimacy was never seen as originating from democracy. Rather, the greater emphasis on the principle of *Rechtsstaatlichkeit* is usually sufficient to overcome doubts over the democratic character of judicial review (Koopmans, 2003: 106). Möllers notes that the constitutional legitimacy of judicial review in Germany was never a topic of interest in the academy or for the people (2007: 95–96). Heun's observation that "self-restraint is considered as self-authorization which is constitutionally prohibited" (2011: 183–184) illustrates the degree to which the Basic Law determines the powers, limits, and obligations of the Court, making the American political question doctrine, and the countermajoritarian difficulty a moot point in the context of German constitutional jurisprudence. Put simply, the Basic Law does not allow the justices of the *BVerfG* to escape their responsibilities through use of Bickelian 'passive virtues' to avoid making a decision in a case.[17] The Court's function is "to resolve even doubtful questions of constitutionality, not to avoid them" (Kommers and Miller, 2012: 68). This point was reinforced by Böckenförde who noted that the *BVerfG* is prevented by statute from falling back on a US style political question doctrine (2017: 403). "If the court has broad authority, as it does with us, it is obliged to make use of it when it is appealed to" (Böckenförde, 2017: 403). The unambiguous affirmation of judicial authority in the Basic Law together with the articulation of the Court's jurisdiction in the Federal Constitutional Court Act help explain why neither original intent nor the notion of judicial restraint are salient issues in German constitutional jurisprudence.

For one thing, the clarity of the Basic Law provides a set of useful principles for separating matters which are properly political in nature, and those (primarily procedural) matters where it would be legitimate for the courts to rule. In the US context this dichotomy might form part of what has come to be called the 'political question doctrine'. The Basic Law is clear on the difference between political and procedural matters: "The decisions of committees of inquiry shall not be subject to judicial review. The courts shall be free to evaluate and rule upon the facts that were the subject of the investigation" (Basic Law, Art. 44(4)). While original intent partly took on more significance in the US due to feelings of reverence for the framers, the German need to avoid undue veneration of political figures after 12 years of the *Führerprinzip* perhaps made the *BVerfG* justices seem more acceptable objects of respect. As Collings observes, "West Germans embraced the Court's immense power at a time when circumstances led them to view constitutional justice as a precondition to democracy rather than a restraint on it" (2015: 305).

Despite the *BVerfG*'s significant role in the emergence of a strong and liberal German democracy, its preeminent position also places significant responsibility on it to use its constitutional authority judiciously. For Böckenförde, the Court "is on a par with the *Bundestag*, *Bundesrat*, the federal government and so on. But it is intended as a constitutional organ that operates in the mode of a court, and only in that mode" (2017: 402). Here, Böckenförde is clear that "the court is not and must not be a parallel legislator" (2017: 401). The danger in the Court's position is that in its role as the Basic Law's supreme interpreter, every decision it makes adds a further complexion to the content of the constitution. The consequence of this accretion of interpretational meaning over time, according to Böckenförde, becomes that "the separation of powers shifts" and the Court can "turn from the servant and guardian into the master of the constitution" (2017: 402). As the analysis of the Court's decision-making in Chapter 6 argues, the Court has sometimes been in danger of crossing this constitutional boundary.

Conclusion

This chapter has highlighted the inauspicious circumstances for democracy in 1950s Germany when the *BVerfG* began hearing cases. The lingering questions at the time over the willingness of so many Germans to support, actively or passively, the Nazi regime reinforced the need to establish not only a resistant militant democracy but a supportive constitutional culture, which would permit liberal democratic values to take root in Germany. In creating its so-called 'Aristotelian polis', the *BVerfG* was attempting to reinforce the German values of community as a force of cohesion in Böckenfördean terms, but without sacrificing the dignity of the individual in the community. What assisted the Court in being accepted was the immense cultural respect for law in Germany which predated the Federal Republic. What was uncertain was how much that respect for law could provide the basis for a democratic culture that respected fundamental rights rather than simply the authority of judges and the courts. Law as it emerged in the Basic Law was no longer rooted in the legal positivism of the Weimar Republic, but in supra-positive principles of justice. The emergence of the Basic Law's 'objective value order' as enunciated by the *BVerfG* built on this conception of justice as it sought to entrench the fundamental values of human dignity and the free democratic basic order at the centre of the constitutional order.

In its first few decades the *BVerfG*'s role was partly to inculcate Germans regarding the majesty of law, but within a hierarchical constitutional order that firmly established individual rights and human dignity as fundamental values. Although German democracy has made impressive strides since 1949, the elephant in the room remains the support of ordinary Germans for Hitler in the 1930s. Neil MacCormick observed that legal authority is "empty without general acceptance in a society of the decisions taken by those in authority" and consequently that "without the backing of political power this cannot practically be achieved" (1995: 4). This has implications for Germany. The authority of the *BVerfG* today is bolstered by the support that it has enjoyed among the German public, the maintenance of which has shielded the institution from more stinging criticism (Amann et al., 2014) or attempts to reign in some of its authority. If Germans continue to realise, as Dirk Kurbjuweit suggests, that "they still have to practice democracy" (quoted in Packer, 2014) and that they are still on the training programme, then they may be less likely to become complacent about protecting their constitutional order.

The question assessed in the next chapter with reference to the European Parliament (EP) electoral threshold cases is whether the balance the Court has struck between the imperative of the militant democracy and the rights of German citizens is the correct one. At issue is the *BVerfG*'s central role within Germany's political and legal order, its decisions and reasoning in the EP cases, and the comments of its president that the Court is on the side of the people. The question posed is whether the Court's position has become so powerful that it has effectively relegated the *Bundestag* to the position of an *ersatz* legislature, as a former *BVerfG* justice put it (Collings, 2015: 288), while overlooking potential threats to stability that are increasingly hard to miss.

Notes

1 See *Life Imprisonment Case* (1977a).
2 The National Socialists emerged as the largest party winning 37 percent of the vote and 230 seats in the *Reichstag*.
3 For example, the language used in Count One of the indictment included the phrases "Instill fear in the hearts of the German people" ('Consolidation of Control' Section B) and "In order to make the German people amenable to their will" ('Consolidation of Control' Section E); (see 'Nuremberg Trial Proceedings', 2008).
4 Prior to the ratification of the Seventeenth Amendment in 1913, US senators were appointed by the states, giving the latter considerable influence. However, that is different to having an institutional role in the federal government, as the German states do in the *Bundesrat*.
5 See, for example, Jasper's seminal study on the question of the culpability of Germans for the Nazi period (2009).
6 The *Sonderweg* thesis—that Germany chose a special path between 1848 and 1933 which did not match that of other comparable European states like France or Britain—is one explanation given for the failure of democracy to take root.
7 This resonates with the analysis in Chapter 1 (see also Koopmans, 2003: 123).
8 See *Der Spiegel Case* (1966) and Walter Murphy's analysis of the case (1979: 752).
9 The criticism of oligarchical tendencies among the established parties was made by Böckenförde in his opinions in *Party Finance V Case* (1986b) and *Green Party Exclusion Case* (1986a), and is discussed in Chapter 6.
10 The principle is used to "justify limits on democratic rights and fundamental freedoms" (see Kommers and Miller, 2012: 67). The Court's use of legal principles (including proportionality and its coherence doctrine) is part of a larger critique of the Court from some scholars and jurists which will be assessed in Chapter 6.
11 Other significant cases where the Court invoked its "image of man" idea include *Life Imprisonment Case* (1977a) and *Mephisto Case* (1971).
12 Schmitt expressed this question in *Der Hüter der Verfassung* (1929: 162).
13 For a useful analysis of the debate on constitutional guardianship, see Kelsen and Schmitt (2015).
14 See Articles 10(2), 21 (2), 11(2), 18, 73(1), 87(4), 91(1).
15 See Robert Dahl, who also notes the connection between a well-functioning economic order and democracy (2003: 94).
16 Stern here cites the words of the Parliamentary Council which drafted the Basic Law.
17 This logic of the law giving judges little room for manoeuvre is more understandable in the German civil law system where the judicial role is to faithfully apply the legal

code to the circumstances of a case so that the law reveals the answer. Judge David Edward noted how this style of decision-making works in the French civil law system: "It's a kind of Aristotelian syllogism. Applying that law to those facts, and there you have an answer" (Interview with author, 2013).

References

State of Missouri v Holland, 252 US 416, 1920

'Nuremberg Trial Proceedings (14 November 1945–1 October 1946) Vol. 1: Indictment: Count One' Lillian Goldman Law Library, Yale Law School, (2008), available at: http://avalon.law.yale.edu/imt/count1.asp [last accessed 3 July 2020].

Socialist Reich Party Case, 2 BVerfGE 1, 1952

Equality Case, 3 BVerfGE 225, 1953

Investment Aid I Case, 4 BVerfGE 7, 1954

Communist Party Case, 5 BVerfGE, 1956

Elfes, 6 BVerfGE 32 (1957), 1957

Lüth Case, 7 BVerfGE 198, 1958

Der Spiegel Case, 20 BVerfGE 162, 1966

Mephisto Case, 30 BVerfGE 173, 1971

Life Imprisonment Case 45 BVerfGE 187, 1977a

Official Propaganda Case, 44 BVerfGE 125, 1977b

Green Party Exclusion Case, 70 BVerfGE 324, 1986a

Party Finance V Case, 73 BVerfG 40, 1986b

NPD Banning Case, 2 BvB 1/13, 2017

Ackerman, B., "The Rise of World Constitutionalism", *Virginia Law Review* (1997), 771–797.

Allott, P., *The Health of Nations: Society and Law Beyond the State* (Cambridge: Cambridge University Press, 2002).

Amann, M., D. Hipp, R. Pfister, and C. Schult, "Is Germany's High Court Anti-European?", *Spiegel Online*, 13 March 2014, available at: www.spiegel.de/international/germany/the-eu-critical-course-of-the-german-high-court-a-958018.html [last accessed 18 October 2016].

Amis, M. "Martin Amis on His Latest Novel 'The Zone of Interest' " [Interview] Charlie Rose, 22 October 2014 (2014), available at: https://charlierose.com/videos/3903 [last accessed 3 July 2020].

Böckenförde, E. W., *Constitutional and Political Theory: Selected Writings*. Vol. 1 (Oxford: Oxford University Press, 2017).

Braunthal, G., *Political Loyalty and Public Service in West Germany: the 1972 Decree Against Radicals and its Consequences* (Amherst: University of Massachusetts Press, 1990).

Brinkmann, G., "Militant Democracy and Radicals in the West German Civil Service", *The Modern Law Review*, 46(5) (1983), 584–600.

Collings, J., *Democracy's Guardians: A History of the German Federal Constitutional Court, 1951–2001* (Oxford: Oxford University Press, 2015).

Dahl, R. A., *How Democratic is the American Constitution?* 2nd edn (New Haven, CT: Yale University Press, 2003).

Eberle, E. J., *Dignity and Liberty: Constitutional Visions in Germany and the United States* (Westport, CT: Praeger, 2002).

Forner, S. A., *German Intellectuals and the Challenge of Democratic Renewal: Culture and Politics After 1945* (Cambridge: Cambridge University Press, 2014).

Frei, N., *Karrieren im Zwielicht: Hitlers Eliten nach 1945* (Frankfurt: Campus, 2001).

Friedrich, C. J., *Trends of Federalism in Theory and Practice* (London: Pall Mall, 1968).

Gellately, R., *Backing Hitler: Consent and Coercion in Nazi Germany* (Oxford: Oxford University Press, 2002).

Heun, W., *The Constitution of Germany: A Contextual Analysis* (Oxford: Hart, 2011).

Howard, A., "A Traveler from an Antique Land: The Modern Renaissance of Comparative Constitutionalism", *Virginia Journal of International Law*, 50 (2009), 3.

Hucko, E. M., *The Democratic Tradition: Four German Constitutions* (Leamington Spa: Berg, 1987).

Jaspers, K., *The Question of German Guilt* (New York: Fordham University Press, 2009).

Kay, R. S., "American Constitutionalism", in *Constitutionalism: Philosophical Foundations*, ed. by Lawrence A. Alexander (Cambridge: Cambridge University Press, 1998).

Kelsen, H. and C. Schmitt, *The Guardian of the Constitution* (Cambridge: Cambridge University Press, 2015).

Kermani, N., "Rede von Dr. Navid Kermani zur Feierstunde 65 Jahre Grundgesetz" [Speech] Deutscher Bundestag, 23 May 2014, available at: www.bundestag.de/dokumente/textarchiv/2014/280688-280688 [last accessed 3 July 2020].

Kommers, D. P., "German Constitutionalism: A Prolegomenon", *Emory Law Journal*, 40 (1991), 837–873.

Kommers, D. P. and R. A. Miller, *The Constitutional Jurisprudence of The Federal Republic of Germany*, 3rd edn (Durham [NC]: Duke University Press, 2012).

Koopmans, T., *Courts and Political Institutions: A Comparative View* (Cambridge: Cambridge University Press, 2003).

Lepsius, R. M., "Institutional Structures and Political Culture", in *Party Government and Political Culture in Western Germany*, ed. by Herbert Döring and Gordon R. Smith (London: Palgrave, 1982).

Loewenstein, K., "Militant Democracy and Fundamental Rights, I", *American Political Science Review*, 31(03) (1937a), 417–432.

Loewenstein, K., "Militant Democracy and Fundamental Rights, II", *American Political Science Review*, 31(04) (1937b), 638–658.

MacCormick, N., "Sovereignty: Myth and Reality", *Scottish Affairs*, 11 (Spring) (1995), 1–13.

MacCormick, N., Z. Bankowski, L. Morawski, and A. Migue, "Rationales for Precedent", in *Interpreting Precedents: A Comparative Study*, ed. by Neil MacCormick and Robert Samuel Summers (Aldershot: Ashgate Publishing, 1997).

Mertens, T., "Nazism, Legal Positivism and Radbruch's Thesis on Statutory Injustice", *Law and Critique*, 14(3) (2003), 277–295.

Miller, R. A., "Germany's German Constitution", *Virginia Journal of International Law*, 57 (2017), 95.

Möllers, C., "'We Are (Afraid of) the People': Constituent Power in German Constitutionalism", in *The Paradox of Constitutionalism: Constituent Power and Constitutional Form*, ed. by Martin Loughlin and Neil Walker (Oxford: Oxford University Press, 2007).

Möllers, C., "Democracy and Human Dignity: Limits of a Moralized Conception of Rights in German Constitutional Law", *Israel Law Review*, 42(02) (2009), 416–439.

Müller, J.-W., *A Dangerous Mind: Carl Schmitt in Post-War European Thought* (New Haven, CT: Yale University Press, 2003).

Müller, J.-W., "On the Origins of Constitutional Patriotism", *Contemporary Political Theory*, 5 (3) (2006), 278–296.

Müller, J.-W., *Constitutional Patriotism* (Princeton, NJ: Princeton University Press, 2009).

Murphy, W. F., "An Ordering of Constitutional Values", *Southern California Law Review*, 53 (1979), 703–760.

Noelle, E. and E. P. Neumann, *The Germans: Public Opinion Polls 1947–1966* (Allensbach; Bonn: Verlag für Demoskopie, 1967).

Packer, G., "The Quiet German", *The New Yorker*, 1 December 2014, available at: www.newyorker.com/magazine/2014/12/01/quiet-german [last accessed 27 November 2014].

Popper, K. R., *The Open Society and its Enemies. Vol 1, The Spell Of Plato* (London: Routledge & Kegan Paul, 1962).

Quint, P. E., "Judging The Past: The Prosecution of East German Border Guards and the GDR Chain of Command", *The Review of Politics*, 61(02) (1999), 303–330.

Radbruch, G., "Gesetzliches Unrecht und Übergesetzliches Recht", *Süddeutsche Juristen-Zeitung*, 1(5) (1946), 105–108.

Schlink, B., "German Constitutional Culture in Transition", in *Constitutionalism, Identity, Difference, and Legitimacy: Theoretical Perspectives*, ed. by Michel Rosenfeld (Durham, NC: Duke University Press, 1994).

Schmitt, C., "Der Hüter der Verfassung", *Archiv des öffentlichen Rechts*, 55(N.F. 16)(2) (1929), 161–237.

Schweitzer, C.-C., *Politics and Government in the Federal Republic of Germany: Basic Documents* (Leamington Spa: Berg, 1984).

Sereny, G., *The German Trauma: Experiences and Reflections, 1938–2001* (London: Penguin, 2000).

Somek, A., *The Cosmopolitan Constitution* (New York: Oxford University Press, 2014).

Steinberger, H., "Political Representation in Germany", in *Germany and its Basic Law: Past, Present, and Future: A German-American Symposium*, ed. by Paul Kirchhof and Donald P. Kommers (Baden-Baden: Nomos, 1993).

Stern, K., "General Asseessment of the Basic Law—A German View", in *Germany and its Basic Law: Past, Present, and Future: A German-American Symposium*, ed. by Paul Kirchhof and Donald P Kommers (Baden-Baden: Nomos, 1993).

Teitel, R. G., *Transitional Justice* (Oxford: Oxford University Press, 2000).

Thornhill, C. J., *A Sociology of Constitutions: Constitutions and State Legitimacy in Historical-Sociological Perspective*, Cambridge Studies in Law and Society. (Cambridge: Cambridge University Press, 2011).

Waldron, J., "Precommitment and Disagreement", in *Constitutionalism: Philosophical Foundations*, ed. by Lawrence A. Alexander (Cambridge: Cambridge University Press, 1998).

Weber, W., *Weimarer Verfassung und Bonner Grundgesetz* (Karl-Friedrich Fleischer, 1949).

Wefing, H., "Der Andere Präsident", *Die Zeit*, 24 March 2016, available at: www.zeit.de/zeit-magazin/2016/12/andreas-vosskuhle-bundesverfassungsgericht-verfassung-praesident [last accessed 16 May 2016].

6 Karlsruhe and the People

Ulrich Wenner observed that "once the majority of voters in democratic elections vote for parties committed to rejecting or attacking the existing constitutional order, a political system no longer stands a chance" (1986: 40; translated from German original).[1] Wenner's statement identifies the danger of democratic failure discussed in earlier chapters, a vulnerability which was manifested most tragically in the collapse of the Weimar Republic. His statement also highlights the challenge to law and constitutionalism in preventing democratic suicide, while also allowing citizens a genuine voice in how they are governed. Achieving this balance in Germany has depended, to a greater extent than in most other countries, on the preeminent role of law.

Donald Kommers observes that "the law of democracy in Germany represents a vast jurisprudence" (2006: 116). That there even is a 'law of democracy' in German constitutional jurisprudence is indicative of a German political system governed much more by law than is the case in the United States. Yet as Germany's democratic culture has matured, the need to maintain the myriad facets of the militant democracy has been questioned. Germany's new constitutionalism as it emerged in the 1949 Basic Law had two main aims: first, to create a stable and democratic government based on the authority of the people derived from regular representative elections; second, to protect the rights and dignity of all individuals against both state power and the unconstrained will of the people. The possibility of allowing voters a completely free choice between all political parties—including those which might abolish democracy—was never entertained because, following Wenner (1986: 40), the post-war German founders saw that rights and human dignity could only exist if the political order committed to upholding them survived. Or, as Murphy construed the *Der Spiegel* Case decision, "survival is essential to dignity" (1979: 752). However, the drawback was that this militant democracy could not be sustained, as Böckenförde identified, without sacrificing the liberal state's *liberalness* (1991: 45).

This chapter considers the relationship between German democracy and the German people as mediated by the *Bundesverfassungsgericht*. As noted in the previous chapter, it was the immense respect for law in German society and culture which bought the Federal Republic some breathing space with the German people in its early years. Also needed, though, was the creation of a supportive democratic culture. What was necessary, then, was for Germany's fledgling democratic institutions to be reinforced through the already deep respect for law in the country. As will be shown, this has been partly achieved through the role of the constitutional complaint mechanism which has made Germans more acutely aware of their democratic and individual rights. The chapter will address how the *BVerfG* has balanced threats to stability within the German political system against the importance it attached to the principles of electoral equality and equal opportunity among political parties. It will do this by examining one important strand of the concept of militant democracy: the constitutionality of electoral thresholds (or hurdles) with respect to German political parties participating in elections within Germany and for the European Parliament.

The chapter will first examine the constitutional role of the Court in dealing with political parties in the German system, particularly through its historical role in managing the integration of new political parties, like the Greens, into the system. It will then assess the historical background regarding the necessity of having electoral thresholds in the context of the failure of the Weimar Constitution and the establishment of the Basic Law, before examining the European Parliament (EP) cases. In the final section, the chapter will examine the changing relationship of the Court with the German people before questioning whether its central role in the country's constitutional order represents a risk to German democracy, or its strongest foundation.

Overview

One of the main puzzles in the relationship between the *Bundesverfassungsgericht* and German democracy is that while its decisions on electoral thresholds in *European Parliament II Case* (2011) and *European Parliament III Case* (2014) (hereafter *EPII* and *EPIII*) highlighted the importance of electoral equality, popular sovereignty, and democracy, each of these opinions was also highly assertive of the Court's power vis-à-vis the German Parliament and federal government. The Court's decisions striking down the 5 percent and, then, 3 percent hurdles for EP elections in 2011 and 2014, respectively, scaled back aspects of the militant democracy, and restored the voting rights of those voting for smaller parties, even while overruling the elected representatives of the German people in the *Bundestag*. Given the crucial role of parties in the German political system as organs of state "in the formation of the political will of the people"[2] (see Basic Law, Art. 21(1)), and the enduring memory of the fate of the Weimar Republic, any change to these thresholds, even at the EU Parliament level, remains contentious. As much as these decisions were criticised by politicians in Berlin, the larger complaint about the Court from a number of German constitutional scholars, some of its former justices, and a former judge of the European Court of Justice is the increasingly inconsistent reasoning by which it has reached some of its decisions.

The European Parliament electoral threshold cases that have reached the Court highlight a number of specific problems related to these cases and broader problems with the Court's methodology over several decades. First, is whether the Court's emphasis on material conditions (or *Verhältnisse*) may have made it overly responsive to a changing context and too reliant on a living instrument means of interpretation that many judges in the ordinary German courts find troubling. Second, the cases illustrate a development in the Court's jurisprudence from the early days of the Federal Republic from the early emphasis on political and legal stability to a Court that has become too 'renewal' focussed, as well as insufficiently attentive to the Basic Law and to the consistency of its decisions with its past case law and reasoning. Third, the cases illustrate a broader tendency of the justices on the court over decades, who have, notes Collings, "seemed to do more as the country has needed them less" (2015: 302). While the *BVerfG* has been, and remains, an impressive and essential institution at the heart of Germany's constitutional order, one question is whether the increasingly tenuous relationship between its decision-making and the text of the Basic Law poses risks to the stability of the political system, and to the Court's position and standing with German citizens?

Some comparison with the jurisprudence of the Supreme Court is also worthy of note. In rejecting any claim to a timeless validity in constitutional meaning with respect to the fundamental value of human dignity, the *BVerfG* has more clearly adopted a living constitution approach to constitutional interpretation. As the chapter will show, although this approach is quite common to modern constitutional courts, some critical observers have argued that the living instrument approach has been taken to such extremes by the Court that it is often difficult to follow its reasoning. As with the decision-making of the Supreme Court seen in the US reapportionment cases which recognised the evolving conception of equality in society and American history, so the *BVerfG*'s decision to strike down the 5 percent, then 3 percent, hurdles for European Parliament elections evidences a shifting balance away from the militant democracy and managing threats to stability, and towards a greater realisation of the value of equality and human dignity in the Basic Law's fundamental rights section. One interpretation could be that the *BVerfG* is edging towards a normalisation of German identity where, at least for European Parliament elections, German citizens voting for smaller parties no longer have to be disenfranchised to protect the integrity of the political system.

Are these developments in the Court's jurisprudence the result of a change in the threats that it perceives to the free democratic basic order (i.e. a change in actual "conditions" [*Verhältnisse*] as it put it in the *European Parliament II Case* (2011)), are the developments the result of the Court re-formulating its decision-making according to a changing conception of equality, or does the Court's willingness to reimagine constitutional principles suggest it is also reimagining its own constitutional and political role? The shift towards constitutional case law in Germany and away from legal positivism is indicative of the effect that the *BVerfG* has wrought on the country's legal order since it began hearing cases in 1951. That effect reflects a shift away from the traditional German legal concept of *Begriffsjurisprudenz*, reflecting the scientific, systematic analysis of law associated with legal positivism, to a less methodologically consistent and more politically aware style of decision-making by the *BVerfG* (see Schlink, 1994: 220–221). The important place given to law in determining whether statutes, the actions of the state, and the judicial decisions of the ordinary courts conform with the Basic Law has led the *BVerfG* inexorably into areas of political and social policy. One of the reasons for this is that some of the Court's most contentious decisions do not actually settle an issue in a way that decisions of the US Supreme Court are accepted as settled even when people disagree over them. As will also be shown, though, this indeterminacy also allows for the possibility of the Court changing course.

Bernhard Schlink's criticism of the Court as a respected German legal scholar, and constitutional court judge of the federal state of *Nord-Rhein Westfalen*, was significant. Schlink argues that the Court's jurisprudence has simply allowed the losers in the legislative sphere to get their policies enacted by submitting to the rule of Karlsruhe (1994: 215). One aspect of this is the abstract review process where recognised organs of state, including parliamentary groups of sufficient size, can challenge political decisions that go against them by appealing to the justices in Karlsruhe. In this way, the parliamentary opposition defeated in the *Bundestag* or the state (*Land*) that sees a decision go against it in the Federal Council (*Bundesrat*) is "given a new chance to challenge the winning majority and to continue to debate their differences of opinion" (Rinken, 2002: 65).

Schlink has also suggested that the methodological consistency of the rulings of the *BVerfG* has been found wanting as it intervenes in ever increasing areas of social and political life based on its sense for what decision might best fit the rubric of society. There are risks here if the Court is calibrating the correctness of its decisions less against the fundamental precepts of the Basic Law and more against what Schlink calls its "feel for what is indicated by social and political life—for what is accepted and 'fits' into the social and political landscape" (1994: 215). If the Court has simply become another actor in Germany's political firmament, the concern would be that it is endangering not only its position as one of the country's most respected institutions, but the respect Germans have for law itself. Moreover, as Collings notes, the Court "cites itself far more often than it cites the constitution" (2015: 302) which raises concerns about whether German constitutionalism is metamorphosing as a result of developing understandings of the Basic Law or the Court's own enormous case law. The threshold between where constitutional understandings end and the *BVerfG*'s repetition of its own case law begins is increasingly hard to define. One example is the rule of optimisation for basic rights, which when subjected to the Court's balancing exercise makes basic rights more of a lottery than a constitutional guarantee.

> The 'rule of optimization'—as much individual freedom as can be realised in accordance with what is legally and actually possible—is such an open-ended concept that it can justify any state intrusions upon freedoms. Although the BVerfG does not actually permit every state intrusion, its

> decision to confirm or reject a particular intrusion may often come as a surprise, pleasant or unpleasant, depending upon one's point of view.
>
> (Schlink, 1994: 213)

Thus, even under the tightly defined structures of the Basic Law, the interpretive methodology of the *BVerfG* has become something of a moving target. The perception that judicial decisions are being made in an arbitrary and unpredictable manner is damaging for the credibility of any court.[3] Decision-making which jettisons the Court's own long-standing case law and neglects actual circumstances in favour of what Schlink calls a "feel" (1994: 215) for preferred or popular outcomes carries dangers, not least that it risks undermining the stability which has underpinned the success of post-war German constitutionalism.

Electoral Thresholds: The Lessons of Weimar

Although the *Bundesverfassungsgericht*'s power to ban political parties that threaten the free democratic basic order is its most prominent power, it is the statutory 5 percent hurdle for electoral success which is the most countermajoritarian element of Germany's democracy. Only political parties that gain 5 percent of the national vote or more will get seats in the *Bundestag*, while individuals voting for parties that fail to reach the 5 percent hurdle see their vote wasted. Since the founding of the Federal Republic, the high democratic cost of electoral hurdles has been viewed as a necessary price to avoid the fate of the Weimar Republic.

The introduction of electoral thresholds in electoral laws in the 1950s can only be understood against the background of the development and ultimate collapse of the Weimar Republic (Wenner, 1986: 5). Wenner notes that the fact that "the collapse of the Weimar Republic was also due to the fragmentation of the party system … is often seen as confirmation of the 'Weimar experience' and an argument—also accepted by the *BVerfG*—for the necessity of a restriction on electoral equality" (1986: 38). The inability of the Weimar Parliament to function due to the fragmentation effect of smaller parties resulted in government's increasing reliance on executive institutions and channels, which were often supplemented by unofficial networks parallel to the state apparatus. It was into these unofficial but well-oiled executive mechanisms that Hitler stepped in 1933. For Germany's post-war founders the tragedy of Weimar was a reminder of how dangerous power vacuums could be. As a consequence the constructive vote of no confidence was enshrined in the Basic Law to ensure that no federal chancellor could be removed without the election of a replacement.[4] During Weimar, the Parliament's inability to agree on replacement chancellors was made more acute by the plethora of small parties which prevented an agreement among more moderate parties taking shape. The lesson that democracy needed to be credible, even at the risk of sacrificing a little democracy to the demands of a stable process, was one that Germany's post-war founders took to heart.

The experience of Weimar and the 1930s demonstrated that aspirational rights provisions were meaningless if the constitutional order which guaranteed them was overthrown through democratic mechanisms. This was the paradox of the constituent moment which created the Basic Law where preserving democracy meant limiting democracy, and preserving the individual rights of the people meant limiting the power of the people. Since political disunity was seen as one of the major flaws that crippled the Weimar Republic, the question for the German framers became how to ensure an electoral system that would be both representative and promote political unity. The rule that parties should achieve a minimum threshold of electoral success in order to enter the *Bundestag* has been a feature of the German electoral system since 1949, and by 1952 a 5 percent rule had been adopted at almost every level of the federal government (Kommers and Miller, 2012: 254). Many of the parliaments of the German states also prescribed electoral hurdles, so the principle of electing a parliament capable of functioning preceded the Basic Law (Wenner, 1986: 90–91).

Nevertheless, at the Parliamentary Council which drafted the Basic Law, there was disagreement over the part played by smaller parties in the demise of Weimar. Some representatives of smaller parties were strongly against the proposal for a 5 percent electoral hurdle which they saw as an effort to permanently stabilise the position of the larger parties (Wenner, 1986: 91). Some representatives "already saw the danger clearly at that time that the vitality of political life could be considerably restricted by the imposition of an electoral hurdle" and that "a young, energetic movement that emerges from the people below and tries to rectify the maladministration of larger parties could be stopped in its tracks by the constitution" (Wenner, 1986: 91).[5] Of course, the smaller parties had a point, which is why the debate over electoral hurdles has never gone away. However, in 1948 when this debate was taking place, the majority of delegates had likely seen enough of young energetic movements that burst forth from the people. When judging the constitutionality of barring clauses—which "justify distinctions between votes"—the legislature's ability to function stands out as a fundamental criterion in the context of the history of the Basic Law and the *BVerfG*'s jurisprudence (see Kommers and Miller, 2012: 256).

While members of the Court and German public figures have perhaps rightly chastised the established political parties for creating a sense of ossification within the system, the maintenance of the 5 percent hurdle at the EU level does not seem to fit into this category. Rather, it seems a reasonable measure to ensure that the only institution to be democratically elected by all EU citizens is able to function. Fourteen EU states currently have electoral thresholds for the allocation of seats in EP elections (Sabbati, Sgueo, and Dobreva, 2019). Recent decisions by the Italian and Czech Constitutional Courts upheld the constitutionality of thresholds for EP elections, with both courts diverging from the reasoning of the *BVerfG* (see, for example, Smekal and Vyhnánek, 2016; Delledonne, 2019). The argument is sometimes made by those opposing the hurdle that many far right parties such as the Front National in France clear the hurdle easily and so it chiefly serves to exclude smaller, esoteric, and generally non-extremist parties such as (in Germany) the Animal Protection Party (*Tierschutzpartei*), and the Pirate Party (*Piraten*), among others. The risk is, however, that too many representatives from smaller parties can prevent the mainstream parties from forming a majority, allowing extremist parties to frustrate parliamentary business. In the Weimar Republic, the fragmentation of the *Reichstag* due to the plethora of smaller parties brought the legislature to a standstill and democracy into disrepute, with terrible consequences.

Striking the correct balance between ensuring a stable and functional democratic system, and the election of a representative parliament which reflects the preferences of the electorate is inherently problematic. Electoral thresholds are always likely to attract criticism from some quarter, particularly from those parties and their supporters which are losing out. The main route for political parties and citizens challenging rules such as the 5 percent hurdle is the constitutional complaint mechanism, allowing complainants to file a petition with the *BVerfG* when they consider one of their constitutional rights has been interfered with. Apart from providing the means by which the electoral hurdles for EP elections were ruled unconstitutional, the mechanism for constitutional complaints (or *Verfassungsbeschwerden*) has played an especially important role in establishing a democratic constitutional culture in Germany.

Constitutional Complaints

The creation of a reliable constitutional culture in Germany has been seen as an important adjunct to the structural safeguards in the Basic Law. It might also be the case, however, that elements of the structure of the constitution have contributed to the forging of a constitutional culture. The ability of German citizens and political and state actors to file constitutional complaints with the *BVerfG* represents an interesting German variation on separation of powers principles. Within Germany's constitutional system the Basic Law confers independent rights on five institutions: the federal government (chancellor and cabinet), president, *Bundestag* (lower house of parliament), *Bundesrat* (upper house of parliament), and *Bundesverfassungsgericht* (Federal Constitutional Court), and are the Federal Republic's highest constitutional organs (Kommers and Miller, 2012: 152). The Constitutional Court is *primus inter pares* among these organs because "it has the authority to define the others' institutional rights and duties when resolving conflicts between them" (Kommers and Miller, 2012: 152). Where conflicts occur, such as between individual political parties, or between political parties and the *Bundestag*, they can become the subject of *Organstreit* proceedings before the *BVerfG*. Constitutional scholars tend to see separation of powers in terms of a "creative tension" between the Parliament and federal government, a view that is anchored in the Basic Law itself (Kommers and Miller, 2012: 152).

Verfassungsbeschwerden (Constitutional Complaints)

The Basic Law allows "any person alleging that one of his basic rights ... has been infringed by public authority" (Basic Law, Art. 93(1) No. 4a) to file a complaint directly with the Court. Although originally existing only as a statutory privilege to petition the Court, the popularity of this direct route to the Court led the German Parliament to amend the Basic Law making the right of petition a constitutional and not merely statutory right. By 1970 the Court had received over 21,000 constitutional complaints, representing 96 percent of its caseload (Kommers, 1991: 841). In 2015, the *BVerfG* received 5,739 constitutional complaints, representing 97 percent of its caseload. (Bundesverfassungsgericht, 2015). Between 1951, when it began hearing cases, and 2001 the Court heard 135,000 constitutional complaints, 96 percent of which came from private citizens (Collings, 2015: 287). The right to petition the Court which is now a constitutional right is significant in two ways. First, the popularity of this complaints procedure among ordinary Germans seems indicative of a German public which, to paraphrase Ronald Dworkin, take their rights seriously, seeing in the *BVerfG* a body which is worthy of respect. As Rinken notes: "by protecting his/her basic rights and enforcing his/her interests, the citizen is also fighting for the realisation of the fundamental principles of the constitution" (2002: 67). Perhaps just as significant is that in the post-1949 period the right to petition was viewed by the Court "as an important means of instructing Germans in the ways of the Constitution and alerting them to their constitutional rights and responsibilities" (Kommers, 1991: 841). Nonetheless, the chances of a constitutional complaint succeeding in Karlsruhe are quite remote. Of the 117,528 complaints submitted between 1951 and 1998, only 3,000 were upheld (2.62 percent) (Rinken, 2002: 68). Insofar as German citizens have embraced the notion of constitutional petition to the *BVerfG* and view the Karlsruhe Court in positive terms it might be suggested that a constitutional culture of sorts has taken hold in Germany.

Organstreitverfahren (Organ of State Law Suits)

The jurisprudence of the Basic Law rests principally on the theory that separation of powers in modern parliamentary democracies "manifests itself most effectively not in the checks and balances among branches of government but in the duty of opposition parties to confront and publicise the misdeeds of the ruling majority" (Kommers, 2006: 116). The Christian Democrats (CDU), which led German governments until the late 1960s, had hoped that there would be strong ties between the federal government and the *BVerfG*; the Social Democrats (SPD) hoped the Court would serve as an instrument of opposition (Collings, 2015: 9). Ultimately it was the SPD hope that was realised. The Court's repeated affirmation of the "constitutional legitimacy and democratic necessity of parliamentary opposition" has, Collings observes, proved to be "one of the early Court's greatest contributions to the democratisation of West German politics" (2015: 9). The *Weltanschauung* of the Basic Law, as enunciated by Karlsruhe, is that opposition forces need the support of law in order to subject state authority to proper scrutiny, and rests on the assumption that without the enforcement of institutional rules, mechanisms, and hurdles, there would be no impediments to the abuse of power. Where such rules and safeguards are solely enforced and applied by the political branches—as seen with the US malapportionment issue—political parties, and disenfranchised or disempowered groups, are left with few, if any, remedies available to them within the parameters of the political system itself. Taking the fight against malapportionment into the federal court system was seen (at the time) as an extraordinary step, whereas under the Basic Law, political actors or individuals going to Karlsruhe to seek redress when rules have been broken or rights violated is seen as axiomatic.

One condition for realising the values of the *Verfassungsstaat* is that there is a vibrant system of political opposition, which the Court has enunciated in a number of *Organstreit* proceedings. Political parties are also recognised as organs of state in the Basic Law, as they are seen as crucial in the "formation of the political will of the people" (Art. 21(1)). Roman Herzog, the former *BVerfG* president (and president of Germany), credits the party system for its stabilising effect on the state created by the Basic Law, at least over the first 40 years of the Federal Republic (1993: 399). Yet, through its decisions regarding the 5 percent electoral hurdle at the EU level—which arose out of constitutional complaints filed by German citizens *and* German political parties—the Court has been controversially prepared to inject new life into the party system where it perceives no credible threats to stability.

Political organs of the state (including parties) will file *Organstreit* complaints with the *Bundesverfassungsgericht* when, for example, they feel that the majority parties have attempted to deny them reasonable representation in parliamentary committees, or have otherwise sought to use their majority position to subvert principles found in the Basic Law. This interesting utilisation of the Court as an ally by German political parties illustrates how Germany evinces a more nuanced picture of constitutionalism than a simple conflict between judicial and political channels. German political parties are only too eager to file an *Organstreit* complaint with the *BVerfG*, such as the Green Party did in the *Green Party Exclusion Case* (1986a) after it was excluded on national security grounds from the committee that controlled the German Secret Service. From the perspective of politics in the UK or the US, it may seem strange and even problematic for the health of political debate when politicians run to the courts every time a political decision goes against them. However, according to the Basic Law, members of the *Bundestag* are "representatives of the whole people, not bound by orders or instructions, and responsible only to their conscience" (Art. 38(1)). Thus, if the rights of parties in the *Bundestag* are not respected, then the implications are that the people's rights are not being respected either.

Compared with the appellate jurisdiction of the US Supreme Court which restricts the way that cases can come before it, there are far more avenues by which cases and questions can come before the *Bundesverfassungsgericht*.

Organstreit proceedings are a form of abstract judicial review, and can originate from the government, from members of the German Parliament (the *Bundestag*), or from political parties, which are specially recognised in the Basic Law as the vehicles by which the popular sovereignty of the people is manifested. Since *Organstreit* proceedings can be initiated at the request of political parties or other parts of the government this means there are also more avenues for the *Bundesverfassungsgericht* to intervene in the political process. Nowhere has this been more apparent than the Court's involvement in facilitating the entry of new political forces into the German party system.

Shaking up the Party System

Within the value system of the Basic Law the principle of popular sovereignty exists in tension with that of representative government. The latter is intended to dilute and limit the vagaries and extremities of popular will, first, through a system of proportional representation and, second, through the exclusion from the German Parliament of parties that fail to break through the 5 percent hurdle. For decades, this adherence to the militant democracy and the inability of any smaller parties to jump over the hurdle meant that party politics in West Germany was limited to a duopoly: the Social Democrats and Christian Democrats.[6] As discussed in the previous section, the role of political parties is prescribed in the Basic Law, making them organs of state responsible for the "formation of the political will of the people" (Art. 21(1)). Since the Basic Law's establishment, the *BVerfG* has played an important role in safeguarding the stability of the party system and slowly integrating newer parties into the constitutional order. With its decisions in the European Parliament electoral threshold cases, however, the Court has demonstrated a distinct preference for renewal over the stability-driven telos of militant democracy.

The de facto two-party system created by the Basic Law remained in place until the emergence of the Green Party as a political force in the 1980s. At the Federal Republic's founding there were possibly good reasons for wanting to keep the German people's political desires more tightly circumscribed, but as German politics and society stabilised into predictability, so came the risk of political and societal ossification. While the principle of free speech was prioritised as a fundamental right in *Lüth Case* (1958), the militant democracy principle as reflected in electoral thresholds and proportional representation made the Federal Republic's political system resistant to new political forces and parties. In his dissent in *Green Party Exclusion Case* (1986a), Ernst-Wolfgang Böckenförde complained about the oligarchical tendency in Germany's established parties, even as federal president Richard von Weizsäcker criticised them for their ossification and lack of creativity (Kommers and Miller, 2012: 237). Yet the Court is itself a product of Germany's party system, given that half of its justices are appointed by the lower house of the German Parliament (the *Bundestag*) and half by the upper house representing the German states (the *Bundesrat*). The

Green Party finally managed to break through the 5 percent hurdle in 1983 and, following reunification, the East German left party managed to do the same in 1998 (Scholz, 2013). Over decades the Court handed down an unambiguous line of jurisprudence that the 5 percent hurdle promoted political unity (Kommers and Miller, 2012: 263), one of the chief goals of the stability-minded German framers following the experience of Weimar. Although the rise of the Green Party changed the configurational complexity of German party politics, it did not affect the overall preeminence of the SPD and CDU in coalition building.

The Court's emerging role in breathing new life into Germany's rather staid democracy can be seen in the example of the Green Party, which went from pariahs in the 1970s—when the party was seen as a threat to stability due to the presence of communists in its ranks—to becoming part of Gerhard Schroeder's government in 1998, with its former leader Joschka Fischer becoming foreign minister and vice-chancellor (see Herzog, 1993: 399). During the 1980s the Greens were excluded from a parliamentary committee handling the German Secret Service on security grounds, leading to the *Green Party Exclusion Case* (1986a). However, their journey from outcasts to the establishment was completed in January 2001 when Brun-Otto Bryde became the first justice appointed to the *BVerfG* on the Greens' recommendation (Collings, 2015: 286). Collings notes that the Greens' "engagement and occasional victories in Karlsruhe played an important role in the party's trajectory towards the constitutional and political mainstream" (2015: 286). It is therefore "a telling example both of the Court's role in integrating the country's political forces and of its related effect of taming the country's political process" (Collings, 2015: 286).

Overall, the Court's involvement in the integration of the Greens into the political system has illustrated that it has often had a better awareness of the changing social context than the political branches or established parties. This awareness has not always come swiftly, as the decisions that went against the Greens illustrate. However, even then, the powerful dissent of Justice Böckenförde in *Green Party Exclusion Case* (1986a) seemingly laid the conditions for future victories for the Greens in Karlsruhe. In his dissent against the Greens' exclusion from the *Bundestag's* Secret Service committee on arbitrary grounds, Böckenförde argued that it is the

> general participation in the formation of the political will of Parliament—a process emanating from general intellectual and political discussion and argumentation—that legitimates the inherent right of a parliamentary majority to decide issues of public policy. One process cannot be separated from the other. … The principle of complete participation of all—including individuals and parliamentary parties—is not merely an axiom but is also an inalienable principle of a representative parliamentary democracy.
>
> *Green Party Exclusion Case* (1986a; quoted in Kommers and Miller, 2012: 225)

Böckenförde's dissent in the *Green Party Exclusion Case* helps explain, I think, why Wilhelm Geck (quoted in Collings, 2015: xxxvi) saw the Court as being so instrumental to the development of democratic understanding in post-war Germany. Six months after the Greens lost in the *Exclusion Case*, they won a victory in Karlsruhe when the Court struck down a provision in a tax statute affecting political parties. Böckenförde wrote a separate opinion in *Party Finance V Case* (1986b) noting that he would have gone further to protect small parties like the Greens, writing that legislation that bolsters the "oligarchical" and "careerist" elements of the established parties erodes Parliament's representative character (quoted in Kommers and Miller, 2012: 226). The Court sees its role in helping the political opposition in the *Bundestag* as an important one, both to ensure that state power is held to account and thus to ensure the representative rights of all German citizens are fulfilled by ensuring that the parliamentary majority meets its obligations.

The Court may well have seen the European Parliament cases in the same context as those from the 1980s onwards in which it supported the Greens in their battles with the established parties. In other words, the EP cases of 2011 and 2014, like the Greens' struggles, were also constitutional battles by smaller parties against the established ones. However, Germany's political position has changed in Europe since the 1980s. There are more significant threats to political stability than in 1979 when the Court last addressed the question of the electoral threshold at the EP level. The European Parliament of 1979 was a much weaker institution than in 2016, yet the Court upheld the 5 percent hurdle then, despite it mattering far less than today whether the Parliament could function or not. Today, the German role is pivotal to the success of European integration and the EU generally. Yet for all the Court's references in *EPII Case* and *EPIII Case* to the importance of changing its reasoning if the context changes, the decisions of a bare majority of justices to strike down the electoral thresholds seemed to ignore the more visible threats to stability in recent years.

The political landscape began to change ahead of the 2005 German federal election when the Democratic Socialist Party (PDS), the post-reunification successor to the (ruling) East German Socialist Unity Party, formed an alliance with disaffected elements of Schroeder's SPD. The new *Linke Partei* (Left Party) represented a significant new political force, polling more than the Greens in the 2005 election. The sudden presence of new parties on the political scene was a challenge to the established dominance of the CDU and the SPD, but it also posed challenges to the *BVerfG*. The Left Party was already comfortably above the 5 percent hurdle after 2005, but the new party political constellation appears to have induced the *BVerfG* to reconsider long-established justifications for keeping the rule in place for elections to the European Parliament. The Court's decisions on the constitutionality of thresholds in *EPII Case* and *EPIII Case*, and the scholarly and political reaction to those rulings are examined in the next two sections.

A "Parallel Legislator"?

Case summary—The European Parliament Cases

In its decision in 1979 the *Bundesverfassungsgericht* had held that the 5 percent hurdle was valid for European Parliament elections. Following *Organstreit* (organ of state) proceedings and constitutional complaints the Court revisited the constitutionality of the electoral hurdles again in 2011. By a bare 5–3 majority in *EPII* the Court ruled that the 5 percent electoral hurdle was unconstitutional. In response, the *Bundestag* passed a revised statute authorising a 3 percent hurdle for European Parliament elections. *EPIII* arose from a combination of *Organstreit* proceedings and individual constitutional complaints from voters. There was no automatic presumption on the *BVerfG*'s part that the 3 percent hurdle would be unconstitutional as its effects might be different; therefore, a separate substantive assessment was required (Pernice-Warnke, 2014: 1144–1145). Since the Court had repeatedly upheld the 5 percent hurdle for the German *Bundestag*, a decision to quash the new 3 percent hurdle would send a clear message "that European parliamentary democracy was inferior to its German counterpart" (Collings, 2015: 291). In its 2014 judgment in *EPIII*, the Court struck down the 3 percent hurdle as well, again with a 5–3 majority despite a change in some of the justices in the interim. One question raised by the EP case decisions was whether it was just a matter of time before the Court struck down the 5 percent hurdle for *Bundestag* elections?

Lisbon Déjà Vu

The *BVerfG*'s rulings in the electoral threshold cases (*EPII* and *EPIII*) retraced some of the terrain covered in its controversial and exceptionalism-heavy judgment in the *Lisbon Treaty Case* (2009), which laid out a state-centric conception of democracy rooted in the *pouvoir constituant* of the German people. Christian Tomuschat argues that in its *Lisbon* ruling the Court seems to have "expressed its wish to prevent the European Union from developing its own democratic legitimacy" (2009: 1261). One critique of the rulings in *EPII* and *EPIII* is that the Court does not regard the European Parliament as a real parliament that possesses genuine democratic legitimacy, thus explaining why the Karlsruhe justices were willing to accept fragmentation in the European Parliament that they would not accept in the German *Bundestag*. Critics of the Court's decisions in *EPII* and *EPIII* can certainly also find evidence in the *Lisbon* ruling to support such a claim.

The Court's ruling in *Lisbon* argued that the "citizenship of the [European] Union is solely derived from the will of the Member States and does not constitute a people of the Union, which could exercise self-determination as a legal entity giving itself a constitution" (2009, Para. 346). The overall reaction from legal and constitutional scholars to *Lisbon* was profoundly negative (see Kommers and Miller, 2012: 349). Many viewed the *obiter dicta*-heavy ruling as excessively hubristic in tone. As Christian Tomuschat puts it: "far from reflecting the views of the framers, the ruling reads like a political manifesto from the judges"

(2009: 1259). Another writer called the judgment "lengthy, repetitive, meandering and sometimes outright fuzzy, [and] often seems to betray an angry acrimony, an uneasy posturing" (Schönberger, 2009: 1207). If the Court's ruling in *Lisbon* seems contradictory by arguing both for and against European integration, and for and against state sovereignty, then the Basic Law itself may be partly to blame. As Kommers and Miller note, in decisions regarding Europe and international law, "the inherent tension between sovereignty and openness that was written into the Basic Law" has often seen the Court attempting to "reconcile seemingly irreconcilable commands" (2012: 351).

In its *Lisbon* judgment, the *BVerfG* articulated an extreme state-centric and German-centric view on what can and cannot be considered 'democracy'. In the Court's view, the European Union was an association of states, not a federal state, and its authority was derived solely from EU member states which were signatories to the various European treaties from Rome to Maastricht to Lisbon. Perhaps the most puzzling aspect of the *Lisbon* ruling was that although the Court ultimately ruled that the treaty was compatible with the Basic Law, its reasoning pointed in the opposite direction. For example, the Court argued that the EU fails to meet the standard of democratic legitimacy found at the nation-state, but that any attempt to increase the EU's democratic legitimacy by becoming a federal state would conflict with the eternity clause of the Basic Law which forbids any constitutional amendments which transgress the principles of democracy, human dignity, and federalism found in Articles 1 and 20. The result of the ruling, then, is that the EU is "trapped in a conceptual and constitutional limbo" and "wedged between its alleged democratic deficit and the prohibition against the transition to a federal state" which could only be solved by the "intervention of the people as the constituent power" (Schönberger, 2009: 1210). The Court also seems trapped, but by its own logic. If the EP is not a real parliament possessing real democratic legitimacy, then the representation arguments it made in *EPII* and *EPIII* would seem to be a moot point. If it *is* a real parliament, then its ability to function seems quite important.

European Parliament II and III Cases

Since the *BVerfG*'s electoral threshold decisions in 2011 and 2014, anti-EU and far right parties have continued to perform increasingly well across Europe, particularly in the EU Parliament elections of 2014. While anti-EU parties did not perform as well in the EU Parliament elections of 2019, the two main party groups[7] in the European Parliament (EP) lost their overall majority for the first time in four decades, delivering a parliament in Strasbourg that is more fragmented than ever before (see Hobolt, 2019).

There are numerous critiques of the Court's decisions in *EPII* and *EPIII* on their methodological grounds, including that the decisions seem to ignore the Court's previous case law, or are based on questionable assumptions. Both of these criticisms are addressed below. However, the larger problem with the Court's decisions is that they are based on the premise that when the conditions change that originally justified the imposition of the hurdle, the decision should be reassessed. This would be reasonable but for the fact that conditions *have* changed, but in ways that run *counter* to the logic of the Court's decisions. Since the *BVerfG*'s previous decision on electoral thresholds in 1979 there has been an increase in the powers of the EP due to the Lisbon Treaty, making it a "co-legislature" on par with the Council of the EU (Hobolt, 2019: 17), while another development has been the greater threat posed by far right parties in recent years. However, according to the logic of the Court's previous decisions—which emphasised the need to maintain stability and preserve the ability of a legislature to function—both of these changes would have pointed to the conclusion that there was *even more* cause to maintain the electoral hurdle (at either 5 percent or 3 percent), rather than strike it down as the Court did. One key question to consider is why the *BVerfG*'s decisions in the two EP cases diverted not only from the Court's previous reasoning, but also from the stability-centric picture of German constitutionalism that the book has advanced so far?

In its decision in *European Parliament II Case* (2011), the *BVerfG* further demonstrated its willingness to jettison long-standing aspects of its jurisprudence in response to a perceived change in circumstances:

> A barring clause once perceived as permissible may not, in consequence, be regarded as constitutional in perpetuity. Rather, a different constitutional judgement may arise if circumstances materially change. If the electoral lawmaker finds him or herself in changed conditions in this sense, so he or she must take them into account. Only the current circumstances are relevant to the question of further retention of the barring clause.
>
> (*European Parliament II Case*, 2011)

The decision to hold the 5 percent electoral hurdle as unconstitutional took many commentators of German constitutional law by surprise. As Strohmeier noted:

> Even though changes in the case law of the *BVerfG*, particularly in the area of electoral law, are by now less the exception but rather the rule, this turnaround is especially surprising.
>
> (Strohmeier, 2014: 352; translated from German original)[8]

Although less direct than Schlink's critique of the Court, Strohmeier's remarks are suggestive of the less methodologically consistent style of decision-making from the Court that Schlink critiqued. Such surprises cut against the grain of what constitutionalism is supposed to be about—to reduce uncertainty (see, for example, Kay, 1998: 22–27). A decision expanding the scope of equality which might be seen by many public commentators as progressive and positive becomes more disconcerting if it has been arrived at through a process that seems arbitrary or has been based on questionable assumptions. Both of these critiques seem relevant to the Court's 2011 and 2014 EP decisions.

Aside from such a significant change in the Court's case law being based on a bare (5–3) majority of the Court, the cases and opinions also highlighted the effect that abolishing the 5 percent hurdle could have on the ability of the EP to form a majority on certain issues. Contrary to the logic behind the *BVerfG* ruling, the existing fragmentation of the EP is already very high, and a majority of the members can often only be achieved through cooperation of both of the largest parliamentary groupings (Strohmeier, 2014: 355–356). As Sara Hobolt notes, the 2019 elections have produced the most fragmented EP to date, with many voters abandoning the traditional centre-right and centre-left parties and opting for smaller right-wing populist, liberal, and green parties (2019: 17). The ghosts of Weimar continue to animate debates over the necessity of particular features of the militant democracy, perhaps none more so than the capacity of a parliament to function, and the political consequences when it is unable to.

Following the decision in *EPII* one CDU member of the *Bundestag* argued that without the 5 percent hurdle, the 13 or 14 parties which would then come from Germany would be those which

> neither belong to the party families, which could join together in political groups in the European Parliament, nor could they be integrated within these. In this respect, without the electoral hurdle, we would produce a number of non-attached parliamentarians who could substantially endanger the increasingly important functioning of cooperation between institutions.
>
> (Grindel, 2013; translated from German original)[9]

The criticism of the decision, then, is that in contrast to when the Court last looked at this question in 1979 and upheld the 5 percent hurdle, the direction of travel has been towards a more powerful EU Parliament where its ability to function matters far more now than it did for the weaker parliament of the late 1970s.

In its ruling striking down the 3 percent hurdle for European elections, the key words in the decision—repeated 37 times each—were '*Wahlrechtsgleichheit*' ('electoral equality') and '*Chancengleichheit*' ('equal opportunity'); the broader context in which the Court invoked these principles—repeated 5 times—was "*die Grundsätze der Wahlrechtsgleichheit und Chancengleichheit der politischen Parteien*" (the fundamental principles of electoral equality and equal opportunities among political parties). According to one commentator, the main principle enunciated in the Court's opinion was nothing less than "the fundamental idea of democracy itself—one man, one vote" (Siedenbiedel, 2014). Justifying its decision in *EPIII*, the majority opinion argued that electoral law was subject to a high standard of constitutional review.

> The design of electoral law is subject to strict constitutional review. This follows from the general consideration that, in a way, the parliamentary majority acts in its own interest with regulations that affect the conditions of political competition, and that the risk that the respective parliamentary

> majority is guided by the aim to preserve its power, instead of considerations of the common good, is especially high in electoral law.
>
> (*European Parliament III Case*, 2014)

The reference to the 'common good' reflects both its Aristotelian *polis* conception of the Basic Law, and the already stated commitment of the Court to maintain a vibrant political opposition.

The Court then argued that while a threshold could be justified "for the election and continued support of a viable government", such an aspiration at the EP level is "still in its infancy" (2014). In other words, the lack of a government attached to the European Parliament meant, the Court implied, that the Parliament could tolerate a level of party fragmentation which would be unacceptable in the *Bundestag*:

> An actual impact on the European Parliament's ability to function is currently not foreseeable, which means that there is no basis for the legislature's prognosis that, without the three-percent electoral threshold, an impairment of the European Parliament's functioning is looming.
>
> (*EPIII Case*, 2014)

Responding to the reasoning of the majority, the dissent by Justice Mueller in *EPIII* sees the Court as having replaced the judgment of the legislature with its own:

> It is not for the Bundesverfassungsgericht to replace the reasonable decision of the legislature with its own reasonable decision. Ultimately, the Senate's decision leads to accepting the risk of an impairment of the European Parliament's functioning for the duration of at least one election period. I cannot perceive this as a constitutional requirement. The impairment of the European Parliament's ability to function is sufficiently important to justify an interference with the principles of electoral equality and equal opportunities of political parties.
>
> (*EPIII Case*, 2014)

Justice Mueller's dissenting opinion evokes Böckenförde's concern that "the court is not and must not be a parallel legislator" (2017: 401). The difference in emphasis between on the one hand, the majority opinion, and on the other, the dissenting opinion and the views of the federal government hinges on the word 'foreseeable'. For the majority opinion, the lack of a foreseeable threat to stability meant that the high cost of interfering with the democratic will of the people through an electoral threshold was unjustified. Yet it was the unforeseeable implications of removing the threshold on the ability of the European Parliament to function which dismayed the dissenting justices, the federal government, and EU officials.[10] Equally perplexing were the Court's highly speculative prognostications (below) in *EPIII* regarding how the decisions might affect voter behaviour.

> It is also possible that clearer political differences between the individual parliamentary groups will increase their internal cohesion. In addition, a changed perception of the European Parliament, resulting from raising the party-specific profiles more strongly, might induce voters more than previously to vote strategically and thus counteract an increase in the number of parties represented in the European Parliament.
>
> (*EPIII Case*, 2014)

The critique of the Court, then, is that it has substituted its highly speculative judgments and knowledge for that of the *Bundestag* with regard to the workings of the European Parliament, while accepting the risk of smaller parties frustrating the formation of a functional majority.

One year after the decision in *EPIII*, the Czech Constitutional Court, which historically has often followed and "approvingly cited" the reasoning of its German counterpart in similar cases (Smekal and Vyhnánek, 2016: 148), diverged from the Karlsruhe line on electoral thresholds. The Czech justices accepted the argument that, following the Lisbon Treaty, it is possible to consider the European Parliament a 'real' parliament, where clear and effective majorities are necessary to ensure its proper functioning, including for the approval and dismissal of the European Commission (Smekal and Vyhnánek, 2016: 157). According to the Czech Court, the 5 percent national threshold was justified because it was a proportionate measure to ensure a European Parliament that was representative and able to function (Smekal and Vyhnánek, 2016: 158).

One particular criticism of the *BVerfG*'s decision to strike down the 5 percent hurdle in European Parliament II Case (2011) is that its justification for the decision painted a picture of the EP not as it was in 2011 but as it was in 1979 (Strohmeier, 2014: 352). What was peculiar, according to Strohmeier, was that the significant expansion of the EP's powers and competencies since the *BVerfG* upheld the 5 percent hurdle in 1979 logically pointed in completely the *opposite* direction to its 2011 decision striking it down (2014: 352). The Court's argument was that the EU Parliament did not have a government attached to it and, thus, it was less dependent on the formation of a stable majority to function. However, as Strohmeier notes, that logic more accurately reflected the weakness of the EP in 1979 when the Court last decided the issue, but not the more powerful parliament of 2011. The whole point of electoral hurdles is to allow a parliament to function by ensuring that splinter parties cannot get into Parliament and so bring the system to a halt. Thus, the 1979 decision upholding the electoral hurdle better fitted the circumstances of today while the 2011 decision better reflected the conditions in 1979 (Strohmeier, 2014: 352).

If the conditions which the Court highlighted to justify its decision actually suggest the opposite—as three dissenting justices also suggested—did the decision simply represent a misunderstanding on the part of the *BVerfG* of how the EP functions and democracy works at the EU level, or was there some other basis for it? Two of the three dissenting justices in *EPII* criticised the decision of the Court's Second Senate for accepting a "possible impairment of the European

Parliament's ability to function in spite of its increased political responsibility" (2011). Directly addressing the point that circumstances supported the 5 percent hurdle even more than in 1979, the dissenting justices noted, first, that the majority on the Court had chosen to strike down the electoral hurdle despite the growth in the EP's competences since 1979 and its increasing political significance, suggesting even more justification for maintaining it than in 1979. Second, they also noted in *EPII* that the Court had taken the decision without explaining how the standards of assessment had changed since the 1979 decision (2011). In its language striking down the 5 percent hurdle, the *BVerfG* has emphasised the heavy toll that electoral hurdles exact on popular sovereignty and the constitutional right of all Germans to participate in their representative democracy. The Court's miscalculation in holding that an impact on the EP's ability to function was not "foreseeable" was illustrated only a couple of months later.

Implications and Aftermath of the Decisions

Alternativ für Deutschland (*AfD*), the anti-immigration party, praised the *BVerfG* decision in *EPIII Case*, calling it "a good signal for democracy in Europe" ('Drei-Prozent-Hürde', 2014a). In the EU Parliament elections of 2014, eurosceptic parties doubled their representation compared to the 2009 elections ('How Eurosceptic', 2014e). Apart from the strong showing of the UK Independence Party (UKIP), France's National Front won 24 out of 74 seats, making it the largest French party in the EP ('Eurosceptic Effect', 2014c). Seven German political parties from the left and right won one seat each in 2014 as a result of the *BVerfG* decisions in 2011 and 2014, including the first neo-Nazi representative to come from Germany. Given these events, both within Germany and at the European level, the Court's view that an impact on the functioning of the EP was not 'foreseeable' seems mistaken. The Court also seemed to understate the risks to stability both within German democracy and at the European level. Instability could ensue at the EU level as a result of increased fragmentation within the EP, and at the German domestic level as more extreme parties are given a higher profile.

The decisions of 2011 and 2014 bring us back to the scholarly critiques of those decisions, of the Court's role in German political life, and of the increasingly unpredictable manner in which it seems to be making decisions. One possible explanation may lie in the increasingly normative bent of German constitutional jurisprudence: that Germans no longer see the Basic Law as "the simple expression of an existential order of power" but as "fundamentally a normative constitution embracing values, rights and duties" (Kommers and Miller, 2012: 45). Notwithstanding the *BVerfG*'s repeated invocation of the term *Verhältnisse* (or 'conditions') as a criterion for determining when a change in its case law may be required due to changing circumstances, the critique is that the Court has in fact been doing quite the opposite by prioritising normative considerations over what the situation and *actual* conditions might require. While the distinctly normative tenor of the Basic Law has been an important feature of German constitutionalism since 1949, without a reasonably consistent *BVerfG* methodology where deviations from its existing case law are convincingly justified, judicially created values may be a fickle orienting star in changing circumstances.

There are several critiques of the Court's decision to strike down the 5 percent hurdle for EP elections. First is that the decision did not sufficiently pay attention to the difficulties that could come from the splintering effect of many smaller parties entering the EP and preventing the formation of a majority within the EP (Strohmeier, 2014). Second is the actual threat to political stability in Germany that could arise due to the higher profile that extremist parties would gain through a seat in the EP. Third was the due respect for separation of powers, and the legislative intent and greater knowledge of legislators regarding the possible effects on the EP of scrapping the hurdle. On this point, two of the dissenting justices in *European Parliament II Case* noted:

> Electoral-law issues are subject to the legislature's political freedom of drafting whose legislative duty imposes restraint on the Federal Constitutional Court with a view to the general nature of the electoral principles.
>
> (*EPII Case*, 2011)

The concern with the Court's jurisprudence regarding the European Parliament decisions—particularly the decision in *EPIII* (2014) which overturned the *Bundestag*'s considered legislative response to Karlsruhe's 2011 decision—is that some of the justices are playing fast and loose with the stability of the European Parliament on the basis of questionable suppositions. Although it's unclear how much attention and weight individual voters attach to decisions by the *BVerfG*, Taylor identifies a further paradox in the Court's reasoning in the EP cases. By implying that the European Parliament was not a proper parliament as the *BVerfG* did, some German voters could be forgiven for wondering whether it was worth bothering to vote at all, or if they did vote, they might see the *BVerfG*'s somewhat disdainful view on the EP as giving them licence to vote for a less serious party (Taylor, 2017: 748) As Taylor notes, while it's perfectly legitimate for voters to experiment with new parties, "that should not happen because they consider the elections or the legislature to be second-rate" (2017: 748).

Some claim that the *EPIII* decision may open up the argument over whether to maintain the (previously sacrosanct) 5 percent hurdle for *Bundestag* elections. One Court observer noted that the *BVerfG* may well have boxed itself into a corner with respect to the *EPIII* decision, committing it to revisit the constitutionality of the electoral threshold at the domestic level.

> Either the *Bundesverfassungsgericht* does not really take the European Parliament seriously, regarding it as a lesser parliament (detractors would say 'a talking shop') for which efficiency is not so important; or the hurdle must also be abolished for *Bundestag* elections sooner or later.
>
> (Siedenbiedel, 2014; translated from German original)[11]

Maximilian Steinbeis argues more directly that the democratic cost of maintaining the 5 percent hurdle domestically has become too high (2015: 45–47). For Steinbeis, the results of the 2013 elections when, as he puts it, 15 percent of the total votes cast or 7 million votes were thrown in the bin, creates a *Bundestag* that does not accurately reflect what Germany looks like politically (2015: 47). Steinbeis believes that as well as simply balancing electoral equality against the ability of a parliament to function, the Court should also include the principle of *Repräsentivität*, and consider in its balancing exercise whether a parliament is a true reflection of a country's political diversity (2015: 47). Fourteen parties achieved between 0.1 percent of the vote and 4.7 percent of the vote and therefore failed to get a seat in parliament, but only four of these parties achieved 1 percent or more (see 'Bundeswahlleiter', 2013). Nevertheless, 15 percent of the vote split between ten or more parties which secure seats in the *Bundestag* would seem precisely the type of Weimar-like situation which would dictate that they be excluded. In other words, while there is undoubtedly an increased democratic cost from a higher percentage of votes going to waste, without a hurdle that would also constitute an even larger proportion of the parliament being fragmented.

The risk if the Court struck down the 5 percent hurdle domestically is that it would make it harder for a parliamentary majority to reach decisions, and would in itself likely prompt further referrals and constitutional complaints to Karlsruhe. The end result in such circumstances might then be a zombie parliament that cannot function, and an ever greater reliance on the Court. A former president of the Court, Hans-Jürgen Papier, sharply criticised the 2014 *EPIII* decision, calling it "correct neither in its result nor in its argumentation" (quoted in "Ex-Verfassungsrichter", 2014d; translated from German original).[12] Papier went on to suggest that a constitutional amendment should be adopted to create clearer conditions for the use of electoral hurdles, possibly with a view to reintroducing the 5 percent hurdle at the EP level and ensuring it remains in place domestically ("Ex-Verfassungsrichter", 2014d).

The 'stability' imperative likely makes the domestic 5 percent threshold safe for now. The *Bundesverfassungsgericht* remains convinced that "whatever its cost in democratic terms, the five percent minimum threshold is still necessary to ensure Parliament's stability and efficacy" (Kommers and Miller, 2012: 263). It is this different standard, though, that has so frustrated MEPs and the federal government in Berlin. In other words, that the *BVerfG* was using the EP as a guinea pig by allowing parties into it that it would not tolerate in the *Bundestag*, and without having to deal with the consequences. Indeed, Justice Mueller's dissent in *EPIII* about the impairment of the EP's function raises this problem. New proposals agreed by the European Parliament and EU Council in 2018 (see Sabbati, Sgueo, and Dobreva, 2019) for an EU-wide electoral hurdle of between 2 and 5 percent for all countries with more than 35 seats in the EP may make the *BVerfG*'s decisions in 2011 and 2014 a moot point, unless the Karlsruhe judges are prepared to initiate a confrontation with the European Court of Justice (CJEU) over the compatibility of the proposals with the Basic Law.

When an ex-president of the Court argues that the 5 percent hurdle should be protected by constitutional amendment from the attention of his former colleagues in Karlsruhe, this suggests at the very least that the justices should re-evaluate their reasoning in the EP cases before turning their attention to the *Bundestag* electoral hurdle. The three dissenting opinions in both *EPII* and *EPIII* provide a good basis for a change of course, which, as noted by Rinken, is what German constitutional jurisprudence allows for (2002: 71–72). Moreover, the increased threats to stability across Europe and the greater fragmentation within German politics with the rise of *AfD* certainly represent a change in material conditions, or (*Verhältnisse*), its oft-invoked word for determining whether a change in its case law is necessary. The rather ossified political edifice that Justice Böckenförde identified in the 1980s may well have needed a shot of adrenalin, which it received with the integration of the Greens and later The Left Party (*Die Linke Partei*) into the German party system. However, whether in terms of reassessing the EP case decisions or any change to the 5 percent hurdle for *Bundestag* elections, the present 'conditions' of fragmentation and far right parties in the ascendancy indicate that a parliament capable of functioning may be more important than judicially administered democratic infusions.

On the Side of the People

In 2013, Andreas Voßkuhle, President of the *Bundesverfassungsgericht* from 2010 to 2020, went to Strasbourg to address around 30 parliamentarians (MEPs) of the European Parliament (Amann et al., 2014b). Voßkuhle's visit followed several high-profile *BVerfG* decisions which were seen as anti-European, including the Lisbon Treaty decision in 2009, and the 2011 decision in *EPII* which abolished the 5 percent hurdle for European Parliament (EP) elections. Decisions were also pending on the constitutionality of the European Central Bank's bond-buying programme, and the constitutionality of the (then) 3 percent hurdle for the EP elections. For two hours, many of the MEPs grilled Voßkuhle about the *BVerfG*'s attitude to the EU, and charged that the Court "doesn't comprehend Europe's idea of democracy" (Amann et al., 2014b). Eventually Voßkuhle hit back, telling the parliamentarians: "Not a single person here has mentioned the words 'citizens' or 'voters'", he said, seeking to rebuke the politicians. "Is your own power the only thing you care about?" (Amann et al., 2014b). President Voßkuhle's comments did not go down well.

Recent constitutional tensions have led to criticism that the role of the *BVerfG* as the ultimate arbiter of all legal and constitutional questions has become too overtly political, based on the perception of it adjudicating in ever increasing areas of social policy and politics (see, for example, Müller, 2014). Responding to these criticisms, including some from the German government in Berlin, Voßkuhle commented that the Court is on the side of the people and that without the aid of the legal system they wouldn't have a voice (Amann et al., 2014b). Such comments from the most prominent judge in Europe's largest country at first seem startling and taken at face value might suggest a lack of faith in Germany's democratic institutions.

Voßkuhle has also argued that the role of the courts is merely to "define parameters within which politics can unfold" (Voßkuhle and Von Rahden, 2013).[13] Even this more 'limited' estimation of the political power of the courts does nothing to dispel the notion of judges as platonic guardians. Although Voßkuhle's comments sound superficially similar to Justice Stephen Breyer's view that the US Supreme Court is the "boundary commission" of the Constitution (Breyer, 2016), they seem to envisage very different judicial roles.[14] Echoing Rostow's idea that "man can be free because the state is not" (1952: 195), Breyer sees the Constitution as creating a vast open space where citizens can live their lives. Based on Voßkuhle's comments, however, the role of courts would seem to be about defining not merely the boundaries of political activity, but the playing field as well. Such an expansive view of the judicial role seems surprising to Anglo-American and common law sensibilities where there is an inclination for senior judges to downplay the significance of their political roles, and to stress their adjudicative function in interpreting law, but not making it.

This effort by judges to downplay the political significance of the judicial role, particularly with respect to the US federal courts, often seems at odds with the commentary of legal and media analysts who rarely if ever underplay the political significance of the courts, often due to the momentary drama of high-profile cases. All decisions of the *BVerfG* begin with the words "*In Namen des Volkes*" ("In the name of the people"). Voßkuhle's view that the Court is on the side of the people may perhaps be more understandable in the historical context of the Karlsruhe Court and the constitutional complaint mechanism. After all, well over 100,000 Germans have petitioned the Court since its establishment, even if only around 2 percent of complaints are upheld. Perhaps this statistic tells its own story about the development of German constitutionalism since 1949. The constitutional complaint procedure, as Rinken notes, "crystallises the importance of the basic rights for the whole constitutional order" (2002: 66), while Stephen Macedo observes that "the language of liberal justice and rights, the logic of respect for persons, and the practice in our politics of public justification can serve as the organising focus of positive liberal ideals" (1990: 5). Thus, the very possibility of the civically conscious German citizen being aware of their fundamental rights and being able to file a constitutional complaint with the Court seemingly represented progress for liberal constitutional government.

However, for the president of the *BVerfG* to view the justices as being 'on the side of the people' would seem unthinkable from a senior judge in the United States. Does Voßkuhle perhaps see the *BVerfG* as having a superior relationship with the German people than they have with their elected representatives, or simply a different one? Certainly Voßkuhle is not the first *BVerfG* judge to find fault with Germany's political institutions, as Böckenförde's complaint about the oligarchical tendency among the established parties indicates. Nevertheless, in a country which has learned the hard way where excessive respect for authority can lead, unqualified respect for either judges or politicians may be equally dangerous. The risk, then, is that if the German people see the *Bundesverfassungsgericht* as the best means of having their political and social needs addressed, they may feel less need to participate in the mechanisms of representative democracy, and so remain engaged and vigilant in defending their constitutional order.

Ivory Tower Decision-Making

One of Bernhard Schlink's concerns was not merely the *BVerfG*'s increasingly opaque methodology but the absence of robust critiques of its decisions among German academics. Following Schlink's earlier critique of the Court and the scholarship surrounding its case law, legal and constitutional law scholars have since launched powerful broadsides against the Court's rulings in the electoral threshold cases and other contentious decisions such as its *Lisbon Treaty Case* judgment (see, for example, Halberstam and Möllers, 2009; Taylor, 2017). The common law practice of dissenting and discursive opinions, which are not part of the German civil law tradition but which the Court has embraced since the Federal Constitutional Court Act (FCCA) was amended to permit them in 1971, has contributed to an improvement in the quality of decision-making. Rinken writes that dissenting opinions have allowed for more transparent decision-making that is "more accessible to journalistic and academic criticism" (2002: 71–72). This leaves open a forum for debate which permits re-evaluations of decision-making and an eventual change in the Court's interpretation (Rinken, 2002: 72). Some observers of the Court think such open debates cause problems of their own though. One is that its open-ended opinions and penchant for lengthy *obiter dicta* often fuel debates and controversies within German politics and society rather than settling them (Blankenburg, 2002: 169–170). Since the purpose of courts is usually thought of as primarily being about resolving issues rather than exacerbating them, such debates then invariably convey, often correctly, that the Court is neck-deep in the creation of policy (see also Schlink, 1994: 198). Overall, though, given that transparency is usually seen as an important facet of the rule of law, open public and scholarly debate which may permit a re-evaluation of the Court's decisions is to be welcomed.

Common to most constitutional courts including Germany's is the tendency for a significant proportion of its justices to be drawn from academia rather than from the ranks of professional judges found in ordinary courts of law. Article 94 of the Basic Law and paragraph 4 of the FCCA specifies that three of the eight justices from each Senate must be chosen from one of the federal supreme courts, leaving the remaining ones to be chosen from the ranks of law professors, bureaucrats, and politicians (Blankenburg, 2002: 170). Judge David Edward, a former UK judge of the European Court of Justice, highlighted one of the critiques of the *BVerfG* from judges on the ordinary German courts of law:

> The German ordinary courts, the courts of law, are sometimes resistant to the way in which the Constitutional Court makes law ...; that this is a sort of dreaming up law, rather than a rigorous analysis.
>
> (Interview conducted by Author, October 2013)[15]

The problem that Judge Edward identifies is the idea that the living instrument view of constitutional interpretation has been taken to extremes by constitutional courts in general, and the *BVerfG* in particular.

> If you go to the case law of the European Court of Human Rights you'll get exactly the same [idea]: that this is a living instrument which we have to interpret in today's light. But the ordinary courts find this troubling because they feel that the law is being made on the hoof.
>
> (Interview, October 2013)

Such constitutional courts are, as Issacharoff puts it, "little detained by concerns over the authority for judicial review" (2010: 964), while the countermajoritarian difficulty becomes "a striking irrelevance" (Somek, 2014: 15).

The very nature of constitutional courts is, of course, that in monitoring the political process and guarding the gates of democracy, tensions are created with the political branches of government. What is entirely absent in the *BVerfG*'s approach to decision-making is any hint of the American judicial tradition of "self-doubt", of "agonising over legitimacy, or 'exercising the utmost care' whenever 'breaking new ground' in constitutional matters" (Sadurski, 2014: xiii). In this respect, as Collings notes, "the court requires sensibility to history as well as dogma" (2015: 395). The danger, then, is that the combination of, what could be called, the Court's normative exuberance, its nonchalance with its own case law, its "less consistent legal methodology" (Schlink, 1994: 215), along with a living instrument approach to constitutional interpretation, may damage its crucial role within Europe's largest democracy.

Over time the Court's case load of constitutional complaints from German citizens grew and, as seen, now represents over 90 percent of its work. Taken together with the potential mutability of human dignity, *BVerfG* President Voßkuhle's comments suggest a Court which believes that the values of liberal constitutionalism have firmly taken root in German society, allowing it to step back from the more electorally intrusive aspects of militant democracy. Does the Court's decision in the *European Parliament III Case* therefore represent a considered analysis on the part of the five justices regarding the circumstances in existence at the EP level, or, as one of the three dissenting justices argued in the case, has the Court merely replaced "the reasonable decision of the legislature with its own reasonable decision" (2014)? The critique from some German politicians after the two EP decisions is that the *BVerfG* simply has no conception of how democracy functions at the European level.

Perhaps a bigger concern for the Court, however, is the suspicion that it does not even understand democracy at the German domestic level. As part of its general equality jurisprudence—which is functionally similar to the US Equal Protection Clause—the *BVerfG* will review legislation if it differentiates between people (i.e. treats them unequally) without any justification.[16] This should be unproblematic. However, the Court has expanded the scope of its general equality jurisprudence to review legislation for "consistency, congruity and coherence" (Collings, 2015: 302). The problem, as Collings notes, is that

> legislation is often inconsistent for a noble purpose: it is the product of a compromise. Ban legislative incoherence and you risk rendering parliamentary compromise impossible. What's more, parliamentary decisions are supposed to reflect the wishes of the citizenry, and those wishes are themselves often inconsistent. Strip parliaments of the right to act irrationally, and you kill democracy.
>
> (Collings, 2015: 302)

Baer notes that general equality jurisprudence is based on the doctrine of *Systemgerechtigkeit* which "posits an internal logical coherence of the *Grundgesetz* and evaluates the constitutionality of a law based on its consistency with such logical coherence" (1998: 265). This is, as Collings hints at, a high standard of rationality for a legislature to meet.

The dangers of such a doctrinaire approach are manifold. If the *Bundestag* can no longer compromise out of fear of running afoul of Karlsruhe's edicts and if it can no longer represent the people's interests politically, the Court runs the risk of bringing legislative processes into a similar sort of disrepute as was seen during the Weimar Republic, but this time due to judicial overreach rather than legislative fragmentation. The potential legitimacy crisis for German constitutional government is that while the Court may maintain the 5 percent hurdle domestically to ensure the *Bundestag* can still function and to keep out smaller extremist parties, if the legislation drafted by German MPs is struck down on the basis of self-reverential Court doctrines like congruence, public confidence in the legislature and in Germany's democratic institutions may suffer if they are seen to be impotent in resolving pressing social and political problems. Extremist parties like the *NPD* and rising forces like *AfD* would certainly be the first to make capital from a perception of legislative impotence.

Germany's post-war recovery has been characterised by the gradual shift from stability at all costs to a greater acceptance of renewal, a trend best illustrated by the journey of the Greens from political pariahs to the centre of the political establishment. Integrating the Greens into German party politics has been one of the Court's undoubted successes and, as with the political reaction to its EP rulings, that shift came against a backdrop of resistance from the established parties. Does this mean that the Court's decisions in *EPII* and *EPIII* can be viewed in the same light? I would argue not. As far as outcomes go, then, the Court's effort to balance stability with renewal and breathe some new life into the German political system through the integration of the Greens and the striking down of the 5 percent hurdle at the EU level can be viewed positively.

However, the repeated complaint—from Schlink's critique in the 1990s to more recent criticisms from legal scholars and a former *BVerfG* justice—is that if the Court arrives at these outcomes "more or less politically" (Schlink, 1994: 198) rather than through reasoning grounded in the Basic Law, it is hard to avoid the conclusion that it has simply become another political institution.

The end result of the *BVerfG* striking down the 5 percent hurdle may be a shot in the arm for German politics, at least in its manifestation at the European Parliament level. What one can criticise is the Court's methodology-light, outcome-driven approach which departed wholesale from the logic of its 1979 decision, but without stating the factors which motivated that departure. When a constitutional court repeatedly delivers surprises—whether pleasant or unpleasant, as Schlink would put it—the suspicion is that it is basing its decisions on some other metric than a constitution. It matters little that the normative outcomes the Court is arriving at are ones which we might agree with if the judicial path to those decisions is arbitrary and opaque.

The danger with such opaqueness in a Court that is upholding a constitution as detailed and specific as the Basic Law is that the justices who today may be promoting electoral equality between voters and equal opportunity between parties may tomorrow be restricting it in an equally ad hoc manner. Richard Kay wrote that "one of the most serious injuries the state can inflict on its subjects is to commit them to lives of perpetual uncertainty" (1998: 22–23). That such uncertainty is currently relatively benign and issues from the ivory towers of the *Bundesverfassungsgericht* rather than the midnight knock at the door from the Gestapo cannot disguise the disconcerting scale of the departure from the stability-centric *Weltanschauung* of post-war German constitutionalism.

Conclusion

In recent decades, the *Bundesverfassungsgericht* has had to continually steer a middle course between its role as guardian of the Basic Law, without it becoming overtly political. It has often steered quite badly. Absent a clear methodology the only real explanation for the Court's decisions in the European Parliament cases is perhaps a changed understanding on the part of the justices as to what sort of guardianship German democracy and society need from Karlsruhe in the twenty-first century. On one level, the Court may have been responding to precisely the type of charge highlighted by Collings: that it has sometimes done more as the country needed it less. The logic of 'less' might well mean striking down those tools of the militant democracy, including electoral thresholds, which a mature and liberal German society has made redundant. This view is certainly implicit in the language of the then *BVerfG* president, Andreas Voßkuhle, whose criticism of the MEPs he addressed in Strasbourg in 2013 was that not once had any of them mentioned 'citizens' or 'voters'.

There is, though, a deep paradox in the *BVerfG*'s rulings in the European Parliament cases. In finding that there was no longer a justification for a 5 percent and then a 3 percent hurdle at the EU level, this change from the status quo looked like exactly the sort of political decision-making the *BVerfG* has so often been criticised for. The Court's problem here is that 'doing less' through removing the electoral hurdles at the EU level actually meant shaking up the political orders at the domestic and European level on a bare 5–3 majority. Much like the over-confidence in its *Lisbon Treaty Case* judgment, the decision in *EPIII* to second-guess the considered judgment of legislators in the *Bundestag*—who had responded to the 2011 decision in *EPII* by instituting a revised 3 percent hurdle—seemed to smack of hubris. Justice Müller's dissenting opinion in *EPIII* argued that "the assessment of the corridor between the purely theoretical possibility and the certain occurrence of an impairment of the ability to function is reserved to the legislature" (2014). The Court's decision seemed as incomprehensible as it was badly timed when, just months later, eurosceptic far right parties from across Europe doubled their representation in the European Parliament.

This chapter has generally offered a critical account of the Court's recent decision-making, particularly with respect to its European Parliament decisions. While one can wholeheartedly agree with the principle—as with the reapportionment cases—that all votes should count equally, the special circumstances of German history require more sensitivity to political stability than the *BVerfG* has shown. This is not a reflection on the German people of today. Liberal democratic values appear stronger in Germany than perhaps any other country in the world at present. The problem is not trust in the people as much as understanding the effects of legislative fragmentation during the Weimar Republic, and recognising the propensity of opportunistic and extremist groups and parties to exploit such a legislative impasse and so bring democratic processes into disrepute.

As noted in this chapter and the previous one, the Court's role in upholding fundamental rights, and the willingness of Germans to launch constitutional complaints, helped cement in the public mind the idea that democratic legitimacy depended on respect for legality and human dignity. However, if the ability to petition the Court has helped make the German people better citizens, the reverse may also be true. It is possibly also the case that receiving 5,000 petitions per year has given the justices in Karlsruhe an insight into the concerns of German society that may not always be as apparent to politicians. The development of dissents and *obiter dicta* in German constitutional law have also played a role in developing a greater public awareness of debates among the justices about the rights and responsibilities of citizenship, potentially influencing the Court to think more carefully about its reasoning in cases. The Court's awareness of the type of concerns and issues animating German citizens may also serve as an early warning system of emerging problems in society or of dangers arising from the misuse or misapplication of state power. In other words, like the canary in the coal mine, the Court's position in fielding constitutional complaints gives it a unique vantage point to identify citizens' concerns and, perhaps, any signs that the value orientations of the German people may be shifting away from the principles of the Basic Law.

As I have argued through the previous chapters, Germany's inspiring moral recovery after 1945 has partly been achieved through the efforts of many Germans in the post-war decades to confront the reality of their country's traumatic past. Such efforts have given real meaning to the liberal values of human dignity and fundamental rights in German constitutionalism, imbuing the Basic Law with much the same cohesive force as traditional "internal bonding forces of society" (Böckenförde, 1991: 46) such as religion, or nation. While that does not mean, as the 2017 German parliamentary elections illustrated, that Germany's constitutional order is completely immune to the current ascendancy of populist forces in the West, one continued strength of the Federal Republic seems to be a citizenry who identify far more with their liberal democratic constitutional values than with traditional, and often more reactionary, sources of identity.

Following the European Parliament decisions in 2014 *Der Spiegel* reported that the *Bundesverfassungsgericht* was "now harshly criticised like rarely before" and that its justices felt "misunderstood" (Amann et al., 2014a; translated from German original).[17] Yet such tensions should perhaps be welcomed if it helps ensure that the Weimar Republic and the regime which followed it remain historical catastrophes to be avoided, rather than political models to be emulated. With liberal democracy seemingly under renewed threat on both sides of the Atlantic, and around the world, the *Bundesverfassungsgericht* remains a fundamental institution of German democracy. Criticism, contestation, and constructive tension are, I have suggested, the essential attributes of constitutionalism that are needed to maintain the constitutional order in a state of equilibrium. Germans know only too well from the 1930s what happens when that tension dissipates and the balance is tipped. That is why, despite the critiques I have highlighted, the German people would undoubtedly reject a Germany without the *Bundesverfassungsgericht* as much as they would reject a Germany without their *Grundgesetz*, a constitution that they did not ask for and were not consulted on, but which, like the red-robed justices in Karlsruhe, they have come to appreciate.

Notes

1 My translation from: "*Wenn die Mehrheit der Wähler in demokratischen Wahlen Parteien wählt, die die bestehende Verfassungsordnung dezidiert ablehnen oder bekämpfen, hat ein politisches System keine Chance mehr.*"

2 The *BVerfG* also uses this phrase in *EPIII Case* (2014).

3 Stephen Sedley, a former senior English judge, notes that "many judges believe, not without reason that certainty is the law's greatest virtue" (2011: 205).

4 This provision was notably used in 1982 when Chancellor Helmut Schmidt was replaced by Helmut Kohl.

5 My translation from: "*Deutlich wurde bereits damals die Gefahr gesehen, dass mit Hilfe einer Sperrklausel die Dynamik des politischen Lebens erheblich eingeschränkt werden könnte, und einer 'jungen kräftigen Bewegung, die unten im Volk aufbricht und sich bemüht, die Mißwirtschaft großer Parteien zu beseitigen', von der Verfassung her ein Riegel vorgeschoben werden könne.*"

6 There were three parties: The Christian Democrats (CDU), the Social Democrats (SPD), and the Liberals (FDP), but the Liberals were only ever minor coalition partners of the CDU or SPD.

7 These are the centre-right European People's Party (EPP) and the centre-left Progressive Alliance of Socialists and Democrats (S&D).
8 My translation from "*Auch wenn Rechtsprechungsänderungen des BVerfG, gerade im Bereich des Wahlrechts, mittlerweile weniger die Ausnahme, sonder vielmehr die Regel darstellen, überrascht diese Kehrtwende in besonderer Weise.*"
9 My translation from: "*die weder den Parteifamilien angehören, die sich im Europäischen Parlament zu Fraktionen zusammenfinden, noch von diesen integriert werden könnten. Insofern würden wir ohne Sperrklausel eine Zahl von fraktionslosen Parlamentariern produzieren, die das immer wichtigere Funktionieren des Zusammenwirkens der Institutionen massiv gefährden könnten.*"
10 Günther Oettinger, Germany's EU commissioner, said "the ruling is backward-looking. … I am certain that Karlsruhe will have to correct its case law in 10 years" (quoted in Amann et al., 2014b).
11 My translation from "*Entweder das Bundesverfassungsgericht nimmt das Europaparlament nicht richtig ernst, betrachtet es als ein Minderparlament (böse Zungen sagen: Quatschbude), für das Effizienz nicht so wichtig ist. Oder: Für die Bundestagswahl muss die Hürde früher oder später auch abgeschafft werden.*"
12 My translation from: "*Das Karlsruher Urteil halte er 'weder im Ergebnis noch in der Begründung für richtig'*".
13 My translation from "*Gerichte können nur den Rahmen abstecken, innerhalb dessen Politik sich entfalten kann.*"
14 See analysis in Chapter 2.
15 For more on this resistance of the German ordinary courts, see Miller (2017: 97).
16 This is grounded in Article 3(1) of the Basic Law which states that "All persons shall be equal before the law".
17 My translation from: "*Nun wird es so scharf kritisiert wie selten zuvor. Die Richter fühlen sich missverstanden.*"

References

Lüth Case, 7 BVerfGE 198, 1958
Green Party Exclusion Case, 70 BVerfGE 324, 1986a
Party Finance V Case, 73 BVerfG 40, 1986b
Lisbon Treaty Case, 123 BVerfGE 267 & 2 BvE 2/08, 2009
European Parliament II Case, 2 BVC 4/10, 2011
European Parliament III Case, 2 BvE 2/13, 2014

Amann, M., D. Hipp, R. Pfister, and C. Schult, "Die Anmaßung", *Spiegel Online*, 10 March 2014 (2014a), available at: www.spiegel.de/spiegel/print/d-125443747.html [last accessed 11 November 2016].

Amann, M., D. Hipp, R. Pfister, and C. Schult, "Is Germany's High Court Anti-European?", *Spiegel Online*, 13 March 2014 (2014b), available at: www.spiegel.de/international/germany/the-eu-critical-course-of-the-german-high-court-a-958018.html [last accessed 18 October 2016].

Baer, S., "Equality: The Jurisprudence of the German Constitutional Court", *Columbia Journal of European Law*, 5 (1998), 249.

Blankenburg, E., "Mobilisation of the German Federal Constitutional Court", in *Constitutional Courts in Comparison: The US Supreme Court and the German Federal Constitutional Court*, ed. by Ralf Rogowski and Thomas Gawron (New York: Berghahn Books, 2002).

Böckenförde, E. W., *Constitutional and Political Theory: Selected Writings*. Vol. 1 (Oxford: Oxford University Press, 2017).

Böckenförde, E. W., "The Rise of the State as a Process of Secularisation", in *State, Society, and Liberty: Studies in Political Theory and Constitutional Law* (New York: Berg Pub Ltd, 1991).

Breyer, S., "Interview with Justice Stephen Breyer—With Charlie Rose (Transcript)", (2016), available at: https://charlierose.com/episodes/29278 [last accessed 6 October 2016].

Bundesverfassungsgericht, "Jahresstatistik 2015" (Karlsruhe: 2015).

Bundeswahlleiter, "Endgültiges Amtliches Ergebnis Der Bundestagswahl 2013" (2013), available at: www.bundeswahlleiter.de/info/presse/mitteilungen/bundestagswahl-2013/2013-10-09-endgueltiges-amtliches-ergebnis-der-bundestagswahl-2013.html [last accessed 25 November 2016].

Collings, J., *Democracy's Guardians: A History of the German Federal Constitutional Court, 1951–2001* (Oxford: Oxford University Press, 2015).

Delledonne, G. "Rationalising Political Representation Within the European Parliament: The Italian Constitutional Court Rules on the Threshold for the European Elections", 20 October 2019, available at: https://verfassungsblog.de/rationalising-political-representation-within-the-european-parliament-the-italian-constitutional-court-rules-on-the-threshold-for-the-european-elections/ [last accessed 23 September 2019].

"Drei-Prozent-Hürde bei Europawahl Verfassungswidrig", 26 February 2014 (2014a), available at: www.welt.de/politik/deutschland/article125211492/Drei-Prozent-Huerde-bei-Europawahl-verfassungswidrig.html [last accessed 12 November 2016].

"Eurosceptic Effect at the European Parliament: Key Issues for the 2015 Parliament", UK Parliament (2014c), available at: www.parliament.uk/business/publications/research/key-issues-parliament-2015/foreign-affairs/european-parliament/ [last accessed 11 November 2016].

"Ex-Verfassungsrichter Sieht Fünfprozenthürde in Gefahr", 8 March 2014 (2014d), available at: www.spiegel.de/politik/deutschland/ex-praesident-von-bundesverfassungsgericht-papier-zu-dreiprozenthuerde-a-957583.html [last accessed 12 November 2016].

Grindel, R., "Plenarprotokoll 17/246, 31432" (Berlin: Deutscher Bundestag, 2013).

Halberstam, D. and C. Möllers, "The German Constitutional Court Says 'Ja Zu Deutschland!'", *German Law Journal*, 10(8) (2009).

Herzog, R., "The Separation and Concentration of Power in The Basic Law", in *Germany and its Basic Law: Past, Present, and Future: A German-American Symposium*, ed. by Paul Kirchhof and Donald P Kommers (Baden-Baden: Nomos, 1993).

Hobolt, S., "European Elections 2019: A More Fragmented Parliament", *Political Insight*, 10(3) (2019), 16–19.

"How Eurosceptic is the New European Parliament", BBC (2014e), available at: www.bbc.co.uk/news/world-europe-28107633 [last accessed 11 November 2016].

Issacharoff, S., "Constitutional Courts and Democratic Hedging", *Georgetown Law Journal*, 99 (2010), 961.

Kay, R. S., "American Constitutionalism", in *Constitutionalism: Philosophical Foundations*, ed. by Lawrence A. Alexander (New York: Cambridge University Press, 1998).

Kommers, D. P., "German Constitutionalism: A Prolegomenon", *Emory Law Journal*, 40 (1991), 837–873.

Kommers, D. P., "The Federal Constitutional Court: Guardian of German Democracy", *The ANNALS of the American Academy of Political and Social Science*, 603(1) (2006), 111–128.

Kommers, D. P. and R. A. Miller, *The Constitutional Jurisprudence of the Federal Republic of Germany*. 3rd edn (Durham, NC: Duke University Press, 2012).

Macedo, S., *Liberal Virtues: Citizenship, Virtue, and Community in Liberal Constitutionalism* (Oxford: Clarendon Press, 1990).

Miller, R. A., "Germany's German Constitution", *Virginia Journal of International Law*, 57 (2017), 95.

Müller, R., "Berliner Gedankenspiele zur Dritten Gewalt", *Frankfurter Allgemeine Zeitung*, 3 April 2014.

Murphy, W. F., "An Ordering of Constitutional Values", *Southern California Law Review*, 53 (1979), 703–760.

Pernice-Warnke, S., "Das Urteil des Bundesverfassungsgerichts zur Drei-Prozent-Sperrklausel im Europawahlrecht–Bundesverfassungsrechtliche und Europarechtliche Fragestellungen mit Prüfungsrelevanz", *JURA-Juristische Ausbildung*, 36(11) (2014), 1143–1152.

Rinken, A., "The Federal Constitutional Court and the German Political System", in *Constitutional Courts in Comparison: The US Supreme Court and The German Federal Constitutional Court*, ed. by Ralf Rogowski and Thomas Gawron (New York: Berghahn Books, 2002).

Rostow, E. V., "The Democratic Character of Judicial Review", *Harvard Law Review*, 66(2) (1952), 193–224.

Sabbati, G., G. Sgueo, and A. Dobreva, "2019 European Elections: National Rules", European Parliamentary Research Service, April 2019, available at: www.europarl.europa.eu/RegData/etudes/ATAG/2018/623556/EPRS_ATA(2018)623556_EN.pdf [last accessed 20 October 2019].

Sadurski, W., *Rights Before Courts: A Study of Constitutional Courts in Postcommunist States of Central and Eastern Europe*. 2nd edn (Dordrecht, Netherlands: Springer, 2014).

Schlink, B., "German Constitutional Culture in Transition", in *Constitutionalism, Identity, Difference, and Legitimacy: Theoretical Perspectives*, ed. by Michel Rosenfeld (Durham, NC: Duke University Press, 1994).

Scholz, K. A., "It's Tough Out There for Small Parties", *Deutsche Welle*, 16 August 2013, available at: www.dw.de/its-tough-out-there-for-small-parties/a-17012475 [last accessed 23 October 2016].

Schönberger, C., "Lisbon in Karlsruhe: Maastricht's Epigones at Sea", *German Law Journal*, 10(8) (2009), 1201–1218.

Sedley, S., *Ashes and Sparks: Essays on Law and Justice* (Cambridge: Cambridge University Press, 2011).

Siedenbiedel, C., "Demokratie Muss Nicht Effizient Sein", *Frankfurter Allgemeine Zeitung*, 2 March 2014, available at: www.faz.net/aktuell/wirtschaft/3-prozent-huerde-demokratie-muss-nicht-effizient-sein-12827235.html [last accessed 24 November 2016].

Smekal, H. and L. Vyhnánek, "Equal Voting Power Under Scrutiny: Czech Constitutional Court on the 5% Threshold in the 2014 European Parliament Elections", *European Constitutional Law Review*, 12(1) (2016), 148–163.

Somek, A., *The Cosmopolitan Constitution* (New York: Oxford University Press, 2014).

Steinbeis, M., "Ist am Sonntag die Fünfprozenthürde Verfassungswidrig Geworden?", in *Gebändigte Macht: Verfassung Im Europäischen Nationalstaat: Verfassungsblog* ed. by Alexandra Kemmerer, Christoph Möllers, and Maximilian Steinbeis (Baden-Baden: Nomos Verlagsgesellschaft 2015).

Strohmeier, G., "Funktioniert Weimar auf EU-Ebene? Reflektionen zur Europawahl 2014 ohne Sperrklausel", *ZfP Zeitschrift für Politik*, 61(3) (2014), 346–368.

Taylor, G., "The Constitutionality of Election Thresholds in Germany", *International Journal of Constitutional Law*, 15(3) (2017), 734–752.

Tomuschat, C., "The Ruling of the German Constitutional Court on the Treaty of Lisbon", *German Law Journal*, 10(8) (2009), 1259–1262.

Voßkuhle, A. and W. Von Rahden, "Die Rolle des Bundesverfassungsgerichts in Europa: Ein Gespräch", *Gegenworte* (30) (2013).

Wenner, U., *Sperrklauseln im Wahlrecht der Bundesrepublik Deutschland* (Frankfurt am Main: Peter Lang, 1986).

Conclusion

> The Americans or the Germans or the French would say: 'Hang on, the state isn't allowed to do that, or if it is to do that, then it must be given the power to do it.' So I think constitutionalism is also a frame of mind.
>
> (Judge David Edward,[1] Interview with author, October 2013)

The central dilemma which this book has addressed is the paradox that the state is dependent on its citizens for its survival, but citizens are ultimately dependent on the state for their liberty. Despite its flaws, representative democracy remains the essential vehicle in the modern state by which citizens can play a role in how they are governed, in order to maintain their own freedoms. Constitutional courts, whether in the guise of the United States Supreme Court's appellate jurisdiction, or the *Bundesverfassungsgericht*'s concrete and abstract judicial review remit, have played an important role in scrutinising democratic processes to ensure the democratic rights of citizens are protected. Such judicial scrutiny can facilitate, support, and protect democratic participation, but it cannot replace civic involvement from citizens.

The particular characteristics of each country's constitutionalism—whether it is more inclined towards liberty or dignity—have shaped the nature of the *polis* that was established. This, in turn, has determined how interventions in the processes of representative democracy occur, and whether the values emerging from civil society struggles are formalised in law, or whether the norms of the state are inculcated in society. The problem, though, is that in establishing the terms and (liberty or dignity imbued-) parameters of the *polis*, constitutionalism creates a civic space, and a 'legal institutional' space. Thus, the net effect, and accepted ideology of the American Constitution, was the creation of a zone of liberty where, as Rostow put it, "man can be free because the state is not" (1952: 195). This liberty, though, created a rupture between the freedom of the citizen, and the activities or "political action" (Somek, 2014: 283) which was required of them to uphold their representative government.

The enquiry undertaken in the preceding chapters has sought to illuminate distinctive aspects of American and German constitutionalism which are particularly germane to democratic and electoral processes. The comparative analysis of the two courts revealed several conclusions about the role of constitutionalism in representative democracies. First, the theoretical distinction articulated in the book between the civic space and the legal institutional space (and between the people and the courts) illustrated differences between the United States and Germany. Crucially, the interaction between the civic and legal institutional spaces works differently in the liberty-centric American constitutionalism compared to the dignity-oriented German constitutionalism. In the former, emerging norms in the civic space have been largely *formalised* by the Supreme Court as constitutional values, whereas in the latter, constitutional values have been *inculcated* in the civic space by the *BVerfG*, particularly through the effects of the constitutional complaint mechanism. The idea of value formalisation by the Supreme Court draws on Tocqueville's view that once a majority of the community comes to embrace new norms or value orientations, those who were previously in opposition fall in behind the new consensus (1998: 103). On multiple issues, the Supreme Court generally lagged behind rather than led democratic debates and civil society struggles regarding human rights issues. This was true with respect to issues including slavery, segregation, and redistributionist policies during the Progressive Era, which were only belatedly formalised in court decisions.

Second, the stability and renewal paradigm used in the book provides a distinctive lens to assess the relationship between legal and democratic institutions in the modern state, and the role of constitutionalism and the courts in sustaining a constructive tension between the need for stability and the demands of a changing society. The Supreme Court has referred to "the evolving standards of decency that mark the progress of a maturing society" in *Trop v Dulles* (1958: 100–101) and *Rhodes v Chapman* (1981), and in the aftermath of *Baker v Carr*, Bruce Terris wrote to Archibald Cox that "the meaning of equal protection is necessarily a changing concept" (Smith, 2014: 161). In *Life Imprisonment Case*, the *BVerfG* rejected the notion of absolute stability in constitutional meaning, arguing that attempts to define human dignity must be based on present understandings of it and "not on any claim to a conception of timeless validity" (1977). The argument advanced in the previous chapters has been that stability and renewal are important principles at the heart of any constitutional system, but that either pushed to an extreme represents a failure of constitutionalism.

Third, the responses of each court to the reapportionment and electoral threshold cases were primarily shaped by the liberty-dignity facets of American and German constitutionalism. Consequently, because democracy in the German context was derived from the Basic Law's architectonic principle, human dignity, and because the *Bundesverfassungsgericht*'s authority is textually grounded in the constitution, the Karlsruhe Court neither faced the scale of criticism that the Supreme Court did in the reapportionment cases, nor did it have to justify its role in restoring its notion of electoral equality in *EPII Case* and *EPIII Case* as the Supreme Court had to in *Baker v Carr* and *Reynolds v Sims*.

The liberty-dignity dynamic also informs another dimension of the comparative analysis of the courts: the views of Associate Justice Stephen Breyer of the Supreme Court, and *BVerfG* president, Andreas Voßkuhle, on the role of their respective courts within society and politics. Breyer's view (2016) of the Supreme Court as the "boundary commission" of the Constitution sees, I have suggested, a minimalist role for the Court within America's liberty-framed constitutionalism that leaves vast space for citizens to live their lives. By contrast, Voßkuhle's view of the role of German courts as being "to define parameters within which politics can unfold" (quoted in Voßkuhle and Von Rahden, 2013) fits, I contend, the more comprehensive dignity-orientation of German constitutionalism, where rights are a necessary precondition for democracy (see Collings, 2015: 219).

The analysis in Chapters 1, 2, 3, and 5 illustrated the theoretical constitutional risks to the liberal state both from unrestricted democratic participation which may permit illiberal autocrats to take control, and from more restricted participation which may lead to an ossified and oligarchical polity. In Chapters 4 and 6, the analysis of the legal cases revealed the practical way that the US Supreme Court and the *Bundesverfassungsgericht* have responded to these 'theoretical risks' in their interventions in US districting policies and German electoral processes, respectively. A particular focus of the comparative analysis was the question of how the Supreme Court and *BVerfG* have dealt either with oligarchical tendencies attempting to exclude certain voters or parties from the democratic process, or with long-standing statutory rules designed to preserve the integrity and stability of the constitutional order. Examples of practices requiring such juridical interventions included the dilution of citizens' votes through malapportionment, the discrimination against the German Greens by larger parties in the *Bundestag*, and the exclusion of smaller parties that fail to achieve a specific threshold for electoral success.

The importance of Ernst-Wolfgang Böckenförde's claim (1991: 45) in 'the Böckenförde Dilemma'—that "the liberal, secularised state is nourished by presuppositions that it cannot itself guarantee"—has been generally understudied outside Germany, yet his insights hold lessons for the health of the relationship between citizens and state in all liberal democracies, and for the balance between democracy and individual rights. As Mouffe notes, it is "only thanks to the democratic logic of equivalence that frontiers can be created and a *demos* established without which no real exercise of rights could be possible" (2000: 10). The continued relevance of Böckenförde's ideas in mediating the tensions between liberalism and democracy in Germany and beyond was highlighted in 2017 by Angela Merkel, who directly referred to Böckenförde and his ideas, and commented on their implications for the role of citizens and civil society in liberal democratic states. Merkel indicated that the implications of Böckenförde's dilemma was that nobody feels they are responsible for their society (Walker, 2017). Merkel praised those Germans taking part in a number of Sunday demonstrations in support of the European idea and said that such civil society involvement was indispensable (Walker, 2017).

Comparing 'Constitutionalisms'

One of the key puzzles which this book has wrestled with is how constitutionalism deals with overt threats to democratic processes, as in 1930s Germany, or more insidious and subtle dangers such as malapportionment. I have argued that the response of American or German constitutionalism is partly contingent on the nature of the original constituent act, the circumstances in which the polity was established, and how that context shaped the constitutional text and norms produced. The circumstances of the US founding, which was effectively a compromise between significantly different interests, created a more general constitutional text. Partly through omission, and part design, the text restrained the state but left the citizen free. It is this 'liberty' consciousness within American constitutionalism which tends to lead to a more tentative application of judicial authority. In Germany—where a predominantly normative constitution was designed to preserve human dignity, establish resistant state institutions, and forge a society of liberal citizens—judicial power was applied more assertively.

Essential for both countries is the need for a vigilant citizenry who are familiar with their constitution, its values, and the principle of "equal concern and respect" (Bellamy, 2008: 104) upon which their liberty and the freedom of others ultimately depends. Moreover, if the principles of the *polis* are accepted and respected by citizens and political actors, it seems unimportant whether that *polis* was created by citizens in a state of liberty or by a constitutional court out of an objective order of values. Rather, what seems to matter most is whether the citizens charged with tending the constitution in the present are equal to the task. John Finn writes that "if citizens are uncongenial to constitutional rights, then we have precisely the kind of citizens the juridic monopoly helped to create" (2014: 223). Yet, are American citizens (or German citizens for that matter) really less congenial to constitutional rights now than they were before the ascendancy of judicial power? Are US citizens today less congenial to rights than they were in the era of segregation and Jim Crow? Are citizens of the Federal Republic of Germany less congenial now to constitutional rights and "the safeguards of law" (Frankfurter, 1955: 437) than in 1949? The evidence for such a claim seems wanting, yet there is no room for complacency.

As stated at the outset, historical institutionalist approaches emphasise a strong connection between the normative understandings held by individuals within a community regarding their courts and legal institutions, and how judges perceive their roles and that of courts institutionally.[2] The understanding of constitutionalism outlined in this book certainly implies an important constitutional role for courts in educating citizens about their individual and civic rights, the rule of law, and in terms of Arendt's idea of *isonomy*, the role of law in making people "equal in the political realm" (Waldron, 2016: 299). This *does* mean that citizens must have a "respect for constitutionalism and legality" (Orwell and Davison, 1986: 397), but does not mean that courts must have a primary role in constitutional interpretation, or that politics must play second fiddle to law. Citizens can perhaps learn just as much about their constitutional system and their own role within it when the courts get decisions wrong as when they get them right. The Supreme Court's decision in *Rucho v Common Cause* (2019) that a solution to the problem of gerrymandering does not lie with the federal courts can serve as an added reminder to citizens of the imperative of collective political action and civic participation.

Due to the inevitable constraints of the book, the analysis has been confined to the problem of citizens being excluded from the civic space by external actors, either unconstitutionally or constitutionally (i.e. the US states, or the German federal government). It has not been possible to directly explore the important question of citizens excluding themselves from the civic space by not engaging in their democratic process. Although the book has looked at this question indirectly through the ability of American and German constitutionalism and the courts to exert influence over the civic space and support constitutional democracy, the motivations of individual voters have not been considered.

This, however, raises the question of whether self-exclusion from the civic space by the citizen is the fault (or problem) of the citizen, or whether it is primarily the state's responsibility for establishing the conditions which are conducive for the citizen to participate in their democracy? America's liberty-centric constitutionalism created a zone of autonomy for the citizen, but then it was up to the citizen, individually or through religious and other forms of civic associational practices to stay involved in public and democratic life. Germany's dignity-oriented constitutionalism had two specific tasks to fulfil in 1949: first, to create a viable and stable constitutional order that could sustain liberal democracy and promote economic prosperity and, second, establish a supportive and inclusive democratic culture based on respect for individual rights, without which, as Dahl saw (2003: 95–96), the first objective would be vulnerable.

Owing partly to the generality of the American Constitution compared to the Basic Law, the struggle over constitutional meaning often generates tensions between the law of the state and that of individuals and groups in society. It is often outlier groups within a polity who are most certain what the constitutional text means. As Robert Cover noted, "there is a radical dichotomy between the social organisation of law as power and the organisation of law as meaning" (1983: 18). Moreover, there is a particular consequence in liberal societies where individuals or groups who do not share a singular cohesive narrative of constitutional meaning may divine significantly different understandings about what law or politics require in a given set of circumstances. In a "liberal society that disclaims control over narrative" the "uncontrolled character of meaning exercises a destabilising influence upon power" (Cover, 1983: 18). Of course, this does not help the judge charged with interpretation, but this is precisely the paradox that Justice Stephen Breyer identified about the document leaving "vast space" for people to decide what kind of a nation they want (2016). Breyer was referring to a civic space within which citizens can participate in building the kind of *polis* that they want. It is *not* primarily a legal space, although, as the reapportionment cases illustrated, the questions posed by citizens in that civic space may ultimately require legal remedies. This is the difference which has been addressed throughout the book between the civic space created by constitutionalism and the more limited legal space in which interpretation occurs.

Nevertheless, as the examples of the United States and Germany indicate, when citizens or groups in the *polis* find their civic space restricted—for example, when politicians or legislatures do not reapportion, or when voters find their vote is wasted because they have chosen a party that does not clear a 5 percent hurdle—it is inevitable that the courts may be called on to decide. In this regard, Tocqueville's observation that "scarcely any political question arises in the United States that is not resolved, sooner or later, into a judicial question" (1998: 110) seems as relevant to German democracy after 1949 as to democracy in America in the 1840s.

The United States

The reapportionment cases offer a picture of civil society actors and individual voters doggedly attempting to uphold the principle of representative government despite the efforts of political actors to hold onto power unconstitutionally. In the United States, engaged civil society actors were involved in the unsuccessful political efforts against malapportionment, and then the successful legal effort to get *Baker v Carr* heard in the federal courts. Sager rightly notes that many observers of constitutional institutions are "strongly inclined to see the insulation of constitutional judgment from ongoing politics as a virtue, not a liability" (1998: 236). The complaint about the *Bundesverfassungsgericht* and the US Supreme Court, however, is that they are not divorced from politics enough. Indeed, Dahl's view of the Supreme Court as a majoritarian and policy-making institution (1957: 285) suggests that the 'insulation' of the judicial branch from ordinary politics is largely an illusion.

Writing about the backlash against judicial constitutionalism in the wake of the social and progressive rulings of the Warren Court, Post and Siegel highlighted the question of whether the public might lose confidence in the authority of the courts to declare constitutional law if they are seen "to yield to political pressure" (2007: 375). There are different ways of seeing this though. In the reapportionment cases, the Court was reacting to widespread concern among civil society actors about malapportionment, yet its decisions certainly found favour with the Kennedy Administration, as they probably would have with the Eisenhower Administration based on the early support from Solicitor General J. Lee Rankin. Notwithstanding Oliver Wendell Holmes' view on the necessity of judicial review to check states' laws and Whittington's analysis of how the Court has often acted as an agent of national power against the states, the Warren Court's decisions on reapportionment were neither dictated by the federal government, nor opposed by the public (see, for example, McCloskey, 1972: 266).

The nature of the civic space created by each constitutionalism has determined how political action and legal interpretation unfold; in other words, the civic space was shaped by whether the original constitution that was established—through sins of omission or design—is an American 'liberty'-oriented *polis* or a German 'dignity'-centric one. As seen in Chapter 3, it was the generality of the Janus-facing constitution that created opportunities, but also problems when it came to interpretation. The US Constitution began with a compact between 13 sovereign states, but just as significant was the compromise between the widely differing interests within those states. Most of the Anti-Federalists who had strongly opposed the Constitution during the bitterly fought ratification process "acquiesced, often without a peep" once they had been outvoted (Amar, 2012: 58). The compromises necessary to bridge the differences between these interests were channelled into a document that few were happy with and which profoundly dismayed Madison. It was from such meagre ingredients, which the compromises of the founding period produced, that the people, representatives, and institutions of the United States were commanded to go forth and fashion a viable constitutional order. While these principles of the American constitutional experiment have remained largely unaltered in theory, the societal context in which they have been interpreted has changed dramatically.

The Bickelian angst over the countermajoritarian difficulty is a result of the original constitutional generality over what the document means. These tensions were behind the Court's problems during the Lochner era, and its subsequent clash with Franklin Roosevelt over his New Deal legislation. Justice Holmes' dissent in *Lochner v New York* (1905) that a constitution is for "people of fundamentally different views" and did not prescribe eternally applicable economic theories rejected both the notion of a unitary constitutional intent, and the presumption that experience and the changing needs of society had nothing to teach constitutional interpretation.

What was common to numerical malapportionment and gerrymandering was seeking partisan advantage. However, while numerical malapportionment tended to be backed more broadly by the social classes benefiting from it, gerrymandering seems to affect all voters equally, since it gives both Republicans and Democrats considerably less power to have a genuine choice between parties. The majority holding in *Rucho v Common Cause* (2019) that "political gerrymandering claims present political questions beyond the reach of the federal courts" seems in the spirit of Felix Frankfurter's opinion in *Colegrove v Green*. Based on the 'political question doctrine' rationale given by Chief Justice Roberts it is hard to believe that his court would even have touched the malapportionment issue that the Warren Court grappled with in *Baker v Carr* and *Reynolds v Sims*, which brought 'one person, one vote' to the United States. Arguing that gerrymandering claims are not justiciable, the Court has effectively allowed political parties to remove the political and legal rights of millions of voters to participate equally in their democracy. A citizen wishing to exercise a genuinely meaningful vote within the American political system would now be best advised to join one of the two major parties, as the Court's green light for gerrymandering will increasingly mean that party primaries will be far more consequential than the general election in many states. Given the founders' profound fear over the dangers of faction[3]—some would say the Constitution's defining leitmotif—the majority opinion's view that partisan gerrymandering is not prohibited by the Constitution is like saying that the document doesn't deal with government. The majority opinion in *Rucho* also neglects John Rutledge's view at the Constitutional Convention that one of the Court's chief functions was to "secure national rights" (May and Ides, 2007: 21).

How, then, can we assess the Court's decision on gerrymandering in terms of this book's discussion of constitutionalism? In terms of stability and renewal, the Court has come down squarely on the side of ossification and political entrenchment which is only likely to make many voters question the point of voting at all if their districts have been drawn so as to make their votes meaningless. Is this, then, stability or renewal? Seen in the light of the American and German experience in the previous chapters, the danger is that the Court's decision will further vitiate the already broken middle ground of US politics. Justice Kagan's dissent in *Rucho* highlighted the pervasive effect that "big data and modern technology" have in making gerrymanders more effective and durable than before, and so "insulating politicians against all but the most titanic shifts in the political tides" (2019: 9–10). As mapmakers for political parties implement gerrymanders based on more sophisticated data models to hold on to legislative power wholly disproportionate to their vote share and carry out policies that advantage some citizens' interests over others, so the potential for political and social instability will only increase.

The most promising signs of change in the United States lie not with the courts but—in the spirit of those who fought malapportionment in the 1960s—with ballot initiatives and other civil society action to take redistricting out of the hands of self-interested politicians. Such efforts may restore balance to a system and force politicians to moderate their positions to reach voters beyond their own political bases. American representative government may then once more become based on the principle of voters choosing politicians, rather than the other way around. Ultimately, while the courts may be able to correct occasional blips in political and electoral processes, concerted structural efforts by parties to tilt the electoral rules in their favour may create a tipping point beyond which the courts may become compromised as a result of the judicial appointments process.

Germany

Understanding the role of constitutionalism and the courts in democratic processes has been central to this enquiry. Yet in both the United States and Germany, constitutional values, traditional sources of cohesion, and the balance between majority and minority interests have affected this institutional narrative in important ways. The emergence of a strong constitutional culture in Germany has been important in sustaining post-war constitutionalism, yet for the first decades of the Federal Republic this change was shaped overwhelmingly by the Basic Law's framers, politicians, elites, and, perhaps most significantly, the *Bundesverfassungsgericht*. However much Germany's weak constitutional culture required this civic pedagogy in 1951, there is an obvious short-term price to be paid in "liberalness" (Böckenförde, 1991: 45) to ensure a citizenry able to uphold their liberty in the future. The 'fine line' is ensuring that political institutions do not become captured by oligarchical tendencies once it is clear that the stability of the state is no longer at risk. As a result of *Organstreit* complaints filed by the Green Party during the 1980s and a series of decisions which criticised the established parties for their oligarchical tendencies, the *BVerfG* was able to inject new life into Germany's party system.

The Böckenförde Dilemma has relevance for how a constitutional order should respond to the forces of renewal in society. As suggested in previous chapters, the constitutional complaint mechanism of the Basic Law possibly gives the *BVerfG* an insight into emerging trends and tensions within German society which politicians may be unaware of. These trends may signal the emergence of new political forces of social cohesion or disruption, or may herald the reconfiguration of existing political constellations. Taking democracy seriously in Germany has hitherto meant German citizens trusting in the Court to maintain stability using the tools of the militant democracy, and deciding whether the forces of 'renewal' are ones which can be safely integrated within the constitutional order of the Basic Law, as the Greens were in the 1980s, or whether they must be resisted as demonstrated in *Socialist Reich Party Case* (1952) and *Communist Party Case* (1956).

The Court's argument in its *Lisbon Treaty Case* judgment (2009) that the EU derived its authority from its member states rather than an as yet undefined European *demos* bears comparison to Patrick Henry's Anti-Federalist rebuke at the Virginia Ratifying Convention: "Who authorized them to speak the language of, 'We, the people', instead of, 'We, the states'?" (Henry, 1986). Both can be seen as critiquing the 'identity credentials' and the constituent authority of any *demos* beyond that currently in existence. Identifying the relevant *demoi* and the key source of constitutional legitimacy has implications for the harmonious inter-relationship between multi-level or multi-layered forms of citizenship and civic identity both within and beyond the nation-state (Krisch, 2016: 676–677). It also directly speaks to the key question that the book has addressed of whether societies within liberal constitutional states can cohere absent other forms of identity or bonding forces. Henry's reprimand can be seen as a last gasp effort to prevent authority seeping away from the states. The *BVerfG*'s hubristic opinion in *Lisbon* can perhaps be seen in a similar light, but in the context of European integration.

Ernst-Wolfgang Böckenförde criticised the "objective system of values" (1991: 45) in the early Federal Republic, which he saw as an uncertain substitute for religion or some other homogenising force as a support for the liberal democratic state. It was dangerous, first, because such a value order compromised liberalism by placing its destiny in the hands of an immensely powerful court rather than with the people. The other danger, though, was that the value order would come to usurp the Basic Law itself, leaving society at the mercy of the changing whims of constitutional court judges. Set against the backdrop of Andreas Voßkuhle's remarks that the Court is "on the side of the people" and the concerns raised by numerous critics of its second-guessing of legislative decision-making, the risk is that some justices on the Court may be seeing themselves as precisely what one of its former justices, Wiltraut Rupp Von-Brunneck, warned: an *ersatz* legislature (cited in Collings, 2015: 288).

If courts become too immersed in policy-making, political issues, or answering important questions that society and political representatives should be grappling with—due to activism on the courts' part or due to legislators using the courts to tackle politically difficult decisions (see, for example, Lovell, 2003)—then voters may get complacent about engaging in democratic processes and taking the trouble to elect representatives who are committed to public life and to solving complex issues. The danger, then, is that apathy can breed carelessness and we risk repeating the mistakes of the 1930s. I am not convinced, though, that this is what has happened, at least in Germany. As Rolf Lamprecht puts it,

> The common civil right in being able to call upon Karlsruhe at any time helped foster democratic self-confidence. Whoever recognised this possibility, and, if necessary, made use of it, no longer had to view themselves as subjects.[4]
>
> (Lamprecht, 1998)

Due to Germany's traumatic history the values and institutions of German constitutionalism have had to bear an unusually heavy burden in restoring the country's moral compass. While Germany retains a strong religious tradition in its culture, the country's impressive moral recovery since World War II seems overwhelmingly driven by secular factors, most especially the willingness of ordinary Germans from the 1960s onwards to acknowledge and debate their country's traumatic past. Had this debate not taken place then "the prescribed state ideology … and the proclamation of an 'objective system of values'" (Böckenförde, 1991: 45) imposed from above could have become a source of tension. Instead, the architectonic values of human dignity and democracy have over time become more deeply entrenched within Germany's constitutional culture, assisted in part by the constitutional complaint mechanism. The mechanism itself gave Germans a greater civic consciousness and created an awareness among individuals and officials about how the citizen should be treated in the constitutional state. The Court played a role in laying the groundwork for the later *Vergangenheitsbewältigung* debate on coming to terms with the past with its decisions in *Gestapo Case* (1957) and *Civil Servants Case* (1953) relating to the Gestapo and the presence of Nazis in the civil service and judiciary. Overall, the values of German constitutionalism seem to have reinforced the process of coming to terms with the past by constantly providing both aspirational values and a reminder of what happens when a country prioritises political ideology or the state's interests above the rights of individuals.

Throughout the previous chapters I have stressed the *sui generis* nature of the German and American historical experiences which have contributed to the development of constitutionalism in each country. While German exceptionalism may represent constitutional and historical conditions as difficult to replicate as those of American exceptionalism, the extent to which both constitutions have been extensively copied by new democracies around the world makes them essential subjects of analysis if we are to understand how judicial scrutiny of representative democracy should or should not proceed. From an outside perspective the perceived juridification of the German political and legal space can seem disconcerting. However, in challenging times for Western liberal democracies where populist and other reactionary forces seem emboldened, it is perhaps useful to observe the institutional and civic conditions which did so much to establish Germany's strong constitutional democracy when circumstances had perhaps never seemed bleaker.

The *BVerfG*'s rejection of any interpretation of human dignity based on a timeless validity is Holmesian in its organic and evolutionary conception of constitutional meaning. The decisions in the electoral threshold cases in 2011 and 2014 represent just such an organic conception of constitutionalism but, I think, taken to an extreme that Holmes would have balked at. The German Basic Law was, after all, not a compromise between different views as was the American Constitution, but rather an unambiguous and assertive normative instrument intended to safeguard the state and inculcate its liberal democratic values in society. One question is whether the Court now sees its role as being to 'normalise' a German identity which it feels, based on the European Parliament decisions, no longer needs the restraints of the militant democracy?

We have come full circle from Böckenförde's dilemma about the liberal, secular state, which illustrated the potential identity deficit between liberal constitutional values and values such as religion or nation. In Germany, those values of liberal constitutionalism, including human dignity, constitutional justice, and the militant democracy which issued forth from Karlsruhe in response to constitutional complaints, defied Böckenförde's fears and became, over decades, important sources of social cohesion and symbols of Germany's moral recovery. Despite all of the critiques of the *BVerfG*'s reasoning identified in the previous chapter—particularly its ivory tower mentality which so frustrates judges in the ordinary courts of law and some politicians—such tensions must ultimately be regarded as the lesser of two evils given the alternative. The fragile 'Bonn republic' founded in 1949 survived the initial challenge from internal anti-democratic forces and the external challenge of its Cold War adversaries to become Germany's longest enduring constitutional order. That Germany remains a stable liberal democratic constitutional order is no small feat in an era when illiberal democracies seem to be gaining traction. The *BVerfG*'s role in the Federal Republic's longevity and stability seems clear, as is the trust which most Germans continue to have in it.

Conclusions

The central claim in the Böckenförde Dilemma that "the liberal, secularised state is nourished by presuppositions that it cannot itself guarantee" (1991: 45) illustrates a problem that is not unique to Germany: how a state can maintain social cohesion and a system of liberal democratic values without imposing them and, thereby, compromising its liberalism. Although written as a warning that Germany probably needed a more socially cohesive value system than the *BVerfG*'s objective value order, it highlighted a vulnerability in liberal democratic institutions that has become increasingly apparent with the rise of populist forces in Europe and the United States since the financial crisis of 2008. Without religion or another value system which serves to reinforce the liberal democratic institutions of the state, the danger is that the citizens start following a value system that is antithetical to the liberal state, or following none at all. An electorate that is, to paraphrase Wolin (1989: 78), unduly lethargic in not taking an interest in politics, may be as dangerous to a tolerant liberal democracy as the concerted few seeking to undermine it. Indeed, the principal danger is that the erosion of democracy and the norms which underpin it may be imperceptible to a state's citizens (Levitsky and Ziblatt, 2019).

Filling the identity deficit and closing the divide between constitutional values and those of social cohesion may be the key to avoiding such democratic demise. The necessity of a vibrant, inclusive, and broad civil society seems an obvious first step in achieving this reconciliation between values, one that can perhaps be supported by top-down and bottom-up initiatives. Here, Robert Putnam has noted in the US context that institutional and individual change are *both* necessary to restore trust and community bonds in America (2000: 413). When Böckenförde first penned his dilemma in the 1960s, his concerns were acutely focussed on the perceived fragility of liberal values in the Federal Republic. While Germany has not been immune to the rise of populist forces, as the increased support for the far right and anti-immigration party the *AfD* illustrates, the political value system created by the Basic Law seems to have created an unusually strong liberal constitutional democracy and culture from the most inauspicious circumstances.

A reformulation of our understanding of the gap between the public and private spheres which opened up in 1789 may be overdue. One lesson from the political turbulence in Europe and the United States since 2016 may be that the liberal constitutional values found in the public sphere—that is to say in government and in the legal control of public authority—may not necessarily be cohesive enough to resonate in civil society. Jefferson feared, as Arendt noted, that a paradox existed in republican government which could undermine it. While government was meant to be representative, it could only work if it was present in the lives of the people, rather than materialising only at election times (Arendt, 1973: 253). Of course, dangers of autocracy exist in attempting to reconcile the values of the public and private spheres if the prevailing sentiment in either is illiberal and reactionary. Arendt alluded to this in terms of "the tendency of public power to expand and to trespass on private interests" (1973: 252) in the pre-modern era. The solution, reflecting "Jefferson's preoccupation with the dangers of public power and this remedy against them" (Arendt, 1973: 252), was the legal bulwark provided by the Bill of Rights. As seen in Chapter 3, however, this was a *legal* wall of separation between the public and private spheres which Jefferson saw as a "legal check" in the "hands of the judiciary" (Jefferson, Madison, and Smith, 1995).[5] But having erected a legal barrier to protect private interests from public power, the question then became how to pierce or break down that barrier to ensure that the 'protected' citizen retained an affinity or even affection for their form of government, and was willing to defend it?[6] Therein lies the problem, though not perhaps an insurmountable one.

Jefferson's concern on protecting private interests from state power while also ensuring the individual stays involved in upholding their government, I contend, is effectively trying to answer the same existential question as Böckenförde posed: how to preserve representative democracy and its constitutional guarantees while retaining the bond between the people and their government? Jefferson saw the answer was through the citizen playing an active role in government at their local level, for, as Arendt notes, "no one could be called either happy or free without participating, and having a share, in public power" (1973: 255). For Böckenförde, the dilemma and the answer lay in how to ensure that the "internal bonding forces" that the state could draw on—whether religion or nation—could support the values of the liberal secular state and the "opportunity for liberty" that provides (1991: 46). In terms of constitutionalism, societies also require an understanding, as McIlwain acknowledged (2005: 32), that there are limits to what politics can accomplish, without allowing public power to encroach unacceptably on private interests.

One of the key challenges for any constitution is whether it can facilitate and respond to changing political circumstances and changing values. Perhaps all constitutions can really do is to establish some parameters within which "a person may construct his or her own life" (Kay, 1998: 23–24), or "establish a moderate politics" (Kautz, 2011: 2) to reduce the chances of a political society from destroying itself. Yet no constitutional government is fool-proof and, as Keith Whittington reminds us, "constitutions cannot survive if they are too politically costly to maintain and they cannot survive if they are too distant from normal political concerns" (2007: 26). One solution suggested by John Finn is that we should direct our efforts "to the defence not of constitutions, but of constitutionalism" (1991: 220). As this book has argued, though, for constitutionalism to be safeguarded and defended there must be a strong normative understanding by a political community regarding the actions and behaviour that law and constitutionalism require of institutions and officials engaged in the application of state power. Therefore, if constitutionalism *is* to be defended, it must be defended first and foremost by citizens themselves.

Notes

1 Former judge, European Court of Justice.
2 This resonates with the point in Chapter 2 regarding the challenges Congress found during Reconstruction in ensuring that the federal constitution and federal laws were carried out in the South. See also (Orren and Skowronek, 2004: 138).
3 In *Rucho v Common Cause*, the majority and dissent agreed on the Framers' fear of faction, but diverge on the implications to be drawn regarding notions of fair representation of political parties (see 2019: 21 and 9, n.1).
4 My translation from: "*Das allgemeine Bürgerrecht, Karlsruhe jederzeit anrufen zu können, schuf demokratisches Selbstbewußtsein. Wer diese Möglichkeit kannte und notfalls auch wahrnahm, mußte sich nicht länger als Untertan begreifen*".
5 See discussion in Chapter 3.
6 As Jefferson put it, "love your neighbour as yourself, and your country more than yourself" (quoted in Arendt, 1973: 253).

References

Lochner v New York, 198 U.S. 45, 1905
Socialist Reich Party Case, 2 BVerfGE 1, 1952
Civil Servants Case, 3 BVerfGE 58, 1953
Communist Party Case, 5 BVerfGE, 1956
Gestapo Case, 6 BVerfGE 132, 1957
Trop v Dulles, 356 US 86, 1958
Life Imprisonment Case, 45 BVerfGE 187, 1977
Rhodes v Chapman, 452 US 337, 1981
Lisbon Treaty Case, 123 BVerfGE 267 & 2 BvE 2/08, 2009
Rucho v Common Cause, 18–422, 2019

Amar, A. R., *America's Unwritten Constitution: The Precedents and Principles We Live By* (New York: Basic Books, 2012).
Arendt, H., *On Revolution* (Harmondsworth: Penguin, 1973).
Bellamy, R., *Citizenship: A Very Short Introduction* (Oxford: Oxford University Press, 2008).
Böckenförde, E. W., "The Rise of the State as a Process of Secularisation", in *State, Society, and Liberty: Studies in Political Theory and Constitutional Law* (New York: Berg Pub Ltd, 1991).
Breyer, S. "Interview with Justice Stephen Breyer—With Charlie Rose (Transcript)", (2016), available at: https://charlierose.com/episodes/29278 [last accessed 6 October 2016].
Collings, J., *Democracy's Guardians: A History of the German Federal Constitutional Court, 1951–2001* (Oxford: Oxford University Press, 2015).
Cover, R. M., "The Supreme Court 1982 Term Foreword: Nomos and Narrative", *Harvard Law Review*, 97(1) (1983), 4.
Dahl, R. A., "Decision-Making in a Democracy: The Supreme Court as a National Policy-Maker", *Journal of Public Law*, 6 (1957), 279.
Dahl, R. A., *How Democratic is the American Constitution?* 2nd edn (New Haven, CT: Yale University Press, 2003).
De Tocqueville, A. and P. Renshaw, *Democracy in America* (Herts: Wordsworth Editions Limited, 1998).
Finn, J. E., *Peopling the Constitution* (Lawrence, Kansas: University Press of Kansas, 2014).

Finn, J. E. *Constitutions in Crisis: Political Violence and the Rule of Law* (Oxford: Oxford University Press, 1991).

Frankfurter, F., "Foreword: Robert H. Jackson", *Columbia Law Review*, 55(4) (1955), 435–437.

Henry, P. "Patrick Henry, Virginia Ratifying Convention, 4 June 1788" [Speech] The University of Chicago (1986), available at: http://press-pubs.uchicago.edu/founders/documents/preambles14.html [last accessed 3 November 2019].

Jefferson, T., J. Madison, and J. M. Smith, "Letter From Jefferson to Madison, 15 March 1789", in *The Republic of Letters: The Correspondence Between Thomas Jefferson and James Madison, 1776–1826*, ed. by James Morton Smith (New York: W.W. Norton and Company, 1995).

Kautz, S., "Introduction", in *The Supreme Court and the Idea of Constitutionalism*, ed. by Steven Kautz, Arthur Melzer, Jerry Weinberger, and M Richard Zinman (Philadelphia: University of Pennsylvania Press, 2011).

Kay, R. S., "American Constitutionalism", in *Constitutionalism: Philosophical Foundations*, ed. by Lawrence A. Alexander (Cambridge: Cambridge University Press, 1998).

Krisch, N., "Pouvoir Constituant and Pouvoir Irritant in The Postnational Order", *International Journal of Constitutional Law*, 14(3) (2016), 657–679.

Lamprecht, R., "Das Über-Ich der Nation", *Spiegel Online*, 1 September 1998, available at: www.spiegel.de/spiegel/spiegelspecial/d-7519479.html [last accessed 2 November 2016].

Levitsky, S. and D. Ziblatt, *How Democracies Die* (London: Penguin Books, 2019).

Lovell, G. I., *Legislative Deferrals: Statutory Ambiguity, Judicial Power, and American Democracy* (Cambridge: Cambridge University Press, 2003).

May, C. N. and A. Ides, *Constitutional Law National Power and Federalism: Examples and Explanations* (Aspen Publishers Online, 2007).

McCloskey, R. G., *The Modern Supreme Court* (Cambridge, MA: Harvard University Press, 1972).

McIlwain, C. H., *Constitutionalism: Ancient and Modern* (Clark, NJ: The Lawbook Exchange, 2005).

Mouffe, C., *The Democratic Paradox* (London: Verso, 2000).

Orren, K. and S. Skowronek, *The Search for American Political Development* (Cambridge: Cambridge University Press, 2004).

Orwell, G. and P. H. Davison, *The Complete Works of George Orwell*. Vol. 12 (London: Secker & Warburg, 1986).

Post, R. and R. Siegel, "Roe Rage: Democratic Constitutionalism and Backlash", *Harvard Civil Rights-Civil Liberties Law Review*, 42 (2007), 373.

Putnam, R. D., *Bowling Alone: The Collapse and Revival of American Community* (New York: Simon and Schuster, 2000).

Rostow, E. V., "The Democratic Character of Judicial Review", *Harvard Law Review*, 66(2) (1952), 193–224.

Sager, L., "The Domain of Constitutional Justice", in *Constitutionalism: Philosophical Foundations*, ed. by Lawrence A. Alexander (Cambridge: Cambridge University Press, 1998).

Smith, J. D., *On Democracy's Doorstep: The Inside Story of How the Supreme Court Brought "One Person, One Vote" to the United States* (New York: Hill and Wang, 2014).

Somek, A., *The Cosmopolitan Constitution* (New York: Oxford University Press, 2014).

Voßkuhle, A. and W. Von Rahden, "Die Rolle des Bundesverfassungsgerichts in Europa: Ein Gespräch", *Gegenworte* (30) (2013).

Waldron, J., "The Constitutional Politics of Hannah Arendt", in *Political Political Theory: Essays on Institutions* (Cambridge, MA: Harvard University Press, 2016).

Walker, B., "Ein Freundliches Signal in Richtung FDP", *Badische Zeitung*, 29 March 2017, available at: www.badische-zeitung.de/deutschland-1/ein-freundliches-signal-in-richtung-fdp-135050655.html [last accessed 6 May 2017].

Whittington, K. E., *Political Foundations of Judicial Supremacy: The Presidency, the Supreme Court, and Constitutional Leadership in US History*, Princeton Studies in American Politics (Princeton, NJ: Princeton University Press, 2007).

Wolin, S. S., *The Presence of the Past: Essays on the State and the Constitution* (Baltimore, MD: Johns Hopkins University Press, 1989).

Index

For Product Safety Concerns and Information please contact our EU representative GPSR@taylorandfrancis.com
Taylor & Francis Verlag GmbH, Kaufingerstraße 24, 80331 München, Germany

www.ingramcontent.com/pod-product-compliance
Lightning Source LLC
LaVergne TN
LVHW052317200926
848481LV00002B/586
9780367609320